Strategies for Smart Car Buyers

**From the Editors at
Edmunds.com**

**By Philip Reed
with Mike Hudson**

Edmunds.com Strategies for Smart Car Buyers

ISBN: 0-87759-691-3
ISSN: 1543-5601

Book Production Team

Publisher
Peter Steinlauf

Editorial Director
Kevin Smith

Editor in Chief
Karl Brauer

Managing Editor
Donna DeRosa

Senior Consumer Advice Editor
Philip Reed

Consumer Advice Editor
Mike Hudson

**Senior Editor,
Content & Syndication**
Erin Riches

Production Editor
Caroline Pardilla

Designer/Illustrator
Jeff Zugale

Director, Creative Services
Guy Schackman

Edmunds.com, Inc.

Chairman & Chief Executive Officer
Peter Steinlauf

President
Jeremy Anwyl

Chief Operating Officer
Avi Steinlauf

Vice President, Consumer Services
Matthew Kumin

**Vice President, Marketing &
Industry Communications**
Bob Kurilko

Editorial Offices
2401 Colorado Avenue, Suite 250
Santa Monica, CA 90404
310-309-6000

Subscription Fulfillment Provider
Nextech Systems Corporation
PO Box 338
Shrub Oaks, NY 10588
914-962-6000

Printed in USA

"Contents at a Glance"

Table of Contents

Acknowledgements

This book was created with the help of many people on the Edmunds.com staff. First of all, much credit is due to Peter Steinlauf, Edmunds.com CEO and publisher for being the one who recognized a unique opportunity to help American consumers. He encouraged us all to put our consumer advice into book form where more people could read and benefit from it. Without his strong motivation, this book would not have been written.

Matthew Kumin, vice president of consumer services, did a great job of coordinating the various elements of the book while being inspiring to—and respectful of—the written word. Ken Levin, executive vice president and general counsel, was especially supportive and helpful. A general thanks goes to the entire Edmunds.com executive team for reviewing the book and contributing their thoughts on its content and direction. Editorial Director Kevin Smith always had time to give this project his full attention at crucial stages of the second edition. Editor in Chief Karl Brauer gave valuable direction to the manuscript and read early drafts while offering essential feedback. Donna DeRosa, managing editor, expertly pulled all the pieces of the book together and moved it forward, day by day, to a successful completion. Book Designer/Illustrator Jeff Zugale's artwork and his graceful book design helped to clearly bring across the messages we were trying to convey. Guy Schackman, director of creative services, also contributed greatly by lending valuable comments about design and content presentation issues. Photography Editor Scott Jacobs also helped with early design ideas and produced some of the graphics. Senior Content Editor Erin Riches' eagle editorial eye, and her probing questions, ensured that all the bases were covered. Scott Schapiro, data development specialist, gave valuable feedback on the entire book and contributed essential information to the leasing section. Production Editor Caroline Pardilla patiently checked and rechecked the book and gave it a final polish. Our publicity department pulled out all the stops to help make the first edition of this book a roaring success and for that we need to thank Vice President of Marketing and Industry Communications Bob Kurilko, Director of Public Relations Jeannine Fallon and Director of Communications Strategy Pamela Krebs. We also have to give a general thanks to other Edmunds.com staff members for contributing in ways too numerous to mention.

And finally, thanks go to you, the American consumer, for giving us valuable feedback through e-mail messages about your interaction with car dealers across America.

Introduction

The process of buying a car has changed enormously over the past five years. The Internet has reshaped virtually every aspect of how consumers shop—from the way they research, select and locate cars to how they negotiate for and finally buy cars. But a few things haven't changed. New cars are still sold exclusively by franchised dealerships, you still have to test-drive a car before you buy it and most shoppers still dread their encounter with the car salesman (we say car sales*man* since most are men).

The New World of Car Buying

If you haven't bought a car in the past five years, you are in for a pleasant surprise. Buying a car in today's market is faster, easier and less stressful than ever before. Furthermore, the new car you buy today will likely cost about as much as your last car and you can probably finance it at a lower rate. It is also likely to be more dependable. Finally, cars today require less maintenance and include many valuable safety features that weren't available until recently.

So if you are one of those people who dreads car shopping, cheer up, it's a whole new ball game. And if you play the game correctly, you'll be the winner. At Edmunds.com we've streamlined the process by breaking it into 10 simple steps to achieve your goals regardless of whether you plan to buy a new or used car, lease a vehicle, buy auto insurance or sell a car you already own. The 10 steps in each chapter are based on extensive research and information provided by industry insiders.

Edmunds.com—From Publishing to the Internet

Edmunds.com has been publishing car-buying guides since 1966 and, with the launch of our Web site in 1995, has grown to become the most trusted source of automotive information. As a leader in the field, we feel it is important to conduct hands-on research. The information in this book was gathered by an investigative reporter who worked undercover as a car salesman at two dealerships in Southern California.

Chandler Phillips Says:

You can follow me through this book, and I'll show you some of the tricks I've picked up as a car salesman and long-time automotive journalist.

How to Use This Book

We know that many of you might not want to wade through a lot of pages just to buy a new car. You probably want to get a good car at a low price and in the shortest amount of time possible. That's why we've created an easy-to-use format for presenting the information. Each section is devoted to accomplishing a specific task: buying a new or used car, leasing a car, buying insurance or selling your old car. The sections begin with background information, and then conclude by putting all this information to work for you in a sequence of 10 easy-to-follow steps. If you are eager to get going, jump straight to the 10 steps and refer back to the other topics as questions spring to mind.

By reading this book you will learn a whole new approach to car buying. It is our hope that when you're armed with the right information, the search for a new car, as well as the negotiating process and final purchase, will be an exciting adventure. Most of all, we want you to reach your goal with the confidence of knowing you did it the right way. We want you to be able to look at that new car in your driveway and feel that, not only did you get the best car, but you got it at a fair price—with no hidden "gotchas" in the deal that will come back to haunt you.

Finding the Right Car for You

So you've made the decision: "I need a car." But that's really where the questions begin. Where do you start? Should you get that fancy luxury sedan, a mid-range SUV or an economy wagon? How about a used car? Should you lease or buy? Sure, it sounds complex, but don't worry, we can help find the right car at the right price. No problem.

Chapter 1

Begin Your Car-Buying Search

One day you are driving down the road when the thought suddenly jumps into your mind. For some people this thought comes when the "Check Engine" light pops on one too many times on the way to work. For others, it's when a hot new car passes on the street or stars in a TV ad, just screaming to live in their garage. But the thought is usually phrased the same way:

"It's time for me to buy a new car."

Following hard on the heels of this first thought is a second. This new thought comes in the form of a question that will lead you in many different directions:

"What is the right car for me?"

Before you go car shopping, you need to decide what you are going to buy. The question of what car to buy should be answered long before you visit the car lot. Don't make the mistake of wandering into a dealership and telling the first salesman who descends on you: "You know, I really need a new car—but I don't know what to buy." Next thing you know, the salesman will be making a huge profit and you'll be driving home in a car you don't want and can't afford. But with our help, a little research on your part and some insider information and professional tools at Edmunds.com, you'll be set up with the perfect car for hundreds or thousands less than others have paid for the same vehicle. Plus, we'll show you how you can use the Internet and the phone to get *rock-bottom deals that salesmen would never offer "walk-up" customers* without hours of unnecessary and uncomfortable negotiation.

First, back to the basics. Need a car? Start by breaking the question into two pieces:

"What do I want?"

and

"What do I need?"

Wanting is pie-in-the-sky dreaming. If you are wealthy—as in "dropping $50,000 on a car won't affect your bank account" wealthy—you can give this question a lot of consideration. But *needing* is where most of us should probably focus.

There are lots of things you would like to have. But your car-buying decision will be a mix of what you can afford and what you really need. There is an old expression that addresses this sticky situation: don't be penny-wise and pound-foolish. In other words, you can make decisions now that look like they will save you money, but they may actually cost you big bucks a year or so down the road. (Please see our sidebar on the long-term costs of car ownership on page 46.) For now, keep in mind that you should be balancing *needs* and *wants* as you move through the car-buying process.

Before we go any farther in that direction, there is a more pressing question you have to address. That is:

"How much should I spend on my new car?"

How Much Can You Afford?

This is a good place to start your car-shopping adventure. If you put a high priority on look and style, you might decide to allocate a larger portion of your paycheck toward a new car. If you think of a car as transportation only, you'll want to spend as little as possible on your next set of wheels.

Financial experts recommend that, before you buy a car, you should review your budget because the cost of a car goes far beyond the monthly payment dealerships advertise. Ask yourself the following questions:

- How much "take-home pay" do you bring in each month?

- How much is your rent or mortgage payment?

- What is the total of your other bills: food, utilities, debts and savings?

- Will you have two cars and two car payments?

- How much will insurance cost for a new car?

- How much will the car cost to fuel and repair?

If you total all your expenses and deduct them from your take-home pay, you will have a clear view of how much wiggle room there is in your budget for a new car. If you can truly afford one, the figure should be more than enough to cover your car payment. We say "car payment" since most buyers will finance a new car, meaning they will take out a loan and pay it off over time. Still other people will lease their new car and make smaller monthly payments. More to come on all that... but back to the finance questions for now.

The 20-Percent Rule

If you want to avoid an IRS-caliber review of your finances, consider this alternative: Your car payment should be only 20 percent of your take-home pay. Same goes if you have two cars; the total monthly payments for both should still be 20 percent of your available household income.

This 20-percent rule may seem rather restrictive. You might be wailing in despair and saying, "I need a car, but 20 percent of my take-home pay won't buy anything!" At least you are confronting that situation now, rather than sitting in a dealership with your pen poised over a contract that will drive you into bankruptcy. But don't fret... there are many, many methods for stretching your car-buying dollar. Leasing is a popular way to make seemingly expensive cars more affordable. Better yet, used cars offer tremendous savings over new, often without sacrificing quality. We'll cover all those options in later sections of this book.

Chandler Phillips Says:

The 20% rule tells you how much to spend on your next car. Remember to figure this out long before you are overwhelmed by new car smell on the test drive.

Worksheet:
How Much Can You Afford?

Begin by listing your monthly take-home pay. This is the amount you have left after taxes and other deductions have been made. Then subtract the expenses as you list them. The amount remaining will be the maximum amount you can afford to pay, per month, for your next car.

Monthly Take-Home Pay: $_____

Monthly Expenses:

Mortgage payment or rent $_____

Utilities $_____

Food $_____

Insurance (home, car, life) $_____

Taxes $_____

Clothing $_____

Personal $_____

Entertainment $_____

Gifts and contributions $_____

Education $_____

Credit card payments $_____

Other payments $_____

Existing vehicle payments $_____

Miscellaneous $_____

Total Monthly Expenses: $_____

Maximum Car Payment: $_____

Deduct total monthly expenses from monthly take-home pay to get your maximum car payment.

Should You Buy a New or Used Car?

Now that you know how much you can spend, your finances will be pointing you toward a new or used car. It might not be clear if you should buy, lease or buy used yet. That's OK. For example, you might have enough money to buy a new car but want to save money by getting a used car bargain. Or, you might find yourself deciding between an inexpensive new car or a high-end used car. How are you going to decide? Here are a few points to consider.

- With a new car you can: Pay more, but save money on financing, get rebates and get a warranty

- With a used car you can: Pay less, but spend time searching for a good deal and researching the history of the car

Chapter 2

New, Used or Lease?

A Case for Used Cars

In terms of economy, there is no decision to be made. Used cars are by far the best deal around. The reason is that once a new car is driven off the dealer lot, it loses 20 to 30 percent of its value. From that point on, it loses 5 to 10 percent more of its value per year. So when it comes time to sell it a few years down the road, that once-shiny new car is now worth substantially less on the market. Sometimes, new car buyers will even owe more on their car than they can sell it for; something dealers call being "upside-down" on a vehicle.

Chandler Phillips Says:

Deciding to buy a used car might make the car of your dreams affordable. This is just one of the benefits to shopping the used car market.

With this depreciation factor in mind, it's easy to see that buying a one-year-old car will be 20 to 30 percent cheaper than a new car. This opens up a new world of opportunities. Now, suddenly, the car of your dreams is actually within reach—as long as you buy it used. Or, you can buy a more upscale used version of the new car you are considering. And just think, after one year of used car ownership, you will be ahead of the new car crowd.

But what about the reliability of used cars? The reliability of cars has risen each year while the required maintenance has dropped. Furthermore, you can now buy a certified used car that comes with a factory warranty. This makes the used car ownership experience nearly identical to driving a new car. Essentially, if something is wrong with the used car you just bought, it will be fixed at no expense to you.

The Benefits of Buying New

Knowing what we now know about used cars, why would anyone buy a new car? Style is a huge part of the answer. Many people want to be ahead of the wave, the first on their block with the newest model car. Along with a prestigious address, or hip fashion, owning the hottest car or newest version of an existing car can be worth the extra cash. But there are also practical reasons to own a new car:

- Interest rates are usually lower for loans on new cars

- Rebates are often available that lower the price of new cars

- All-new cars include warranties, maintenance plans and roadside assistance

- The most advanced safety features are available on the newest cars

- New cars are in perfect condition, free from dings and scratches

There is one other financial question to be considered before we can move on to the consideration of specific models. Besides buying new or used, you should also decide, ahead of time, whether you plan to lease or buy your next car.

Leasing vs. Buying

In a nutshell, leasing makes it easier to get more car for less money. You are essentially paying for a portion of the car, instead of buying the entire vehicle. So, like many things, leasing looks great in the short run. But if you take the long view of economics, you will see that leasing will eventually be more expensive. It is more costly because, once you begin leasing, you usually wind up leasing

Chandler Phillips Says:

Some people choose their car by finding the biggest incentive or the best lease special. Shopping this way can lead to some screaming deals.

again. And again. And again. This means you always have a car payment and never own anything.

Now consider the person who buys a car. At the end of five years of car payments, the car now belongs to him or her. It might not have much value on the open market, but if you're willing to drive it for several more years, it becomes nearly free transportation until the wheels fall off.

A major appeal of leasing, on the other hand, is the ability to get a new car every three or four years. If you love cars, and lust after the latest models, leasing is a way to feed your habit at the lowest monthly cost.

Chandler Phillips Says:

People who enjoy managing their money are good candidates for leasing. Consumers with a strong need for ownership usually shy away from it.

The first year of new car ownership is expensive. After that, the costs level off but remain high until the car is paid off. Leasing is inexpensive at first, but

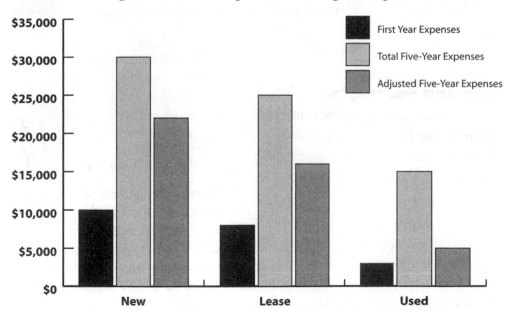

remains high each year for as long as you continue leasing. Used car ownership costs less to start with, and is less each year (provided you don't run into expensive repair bills after the vehicle is out of warranty). When you figure in the value of the cars that the new and used car buyers have at the end of five years, the true price tag of leasing is revealed.

There is a lot more to be said about leasing vs. buying and new vs. used, but we will save those discussions for future sections. With these thoughts in mind, let's get back to the fun stuff: what new car are you going to buy?

Examine Your Needs

The biggest potential savings on your new vehicle can be made before you even buy it. And the key is taking an honest appraisal of what kind of car you need to avoid buying more options, styling and performance capability than you need. The answer to what car to buy next can be found in your past driving habits. Here is a list of questions to get you started:

What is your driving style? Do you enjoy performance driving? Can you drive a stick or do you need an automatic transmission? Is style important to you? Or do you want to just get where you need to go?

Chandler Phillips Says:

If you shop for a car that fulfills your needs rather than your wants you will wind up in a car that satisfies you for a long time.

Where do you go? Will your car be used mainly for commuting? Will you take family vacations in it? Do you drive in the ice and snow? Do you like to drive off-road? Do you live in a hilly or mountainous region?

Who goes with you? Do you spend most of your time alone in your car? Or will you use it to transport a basketball team? Do you have (or are you expecting) a baby who will need to ride in a child safety seat in the back? Do you have to transport clients who you want to impress?

What do you carry? Are you a salesperson who needs to carry large sample cases? Are you a contractor with heavy equipment? Do you have a big family and need to take along a lot of people and luggage? Do you have a boat you will be towing?

By reviewing these questions, a picture of the car you *need* to buy will begin to emerge. If the picture of the car you need to buy begins to clash with the car you *want* to buy, you have a problem. While it's important to "get real" and decide what you need to buy, you could make a list of several cars—even types of cars—and let other factors decide for you. Maybe a test-drive will provide the final answer. Or maybe price will steer you in one direction or another. The point is to narrow your thinking as much as possible before you move forward in the process.

A Car's Vital Statistics

It's likely that, by now, you have several candidates for vehicles you would want to buy. But don't just run out and ask for a test-drive. If you do that, you might fall in love with the wrong car, or get pressured into buying something you don't really want. What you need to do is go to the next level of research—check the car's vital statistics. This means you should consult the experts and review information pertaining to the car's strengths and weaknesses.

If you're saying, "But I don't want to read about horsepower and cargo capacity!" don't worry. You won't be digging too deeply into factory specifications unless you'd like to.

Try to judge prospective vehicles based on how you absorb information.

- Are you visual—do you like to see pictures of the cars you want to buy?

- Are you data-oriented—do you want the vital statistics about a car?

- Are you an auto enthusiast most interested in the way a car performs?

- Are you most concerned about cost?

Vehicle Types and Uses

Cars and trucks are designed and built in a number of different configurations. You've probably heard these terms all your life, but it's good to be clear on them before you begin shopping. Here is a quick list of vehicle types along with a short definition:

Convertible: Convertibles have either soft or hardtops. The hardtop roof automatically folds into sections and stores in the trunk when it is put down.

Coupe/hatchback: A two-door car that has either a fixed glass rear window and trunk or a larger rear hatch that opens up to a cargo area.

Crossover: A vehicle that combines the characteristics of two or more vehicle types such as a car and SUV or an SUV and a truck.

Minivan: A vehicle with a short hood and a box-shaped body enclosing a large cargo/passenger area.

Pickup truck: A vehicle with two or four doors and an exposed cargo box.

Sedan: A car with a four-door body configuration and a conventional trunk.

Sports car: Two doors, low slung, big engine. Definitely sporty.

SUV: Sport-Utility Vehicle. This vehicle has high clearance and was initially made for off-road driving. SUVs now come in two-wheel drive, four-wheel drive and all-wheel drive.

Wagon: A car with a roofline that extends past the rear doors but is otherwise similar to the sedan.

Additionally, many of the above car types break down into subcategories according to size (compact, midsize and large) and market segment (luxury, performance and sport).

Ideally, you want to consider all of these elements of a car as you move through the research process. But pick your favorite and start there. Before you know it, car buying will become fun and entertaining instead of being a chore and you'll end up with a car you love.

Every aspect of different cars is covered on our Web site at www.edmunds. com. And we also offer this information in hard copy form in the *Edmunds.com New Cars & Trucks Buyer's Guide.* You can also browse the car magazines you'll find at the local newsstand or watch television shows that focus on current models. Whatever your favorite source of information, consider evaluating the car in the following ways:

Cost of Ownership: Some cars depreciate quickly. Others hold their value. If you plan to keep the car for three years and sell it, you will want to choose one that has a strong resale value. If you plan to drive the wheels off the car, then don't worry about residual value. Edmunds.com computes the expected depreciation of every car and presents this as the "True Cost to Own^{SM}" (TCO) along with related expenses.

Performance: This is usually a blend of three elements: engine performance, handling and braking. While specifications will tell you about engine size and suspension design, editorial reviews can show how all these attributes actually feel. Experienced drivers writing in Edmunds.com reviews and in magazines describe the driving experience and compare it to cars from other manufacturers. You will, of course, make your own decision about how a car performs when you go on the test-drive.

Reliability: In general, the reliability of cars has improved across all brands. However, some differences remain. Even if repairs are covered by a warranty, it's a hassle to have your car in the shop all the time. Research your potential vehicles with attention to the manufacturer's reliability history. You can also check the maintenance section of our Web site to see if any recalls are in effect for the current model year you are considering. J.D. Power ratings are also available on our Web site going back to the early '90s for some cars.

Luxury car buyers should consider that many cars come with free maintenance for the first four years which, along with the basic warranty, should spare owners the expense usually associated with high-end cars.

Safety: Does it have safety features such as antilock brakes, traction control and side airbags? What crash test scores has this car received? Most new cars are crash tested by the National Highway Traffic Safety Administration. The results can be reviewed at http://www.nhtsa.dot.gov/.

Specifications: This information is generally listed in chart form and is cluttered with numbers. Some will be important to you (horsepower, fuel economy, legroom and cargo space) and others may strike you as being academic (curb weight, wheelbase and shoulder room). As you

Chandler Phillips Says:

New technology has made cars safer than ever before. Take a moment to understand the importance of such features as ABS, stability control and side curtain airbags.

begin to compare cars, these numbers can reveal the real story about which vehicle is the best buy.

Styling: This is the part that everyone loves to talk about. But there are practical considerations to be aware of. For example, you need to think of what kind of resale value your car will have. If you are considering getting the newest design, one that has just emerged in the marketplace, the styling may prove unpopular in the long run. This means the resale value may be lower. The same is true of unusual colors. Of course, if you are going to drive this car until it falls apart, none of this matters to anyone but you.

Arranging a Test-Drive

So far, we've recommended you do "on-line research" to narrow down your choices. Pick a couple new and a couple used models and make a list of your options and general prices. Soon, it will be time for "hands-on" research. You need to actually touch, feel, sit in and, of course, drive the car you are considering buying. If you are lucky, and you have a friend who owns the car you want to buy, perhaps you can test-drive your friend's car in a relaxed environment. But, if you are considering several cars, you will need to test-drive each car in close succession so you can compare your feelings about each one.

First, a word of warning: car salespeople are taught to use the test-drive as the ideal time to seduce buyers into taking the plunge. Old-school dealers tell young salespeople: "The feel of the wheel will seal the deal." We know of another sales manager who counseled his sales staff: "You have to get buyers to register high on their excitement meter. If they are excited, they will buy and pay more for the car than if they are rational."

So, how do you get through the test-drive without committing to a car that may not best serve your needs? We recommend that you initiate your contact with the dealership by going to Edmunds.com and selecting the car you are interested in buying. (If you don't have access to the Web, call local dealerships and ask for the Internet or fleet

Chandler Phillips Says:

Many buyers don't realize that they can easily arrange a test drive through the fleet or Internet manager.

sales manager.) Then follow the prompts on Edmunds.com to send simultaneous e-mails to the Internet managers at competing dealerships. In return you will receive e-mails with the contact information for the Internet departments at the various dealerships.

Now, it's time to make a few calls. Make sure you ask for the Internet sales department. Internet salespeople are accustomed to buyers who are research-oriented and not prone to impulse buying. If you live in a city where there are many dealerships competing for your business, you are in a strong position. If you live in a rural area, be prepared to travel to get your best deal. The time you spend shopping around will save you money.

Whether you e-mail or call the dealership, tell the Internet manager you are cross-shopping several different brands. You need to test-drive them all before you can make a decision. You will test-drive the car and leave. If you like the car, and like the way you are treated by the dealership, you will return and buy the car from them.

During this opening discussion with the salesperson at the dealership, you are, in a sense, "test-driving your salesperson." Is this someone you want to deal with as you make a major economic decision that will impact you for years to come?

Here are a few questions to ask yourself as you evaluate your salesperson:

- Has the salesperson responded to my phone call/e-mail within a responsible amount of time?

- Was the salesperson listening to my needs? Or was he trying to sell me a car he wanted to move?

- If the car I want isn't available, has the salesperson suggested a reasonable alternative?

- Was I treated with respect?

- Do I trust this salesperson to be open and honest when arranging the sale of this car?

- If a disagreement arises, will I feel comfortable voicing my concern?

Action Script: Arranging an Appointment for a Test-Drive

After you initiate contact with the Internet department by sending e-mail messages through the Edmunds.com Web site, follow up with a phone call. Here's how the conversation might go.

While you have the Internet manager on the line, you can also ask for a cell phone number to reach them for follow-up questions. If you get the hard sell on the phone, you might try calling another dealership until you find a salesperson you feel comfortable dealing with.

```
               Phone rings:
               RECEPTIONIST
     Joe Covo Matsura. How can I help you?

             SMART CAR BUYER
     What's the name of your Internet manager?

               RECEPTIONIST
                Mike Austin.

             SMART CAR BUYER
           (Writes down the name)
     Would you connect me with him, please?

     The phone rings and is answered by voice
     mail. The Smart Car Buyer presses "0" for
     the operator. The receptionist picks up
                   again.

             SMART CAR BUYER
     Would you please page Mike Austin for me?

            The phone is answered.

                   MIKE
        Hello, this is Mike Austin.

             SMART CAR BUYER
     Hi. I'm looking for the '04 Matsura
                  Accell.

                   MIKE
     Great car! Come on down, we've got plenty
          of 'em on our lot right now.

             SMART CAR BUYER
     Good. But I'm cross-shopping the Accell
     with other cars and I need to test-drive it
             before I can decide.

                   MIKE
     Of course. We always give a test-drive
     before we sell our cars. But you're gonna
                   love it.

             SMART CAR BUYER
     What I'm saying is I'd like to drive the
     car in a relaxed atmosphere. If I like the
        Accell best, I'll buy it from you.

                   MIKE
     You don't want a hard sell. Okay. The only
      pressure you'll get here's in the tires.

             SMART CAR BUYER
     Great. I'll drive the car, then leave and
           make a decision later.

                   MIKE
        I look forward to meeting you.
```

How to Test-Drive a Car

Once you are at the dealership, ask for the salesperson you spoke with. In some cases, you might be directed to another salesperson who will help you with the test-drive. Some dealerships use the Internet department to funnel leads to the normal salespeople. If you are dealing with a new salesperson, you should repeat what you told the Internet salesperson: you are going to test-drive the car only; you will be leaving after the test-drive. If you like the car and like the way you are treated, you will return to buy the car.

The salesperson will probably make a photocopy of your driver license. This is standard operating procedure that protects them from carjackers. Don't worry, they won't run a credit report with the information on your license (but you might receive follow-up calls from salespeople). Furthermore, if you are going to be driving one of their cars, the dealership has the right to verify that you are a licensed driver. But you can ask for the photocopy back if it appears you won't be doing business with them.

If you have only been reading about a certain car, and have never seen it up close, you might be very surprised by how it looks in person. In pictures, with no frame of reference, cars sometimes look much larger or smaller than they actually are. Open the door and you are in for another surprise; no photo can do justice to the interior of a car. And, certainly, no amount of description is a substitute for sitting in the driver seat.

Chandler Phillips Says:

Take your time on the test drive. You're making a decision that you'll have to live with for years.

Once you get settled, here are a few questions that will help you define your feelings about the car you are considering before you even start driving:

- Do you "fit" in this car? Is there enough legroom/headroom? Remember to check the backseat, too.

- Is the driving position comfortable? Do you feel like you're sitting too low or too high in the car?

- Can you tilt or telescope the steering wheel or adjust the pedals for a better fit?

- Are the controls easy to operate?

- How is the visibility? Check the rearview mirror and the side mirrors.

- Consider bringing your kids along to make sure there is enough room for everyone in the car.

- Bring a child's safety seat to make sure one can easily be installed if necessary.

Evaluating Driving Characteristics

Sometimes the salesperson will drive the car off the lot and then turn the wheel over to you later. While they are driving you can evaluate the car from the passenger's standpoint. Pay attention to the noise and visibility. Once on city streets the car salesperson will try to direct you to drive along a predetermined route. This is often a 10-minute ride involving a series of right-hand turns that leads back to the dealership. This might be convenient for the dealership, but it's not the best way for you to evaluate the car.

Your test-drive should match your driving requirements. If you drive into the mountains, find a hill and see how the car climbs. If you have a highway commute, see how the car accelerates into traffic and performs in the 60-70 mph range. Tell the salesperson what kind of test-drive you want and they will probably accommodate you. However, the salesperson may need to clear it with their manager first.

What to Look For

Before you start driving, adjust the seat, the mirrors and the seatbelt. Turn off the radio so you can hear the engine and concentrate on the driving experience. You can check out the sound system later.

On the test-drive evaluate these specific points (a more detailed checklist is included in the sidebar on page 33):

- **Acceleration:** Is acceleration good throughout the power range?

- **Braking:** Are brakes easily modulated?

- **Cornering:** Does the car lean excessively? Is the steering responsive?

- **Engine noise:** Is there a lot of noise in the passenger compartment?

- **Hill climbing:** Is there enough power?

- **Passing acceleration:** Does it downshift quickly?

- **Rattles and squeaks:** Does the car feel tight?

- **Suspension:** How does it ride?

- **Transmission:** Does the car shift easily from gear to gear or make unnecessary noise?

- **Visibility:** Check for blind spots.

During the test-drive, the salesperson may begin asking you leading questions. No matter how much you love the car, remain noncommittal. If the salesperson senses interest, they will start to pressure you—and you don't want that at this point.

When you're back on the car lot, remember to check the trunk space. You will probably be shown the engine, too. Unless you are mechanically inclined, there is not much to look for. If you want to test your salesperson, ask if there is a timing belt or a timing chain. Timing belts often need to be changed after 60,000 miles, while chains last longer.

If you are interested in buying the car you've driven, you should copy the figures on the window sticker—the base price and all the options and their costs. Also, look for the stock number of the car (a number posted in the windshield) so you can locate it again when you return.

It's likely the salesperson will try to get you inside to begin negotiations. Don't go there. Specifically, don't get into "how much can you afford?" discussions. Once they know how much you can pay, chances are you'll never get below that number again. Resist offers of brochures, coffee or promises to "see what kind of payments we can put together." Take a business card from your salesperson and leave.

Then, go on to the next test-drive. Who knows? You might like the next car a lot better. And, if you like more than one car, you will be in a stronger bargaining position when it comes time to buy.

Chandler Phillips Says:

Keep in mind that the salesman will try to move you to the negotiations phase after the test drive. Don't start dickering until you've done all your research.

After your final test-drive you will have reached the end of the research phase of car buying. You should know what the right car is for you. In the next section, we've taken the information you've just read and put it together into 10 steps. The information may seem repetitive, but it will ensure that you cover all the bases and proceed with your shopping in the right order. The steps are easy to follow and easy to remember. So read on and get ready for the best car-buying experience of your life.

Test-Drive Checklist

Copy this checklist and take it to the dealership with you when you are test-driving prospective vehicles. *There is a detachable copy of this list in the back of this book.*

Make/Model:	Good	Fair	Poor
General Impressions			
Exterior: styling, finish, paint, body panel gap tolerances			
Interior: upholstery and ergonomics			
Materials quality: plastics and leather			
Interior			
Ease of entry to front and backseats			
Headroom in front and backseats			
Legroom in front and backseats			
Comfort of seats			
Layout of controls			
Visibility out front, side and rear windows (in convertible, check with top up and down)			
Effective mirrors, both inside and out			
Storage space			
Trunk space			
Convenience features, cupholders			
Drivetrain, Handling and Braking			
Acceleration			
Passing			
Hill climbing			
Engine noise			
Transmission: smooth shifting			
Transmission: downshift without hesitation			
Cornering			
Suspension			
Braking			
General Driving Impressions			
Wind and road noise			
Rattles and squeaks			
Stereo performance			
Safety Features			
Airbags: driver, passenger, side torso, head curtain			
Antilock brakes (ABS)			
Traction control			
Stability control			

Chapter 3

10 Steps to Finding the Right Car for You

If you are undecided about what car you want, read the following "10 Steps to Finding the Right Car." Once you decide on what car you want, read either the buying new, buying used or leasing 10 Steps to get your car. If you find some jargon along the way, consult our glossary at the end of this section.

The following steps are devoted to helping you price, locate and test-drive the vehicle that is best for you.

1. What kind of car do you need?

If you examine your *needs* you will quickly discover what kind of car is right for you. Take a moment to think about what you use your car for. How many people do you need to transport? What kind of driving do you most often do? How long is your commute, and is it important that your next vehicle get good gas mileage?

Here are a few other questions to keep in mind when you begin your car-buying process:

- Do you want a manual or automatic transmission?

- Do you really need four-wheel drive or all-wheel drive?

- What safety features do you want?

- Do you require a lot of cargo-carrying capacity? Will you be doing any towing?

- Will the car fit in your garage or parking area?

2. How much can you afford?

Regardless of whether you decide to buy or lease your next car, establishing a realistic monthly payment that will fit into your budget is a crucial step. How much should this be?

A rule of thumb is your total monthly car payments—whether you own one car or more than one—shouldn't exceed 20 percent of your monthly take-home pay.

The Edmunds.com Web site has a variety of calculators to help you estimate what your monthly payment will be based on purchase price, down payment, interest rate and length of loan. Take the time to run the numbers now, before you go car shopping, and put this information into your car-buying folder. It will not only show you what you can afford, it will also help you control the numbers when you negotiate with a car salesman.

3. Should you lease or buy your next car?

A lease requires little or no money up front and offers lower monthly payments. But when the lease ends you are left without a car and need to replace it.

Advantages of Leasing

- You can drive a better car for less money.

- You can drive a new car every few years.

- No trade-in hassles at the end of the lease.

Advantages of Buying

- When interest rates are low, it makes more financial sense to own a car rather than lease it.

- No mileage penalty.

- Increased flexibility—you can sell the car whenever you want and make aftermarket modifications if you wish.

4. Have you considered all vehicles in that class?

Today's new car and truck market is filled with great models to choose from. Most shoppers have difficulty keeping up with all of the vehicles manufacturers introduce and the changes they make to their older vehicles. Therefore, it's important to do thorough research.

5. Have you considered all of the costs of ownership?

Before you commit to one car, you should estimate the long-term ownership costs of the vehicle you are considering. These include depreciation, insurance, maintenance and fuel costs. The Edmunds.com Web site has a feature called True Cost to Own^{SM} (TCO). Take this into account when considering prices and affordability.

6. Avoid the dealership until you are ready to test-drive.

Car buyers have been trained to visit their local dealer lots to find the car they want. In the Internet age, this is unnecessary and can cost you money. In the Internet age, you can arm yourself with pricing information before you set foot on the lot. Car dealers are slowly waking up to a new breed of shopper and have created the Internet department, which is a separate department within a dealership dedicated to the educated buyer who already knows what he or she wants and is willing to pay. The only things you have to do in person are test-drive the car and sign the contract.

7. Scheduling an appointment for a test-drive.

It's a good idea to make your initial contact with a dealership by e-mail or telephone before going there in person. One option that won't cost you anything is to visit the Edmunds.com Web site and select the car that interests you. Follow the prompts to send out simultaneous e-mails to competing dealerships in your area. In return, you will get contact names and numbers for Internet managers at each local car lot. Make follow-up phone calls to get a sense of the atmosphere you will be dealing with throughout the buying or leasing process. If you can establish a rapport with a specific salesperson, it can boost your confidence when you arrive on the lot.

Ask the salesperson if the car you're looking for—in the right color and trim level—is actually on the lot. If the car is available, tell the Internet salesperson that you want to set up a test-drive—but that you won't be buying right away. However, assure them that you will buy there if you decide to purchase this particular make and model, and if they can offer the vehicle at a price you feel is fair.

8. How to test-drive a car.

The goal of a test-drive is to experience—as closely as possible—the same type of driving conditions the car will be used for after purchase. If you commute, take the car on similar roads, be they stop-and-go traffic or freeway driving (likely both if you live in an urban area). If you frequently go into the mountains, try to find some steep grades to climb. Drive over bumps, take tight corners at aggressive (but not dangerous) speeds and test the brakes in a safe location, such as a deserted parking lot. Get in and out of the car several times and be sure to sit in the backseat, especially if you plan on carrying passengers. In short, ask yourself what it will be like to live with this car for a number of years.

While you are evaluating the car, don't be distracted by the salesperson's pitch. Don't drive with the radio on—you can evaluate that later. A new car is a big investment; make sure you spend enough time really looking at it. And then, consider one last thing: your intuition. If you are uneasy about this car, follow your instincts. A vehicle purchase decision is too important (and expensive) to undertake without total confidence.

9. After the test-drive.

After the test-drive, you will need to leave the car lot. Why? Because you will probably need to drive other cars at other dealerships. It's a good idea to do all of your test-driving in one morning or afternoon. Driving the cars back-to-back will help you uncover even minor differences, which will lead to a more educated purchase decision.

So, how do you get out of the clutches of the salesperson? Just remind them you still have other cars to drive and you can't make a decision yet. Most good salespeople will respect that. If they don't, you probably shouldn't be coming back to make a deal with them anyway.

10. Getting ready for the buying cycle.

At this point you should have considered all the cars in the class that interest you. You should have a good idea what you can afford. You should have test-driven your top choices. You should also know if you want to buy or lease your next car.

Now it's time to narrow down your choices to one car and make a deal. If you plan on leasing, read the "10 Steps to Leasing a New Car." If you are going to buy your next car, read "10 Steps to Buying a New Car." In either case, take a moment to congratulate yourself. You have done your homework to find the right car for you. Now you can move forward with confidence.

Buying a New Car

So you've decided what car you want to buy. Now it's time to locate the actual car and make a deal. This means you will have to negotiate for the car—a scary thought, right? Actually, we can show you how to make this process easy and even fun. We'll even show you some alternatives to going to the dealership that will get you on the road to new car owner paradise.

Chapter 4
What Kind of Buyer Are You?

We were talking to a friend one day about car buying when he suddenly said, "I invented my own strategy for buying a car."

Naturally, we wanted to know what his method was.

"See, I clip out ads from a bunch of different dealers and paste them into a notebook," he said. "Then, I scrawl notes all over the page as if I've really gone to all those dealerships. I write in the invoice price, cross it out and write in two or three hundred dollars over the invoice price to make it look like I've negotiated aggressively for the car."

"What's the point of all that?" we had to ask.

"You'll see," he said, becoming excited. "Now, I'm ready to deal. I go to the nearest dealership, carrying this notebook, and I say, 'Look, guys, I've been to five dealerships and gotten prices. If you can beat their price, I'll buy the car from you, here, today.' Then I open my notebook and pretend to be looking at price quotes from other dealerships."

"How does it work?" we asked.

"Great! I get cars—high-end luxury cars—for less than anyone else I know."

"Because of your notebook?"

"Because of my notebook."

Different Strategies for Different Buyers

We're not recommending that you use our friend's notebook strategy. You really don't have to go to those lengths just to get a great deal. The reason we brought it up was that we wanted to make an important point. There isn't just one path to buying a car. There are many different routes to achieve new-car happiness.

Now, you might be asking, what is the right method for me?

Well, that depends on what kind of a buyer you are. At the end of this section, we've included our "10 Steps to Buying a New Car," which we think is the best way for most people to buy a car. It is fast, easy and will save you money. But before you take our word for it, you should ask yourself this question:

"What kind of a car buyer am I?"

To answer this, consider the following questions:

- Do you hate negotiating?

- Do car salespeople give you the creeps?

- Do you simply want good reliable transportation—or are you searching for a specific make, model and color?

- Will you be satisfied with a "fair deal"? Or do you expect rock-bottom prices?

- Do you like doing hours of research and crunching numbers?

- Do you have several days to devote to car shopping? Or do you need wheels now?

It's a good idea to clarify your goal and your intentions right now because different outcomes will require a slightly different path. Let's look at these questions one by one.

Do you hate negotiating?

Most people hate negotiating. However, keep in mind that our 10 Steps removes most of the haggling while letting you arrive at a good price for the car you are buying.

Do car salespeople give you the creeps?

There are some truly creepy car salespeople. But there are also some excellent, professional car salespeople who can make the car-buying process easy and enjoyable for you. We'll help you find these salespeople and make the most of their abilities.

Do you just want good reliable transportation—or are you searching for a specific make, model and color?

If you want a good reliable car at a low price, it will be difficult to narrow the field to the right make and model (make sure you read the "Finding the Right Car for You" section of this book). If you already have your heart set on a specific car, in a hard-to-find color, you will have the opposite problem. You may find yourself having to issue a statewide all-points bulletin for the one car in your area that matches your criteria. It can be done, but it could be a challenge.

Will you be satisfied with a "fair deal"? Or do you expect rock-bottom prices?

Not surprisingly, price has plenty to do with your level of satisfaction in the car-buying experience. Your expectations at the outset will guide you through the process. If you are like most consumers, you want to know you got a "fair deal"— about what other people are paying. You definitely don't want to walk away with

the feeling that you've been taken. Ed-munds.com's True Market Value price (TMV®) will tell you what other buyers in your area are paying for the same vehicle. Later in this section, we'll show you how to use TMV® pricing to get your "fair deal." If you want to try to squeeze every penny out of the deal, we'll give you some pointers there, too.

Chandler Phillips Says:

Choose a shopping and negotiating style that fits your personality.

Do you like doing research and crunching numbers?

Getting a great deal is really a combination of elements: getting the right car at a good price with the right financing and a competitive interest rate. So, if you focus too much on one aspect of the deal, another may go unnoticed and bite you. It's a good idea to review the numbers carefully, but always keep the big picture in mind.

Do you have lots of time to devote to car shopping? Or do you need wheels now?

Many people turn car shopping into a week-long event. Others become so obsessed with finding the perfect car that they remain in the research phase for months, like the perennial student who can't face real life so he keeps taking college classes. If you need wheels now, and you work full-time, you might have only a weekend—or several weekday evenings—to shop for your next car. That's plenty of time to get the done job correctly.

Hopefully, the above questions and answers have helped you to recognize your shopping tendencies. Keep this information in mind as you move forward to the next all-important consideration: pricing the car you want to buy.

Chapter 5

Car Prices—How Much Should You Pay?

Until recently, people had no idea where to start when making an opening offer for a car. Consumers knew they weren't supposed to pay MSRP (or "sticker price") for the car. But they didn't want to make an offer that was so low the salesperson would laugh in their face or get angry (or pretend to get angry). The situation is further complicated by incentives, rebates and fluctuating interest rates. Many buyers know there are amazing incentives and rebates, but they are unsure of how to use them for maximum savings.

Edmunds used to recommend that consumers make an opening offer that was 4 percent over the invoice price of the car—in other words, the dealer made roughly 4-percent profit. The problem with this tactic is that some cars are in high demand and will sell for MSRP and above; other cars go for close to invoice. How could the average car buyer, who had no special knowledge of the marketplace, be expected to know which cars fit into what category?

Introducing Edmunds.com True Market Value® Pricing

Recognizing the confusion about pricing, Edmunds.com devised a new approach to car buying. Using a huge databank of actual car transactions, and testing figures with a network of dealers, Edmunds.com began posting True Market Value® (TMV®) prices on our Web site. These prices represent the *average price at which specific cars are sold.*

This means that, if you are buying a certain car, you can look up the TMV® price for the car (adjusted for a variety of elements including options, colors and region) and get a specific price to offer to a car dealer. When the offer is made, there is a high likelihood that it will be accepted. In case you missed it, the Edmunds.com TMV® figures are intended to be "transaction prices" not "asking," "listing" or "starting" prices. TMV® prices are also computed for used vehicles and trade-ins.

Important Pricing Terms

You should become familiar with these pricing terms before you go car shopping:

INVOICE PRICE: This is the amount the dealer paid for the car. There are other elements influencing how much the dealer actually paid, including the "holdback" amount (see "Dealer Holdback" sidebar, page 49). Invoice is generally considered to be the rock-bottom price for the car and all the options including destination charge.

STICKER PRICE: Also called MSRP (manufacturer's suggested retail price) and the "Monroney." This is the amount that the dealer would like you to pay for the car. This price is proudly displayed in the window of a new car. Often, the salesperson will begin negotiations at the sticker price. While you should usually not pay the full sticker price, there is a lot of good information on the "window sticker" such as what options are included and the breakdown of all the extras plus the destination fee. Note: tax and title fees are not included on the sticker.

EDMUNDS.COM TMV® PRICE: Using a database of actual transactions, Edmunds.com sets the TMV® price for every car currently for sale. This price is adjusted for specific regions, colors and, if you want, options. We also show prices for the vehicle with "typical options." This is handy because it lets you know the price of cars you are likely to find for sale on the car lot. Our TMV® prices are tested by calling dealer contacts and confirming the price with them. The TMV® price is the average amount that other buyers in your area are paying for a specific car.

Car buyers across the country began printing out TMV® prices from the Edmunds.com Web site and presenting them to car salespeople for the car they were negotiating to buy. In other cases, we received reports from car dealers saying that they would lead consumers to a computer terminal on the showroom floor, log on to Edmunds.com and show them the TMV® prices. Still other dealers resented the fact that Edmunds.com was telling consumers what a "fair" price was for their cars. Clearly, the reception of TMV® took many different forms, but one thing was clear: TMV® was the wave of the future, because it made the car-buying process easier for consumers.

How to Use TMV®

In the heat of the moment, the figures may blur in front of the average car shopper's eyes. As the salesman begins his tap dance, and the excitement rises, even the savviest shopper might lose control of the numbers. It's important to do your research ahead of time and determine how much you should pay.

Further complicating the process is the fact that, when you actually get to the car lot, you might decide to buy a different car than the one you priced out. You might find a car with different options than what you initially configured. All these things will change the price you should pay for the car. But here's a way to stay in control as the variables change.

Before you ever set foot on the lot, look up the price of the car on the Edmunds.com Web site. Take note of where the TMV® price is in relation to the invoice price. Is the TMV® $200 over invoice? Or is the TMV® a thousand over invoice? Or, is it basically sticker price? Once you answer this question, it is relatively simple to move from one car to another car with different options (as long as it's the same trim level). Just keep in mind that if the car sells for $500 over invoice, or whatever the actual TMV® is, you can't go wrong. (Note: there may be some exceptions in hard-to-find option packages such as all-wheel drive. Whenever possible, always check TMV® on our Web site for the latest prices. And take a moment to use the "Price with Options" feature to arrive at a specific price.)

Chandler Phillips Says:

Knowing TMV® is like seeing someone else's cards while you're playing poker.

Revealing the Hidden Costs of Ownership

Edmunds.com has created a powerful feature called True Cost to Own℠ (TCO) that reveals all the related costs of car purchasing and ownership. This clearly shows that while some cars can be purchased for less, they will be more expensive to own in the long run due to related costs. Consumers rarely consider these additional costs (depreciation, insurance, maintenance, repairs, etc.) during the buying process. We suggest you carefully review the figures in our TCO tables. Go to the Edmunds.com home page and look for the link to TCO. If you are considering several cars, put them all to the TCO test. What you discover may surprise you.

Checking Incentives and Rebates

Incentives, in several different forms, are increasingly used by car manufacturers to lure car shoppers into the marketplace. In some cases, these inducements are so strong they catch the eye of consumers who intended to put off buying a new car for several years. The deals are just too good to pass up, so they jump at a "limited time offer."

The word "incentive" is the most general of several methods used to attract shoppers. It can be anything that provides an added incentive to buy one manufacturer's car or a specific model. Typically, incentives are used for cars that aren't selling well. By offering a $500 customer cash rebate, the models would often begin to fly off the showroom floor. Another popular incentive is low-interest—and even no-interest—financing. Still another incentive might be the offer to allow a current customer to terminate a current lease prematurely, with no penalty, as long as they jump into a lease or purchase for a new car from the same manufacturer.

Finally, there are certain incentives that are offered from the manufacturer to the dealer—without notifying the public. This "dealer cash" used to be difficult for consumers to find out about. Now, however, dealer cash rebates are listed on the Edmunds.com Web site as "Marketing Support."

How to Use Incentives

A certain amount of confusion revolves around how to use the incentives offered by dealers. First, keep in mind that the incentives are actually offered by the manufacturer to the dealer to help move cars. Therefore, many exceptions and qualifications exist. And some rebates may not be available in your region. At Edmunds.com we try to be as specific as possible about who can use the incentives. However, the final determination is up to the dealer. Furthermore, when you talk to the salesperson, they might be as confused as you are about what is available and how it can be used. Be patient. Do your research. Check with other dealers.

On the other hand, incentives are sometimes used by car salespeople to maximize profit for the dealership (what a surprise!). Offers of low-interest financing bring buyers into the dealership. But once they are on the lot, and excited about buying a new car, they find that they don't qualify for the lowest interest rate. They are at the dealer, ready to take the plunge, so they buy the car anyway. In another case, the sales manager might use a $1,000 customer cash rebate to drive the price down to TMV® or invoice. In truth, the price should have been TMV® less the rebate.

At this point you might be thinking, "But if it's a rebate, why don't I just get the cash back?" You can do this if you want since the cash belongs to you. But most shoppers apply the rebate as a down payment to reduce their monthly payments. In any case, remember that you should negotiate your best purchase price for the car based on the latest TMV® price on our Web site, then *remove the amount of the rebate*. As you negotiate, keep repeating: "So you are proposing I pay $20,000, minus the $1,000 rebate, so that would be $19,000 total cost for me. Right?"

Incentives are a powerful buying tool. Make sure you check Edmunds.com for the very latest incentives so you know what is available before you make your final decision about what to buy—and what you can afford. With low-interest rates and cash back, maybe you can afford a better vehicle than you thought possible.

Chandler Phillips Says:

Rebates are great but remember that they make the car you've bought depreciate more quickly. Your resale value won't be as high.

Dealer Holdbacks

Dealer holdback is a percentage of either the MSRP or invoice price of a new vehicle (depending on the manufacturer) that is repaid to the dealer by the manufacturer. The holdback is designed to supplement the dealer's cash flow and indirectly reduce "variable sales expenses" (code words for sales commissions) by artificially elevating the dealership's paper cost.

Contrary to what some consumers think, the holdback itself can't really be used as a bargaining chip. However, knowing about it might help you get a better deal on a new car. How?

Dealerships must have an inventory of cars on hand so that consumers can browse and ultimately select a vehicle. Dealerships pay for their cars when they come from the manufacturer, and the amount paid is the price reflected on the invoice, the so-called "invoice price."

Now the twist: when holdbacks were introduced some years ago, most manufacturers inflated the invoice prices for every vehicle by a predetermined amount (2-3 percent of MSRP is typical). The dealer pays that inflated amount when it buys the car from the manufacturer. But later, at predetermined times (usually quarterly), the manufacturer reimburses the dealer for that excess amount. This is the "holdback," so named because funds are "held back" by the manufacturer and released only after the vehicle is invoiced to the dealership.

Why the sleight-of-hand? Holdbacks can benefit dealers in three ways:

1. Dealerships borrow money to finance cars based on an invoiced amount that includes the holdback. So the higher the invoiced amount, the more the dealership can borrow.

2. Inflating the dealership's "cost" can increase profit, since sales personnel are paid commissions based on the "gross profit" of each sale. Holdbacks lower the gross profit and thus the sales commissions.

3. Holdbacks enable dealerships to advertise "invoice price" sales and sell their vehicles at or near invoice and still make hundreds of dollars on the transaction.

Dealers consider holdback money "sacred" and are unwilling to share any portion of it with the consumer. Don't push the issue. Your best strategy is to avoid mentioning the holdback during negotiations. Mention holdback only if the dealer gives you a song-and-dance about not making money on the proposed deal when you know that isn't true.

In summary, holdback is nice to know, but is just one small piece of a complex puzzle.

Chapter 6

Should You Trade in Your Used Car?

Many people want to take care of all their car-related transactions in a single session: buy a new car and trade in their old one. However, if you trade in, you will not be paid the full value of your car. This may mean you are losing three, four or five thousand dollars, sometimes even more.

Check the Edmunds.com used vehicle prices and you'll see that the difference between the private party sale price for a car and the trade-in price is often $3,000 or more. Furthermore, the actual trade-in figures offered by dealerships are often substantially lower than those listed by popular pricing guides. Dealerships deduct value for extra miles, and they also have a "reconditioning" fee to clean, inspect and possibly repair your car (from $500 to $1,000).

Assuming that the dealer actually gave you the published trade-in price of your used car, you could still easily save $3,000 by selling the car yourself. You may be surprised to find out that dealerships actually make more money selling used cars than they do selling new cars. Furthermore, they make more money selling parts and service than they do on new and used vehicles combined.

So you see, the dealer makes lots of money on used cars even though, from your point of view, they seem less valuable. But there's another reason not to trade in your vehicle. Trading in your used car makes the deal more complicated. You have several different numbers to negotiate on: the down payment, monthly payment, value of the trade-in and the purchase price of the car. This allows the dealers to hide profit and give you what might look like a good deal when, in fact, it isn't.

Chandler Phillips Says:

Dealers will act like they are doing you a favor taking your old car as a trade-in. Don't be misled—they will charge thousands more for it on their used car lot.

If You Must Trade in

Despite our warnings, there are still those people who feel trading in their old car is the only way to go. Furthermore, in some states, trading in will allow you to avoid paying some sales tax on a portion of your new car transaction. There are even times when a dealer will accept a car in trade that you don't think you could sell on the open market at any price.

If you decide you must trade in, here are some guidelines to follow:

- **Check the Edmunds.com TMV® trade-in price for your vehicle.** The Edmunds.com "Used Car Appraiser" will give you a specific, accurate price for a used car. Include all options and record your mileage so value can be added or deducted accordingly. Be realistic when evaluating the condition of your car.

- **If you owe money on the trade-in, make sure you call the bank for the exact payoff amount.** Find your payment stub and call the 800 number of the finance company. Bring payoff information with you to the dealership.

- **Clean your car thoroughly and fix anything that is broken.** Remove all personal clutter (including the petrified French fries under the seat). The money you spend washing and detailing your car will increase "curb appeal."

- **Change the oil and oil filter.** The dealer may check the dipstick to make sure the car's engine has been properly cared for.

- **If larger repairs are needed, get a cost estimate.** The value of your car is reduced with every flaw, so know exactly how much repairs will cost.

- **Be prepared to "sell" your car to the dealer.** They may ask you to justify the price you are asking.

- **If you are seriously "upside down" on the car, consider postponing your new car purchase.** Being upside down means you owe more on a car loan than your vehicle is worth.

- **It is possible to shop your trade-in by going to several dealerships to get the best bid.** If the new car you want to buy is easy to locate, make your trade-in the focus of your shopping. Go to several dealerships and get their best offer on your trade-in. Ask for the "actual cash value" price of your car. Once you get three trade-in offers, this could tell you where to go to buy your new car. A note of caution: If one trade-in quote is exceptionally high, beware—they may be teasing you into negotiations.

- **See if your state offers a tax advantage to trading in.** See if you live in one of the states that allow you only to pay tax on the difference between your trade-in and the new car purchase.

Using the information here, you might be able to make your trade-in work to your advantage. It's unlikely you will receive the full value for it, but the convenience of getting everything out of the way at one time is worth every penny to many consumers.

Chapter 7

Dealerships: Where Will You Buy Your Car?

By now, you're probably itching to hit the dealership lot and find the car you're after. But before you go any further, you should decide what kind of a dealership to shop at.

Evaluating Dealerships

Not all dealerships are created equally. Of course you want to go to a car lot where you will be treated fairly and get a good price. How do you know—ahead of time—what type of business you will be dealing with?

Here are the different types of dealerships you may encounter:

1. High volume/high pressure

2. Turnover houses

3. Mom and pop-style or small-town dealerships

4. Straight-sale car lots

5. "No-haggle" dealerships

High-volume dealerships are often found in auto malls and usually have the widest assortment of cars to choose from. It is assumed that, because there is a big inventory, you can get big savings. However, with the high volume seems to come high-pressure salespeople. Bargains can be had here—if you can take the heat.

"Turn-over houses" are dealerships where you are turned over from one salesperson to the next. The salesperson who greets you is the first of many people you will interact with. If salesperson #1 feels he or she is not moving you toward a sale, you will be turned over to salesperson #2. That salesperson will eventually turn you over to a "closer." This is no fun for you. And it doesn't help you select the right car or get the best price. High-volume dealerships tend to use the turnover method of selling.

Who's Who at the Dealership

It will help you to know who the cast of characters is at the dealership. And who holds the power.

The Salesperson: At some dealerships, the salesperson has little power to approve a deal. They usually take your offer to the sales manager for approval. Some sales-people are "green peas" who have just started. In other cases veteran salesmen have lots of negotiating experience and the power to approve a deal.

The Closer: At some car lots a closer is used to try to sweeten the deal that is roughed out by the salesperson. If you have been negotiating for some time and a second salesperson suddenly appears, this is probably a closer.

The Sales Manager: Deals are taken to the sales manager for approval. The sales managers will also serve as closers to try to sweeten deals or bring commitment from hesitant buyers.

The GM: The GM or general manager is the highest ranking person at the dealership on a day-to-day basis. Usually, the GM doesn't get involved in specific deals but will step in if there is trouble.

The Internet or Fleet Manager: These salespeople work separately from the sales-people "on the floor" (the showroom floor). They handle deals that come through the Internet or deals involving fleet vehicles. Usually, buyers can get better prices through the Internet and fleet department than by going the traditional route through the showroom.

Mom and pop-style dealerships might be found in a small town. They are usually responsive to local customers because they know they will likely be repeat customers. You don't necessarily get the lowest price here, but you will probably have a decent sales experience.

Straight-sale dealerships are those where you are with your salesperson through the entire transaction (you might have an additional person draw up the contract in the finance and insurance department). This is good news if you have a rapport with your salesperson.

"No-haggle" dealerships were pioneered by Saturn, but there are other such car lots cropping up across the country. You simply pay the price listed on the car's window sticker—supposedly already a rock-bottom figure—without negotiating. Some people feel the relaxed buying experience is worth it even if they end up paying a little more. Furthermore, the buyer can concentrate on his or her needs, and not the dealership's income requirements.

A Word About Small-Town Dealerships

Most car-buying literature is focused on urban and suburban car buying, leaving rural shoppers to fend for themselves. But we've picked up some insights into the differences between the country and the city dealerships— and come up with some tips to save you money anywhere.

Chandler Phillips Says:

If you feel uneasy about the way you're being treated at a dealership, negotiate with your feet by walking out. Try another car lot where you're treated with respect.

The key as a rural shopper is to not limit yourself just to the local dealership. The phone and Internet are tools that can help a person in the boonies get as good a price as someone in the middle of Metro Los Angeles where there are hundreds of competing stores.

And it's not just rural shoppers who can save. In some cases, city dwellers can spot deals at smaller lots and get a better deal than they could at their bargain basement auto mall.

Knowing that an urban dealership is more dependent on volume than high profits on their cars doesn't necessarily mean you will get your best deal in the city and the worst deal at a rural store. But knowing generally how they are set up will position you to get the best deal possible by being familiar with how the business works.

Let's first approach this question from the rural buyer's point of view. Small-town dealerships are set up to generate as much repeat business as possible. As the old saying goes, "We don't want to sell them one car, we want to sell them five cars over the course of 20 years."

As such, rural dealerships are:

- Often deeply rooted in the town's culture. They sponsor the town's football scoreboard or buy Little League jerseys for kids.

- The owners are pillars of the community and members of social groups and city government boards.

- Their customers have bought many cars from the same dealership over the years.

- The customers have usually dealt with the same salesman or sales manager every time.

- Customers aren't pressured because there is an existing relationship between the dealer and the buyer.

Compare this with a city or suburban dealership:

- The owner is likely a corporation, reclusive sports star or distant businessperson.

- In the pursuit of profits, they are as lean and mean as possible, cutting extra costs.

- Turnover among the sales staff is high—you won't see the same guy you bought from four months ago, let alone four years ago.

- A person who buys a car might be one of several dozen buying that day.

- The dealership at peak hours is a circus—personal attention has given way to pressure to get deals closed quickly.

- Because of their large volume, larger dealers often get more special models of popular cars.

With these factors in mind, a person in rural areas can bargain with their local dealership by using prices they got from a larger dealership in a metro area. Simply use the Internet to locate and price the car you want and take that price to your local dealer. That way, you get the "down home" service and a great price. If the locals can't beat city price, and it's worth it to you, then drive to the city to get your deal. You can always have it serviced close to home—and they will be happy to get your repair business.

Conversely, a person in the city can sometimes find a particular car cheaper at a rural dealership. One Utah dealership we talked with had been holding on to a Pontiac GTO for months after it arrived because it had an automatic transmission. The owner said he would likely have to sell it for less than a dealership in a larger market just to clear out space for new inventory.

Fees can also vary between city and rural dealerships. Often, a smaller dealership in a more rural city can get cars delivered more easily, leading to lower transportation fees.

At the same time, many small-town dealerships we visited had hundreds of dollars of dealer extras added on to the price of the car. These things like "clear-coating" or "paint protection" and nicer rims or chrome detailing are valuable additions to a car, but they are rarely worth what the dealers are charging for them. Make sure to negotiate these out of the price, or at least down to market value.

Chandler Phillips Says:

Sometimes having a personal relationship with the salesman makes it harder to negotiate. But take a close look at the numbers to make sure you really are getting a good deal.

Your Shopping Checklist

When heading for the car lot, make sure you bring the following:

1. Notebook, pen, calculator

2. Valid driver license

3. Edmunds.com printouts of TMV® prices for car's make, model and options

4. Edmunds.com printouts showing the price of your trade-in

5. Preapproved financing (a blank check from credit union or on-line lender)

6. Any dealer ads that show incentives and rebates

7. Account number and buyout information for loan on your trade-in

8. Proof of insurance or the number for your insurance agent

9. Checkbook or credit card for making a down payment

10. Take along a trusted friend for moral support

Chapter 8

Locating the Car You Want to Buy

If you are flexible about the options and color you want, and the car you are considering is widely available, you won't have much trouble finding the exact car you want to buy. Furthermore, your flexibility will also put you in a stronger bargaining position since you can easily go to another car lot and get the car if you don't get fair treatment at the first dealership. We'll call this person the *"flexible shopper."*

However, if you are seeking a car with specific options and in a hard-to-find color, you might have a real search on your hands. And, when you do locate the right car, you won't be in a strong position to bargain since there is nowhere else you can go to get it. We'll call this person the *"specific shopper."*

The "Flexible Shopper" Approach to Car Buying

The "flexible shopper" will probably want to use Edmunds.com's tool for soliciting quotes from different dealerships in your area. Send the quotes in and wait for either e-mail or phone replies. In many cases you will have to follow up with phone calls. Consult the e-mails you have received for the name and contact information for the Internet dealerships.

When you reach the sales or Internet manager, say something like this:

"I'm looking for the '04 Matsura Accell. I'm not fussy about the color, but I don't want black or white. I want the LE trim level without many options. Can you tell me what you've got on the lot?"

At this point, the Internet manager might say, "We've got Accells all over our lot. Come on down and we'll get just the right car for you."

This is a typical ploy by car salespeople who don't think you are "for real" unless you are standing there in front of them. So, you might want to get a little more specific and say, "Wow, that's great. You know, my favorite color is that

Mystic Blue. Do you have any of those in the LE trim level?"

At this point, a good salesperson will probably go to the computer and look through their inventory. If they do, in fact, have the car you have named, then ask: "What options does the car have on it?" After you write down all the options, you should then ask, "What's the sticker on that car?" Salespeople are willing to give you the sticker, but many of them will hesitate to give you an actual selling price over the phone.

By this time you have had a chance to interact with the salesperson for a few minutes. You may have some feeling for how well he or she responds to your questions and how knowledgeable they seem. Think of this as a "test-drive" for the salesperson. Now, you not only know if it is worth driving down to this car lot, you also know if you want to continue working with this salesperson. After only a five-minute phone call, you are a much better prepared shopper.

The "Specific Shopper" Approach to Car Buying

The task for the "specific shopper" is somewhat more difficult. You should throw a wider net and contact more dealerships via email using Edmunds.com. After receiving the name and contact information of the Internet manager, call and ask for what you are looking for in the following manner:

"I want to buy the '03 Matsura Accell LE in Sunblast Orange with side airbags and adjustable pedals. I'd also like the Convenience Package and rear-sensing feature. The Convenience Package is 'must-have,' but the rear-sensing feature isn't a deal breaker."

Now, in the shortest amount of time, you've conveyed what you want on the car and what, if anything, you are flexible about. If the salesperson is good, he will take careful notes and offer to call you back with the result of his search. In some cases, a computer search will turn up what you are looking for. In still other cases, a salesperson might offer to try to obtain the car from another dealership.

Chandler Phillips Says:

Remember that being overly specific about the kind of car you want may make it harder to negotiate a low price.

If the dealership is nearby, and you particularly like the salesperson helping you, this might be an attractive option. However, you should reach an agreement on the selling price before you let them do this for you. In most cases, you will get a

---

Dodging Dealer Trades

When you ask a salesman if they have a specific car in stock, they may answer, "No, but I can get it." What they are intending to do is arrange a "dealer trade." This means that they will trade a car of equal value on their lot for the car you want to buy that is on another lot. Often, car salesmen will claim they can get you a car before they even look into it. They do this to "take you off the market," to stop you from shopping elsewhere.

Is a dealer trade in your best interest? Not if you are in a hurry, since it could take several days for the trade to be completed. And when it does arrive it will have more miles on it since it is usually driven to the new dealership rather than trucked there. Also, a salesman might quote you a certain price for a car but then find out that the trade was more costly for the dealership than expected. In this case they might renegotiate the deal and ask you to pay more.

It's a good idea to avoid dealer trades if you can. For many reasons, it is easier for you to go to the car than to have the car brought to you.

---

better price buying from the available inventory of a dealership.

More About Using Dealer Locator

When the Internet was first used as a tool for buying cars, it had high promises and low delivery. In the past five years the process has been streamlined to the point where you can easily accomplish all the steps of car buying on-line.

Start the process by going to Edmunds.com and looking for the link at the top of the home page that says, "Free Price Quotes." Answer the prompts to configure the car exactly the way you want it. A pop-up screen will then ask you if you want a free quote from local dealers. Click on as many local dealers as

Chandler Phillips Says:

A call to the Internet manager is a good way to begin the relationship. You can usually get a sense of whether this is someone you want to deal with.

Action Script: Calling Dealerships

If you know what car you want, there's no point in driving all over town to find it. Calling the dealership is a faster way to locate your car—and avoid pushy salespeople. Here's how to get the information you need.

(Phone is answered by the receptionist.)

RECEPTIONIST
Welcome to Joe Covo Matsura. How may I direct your call?

SMART CAR BUYER
I'd like the Internet manager, please.

(Phone rings. Someone picks up.)

SALESMAN
Internet sales. Mike Austin.

SMART CAR BUYER
I'm looking for a Matsura Accell. I wonder if —

SALESMAN
We got Accells all over the lot. When can you come in?

SMART CAR BUYER
Actually, I'm looking for the Deja Blue, in LE trim.

SALESMAN
Got plenty of 'em. You want to come in at 4 o'clock or 5 o'clock?

SMART CAR BUYER
I've already test-driven it. I'm trying to find the blue LE with side airbags and CD changer. Do you have one on your lot?

SALESMAN
Hold on. (The sound of computer keys rattling.) I have two.

SMART CAR BUYER
Could you read me the options, please? (Salesman reads the options.) That's pretty close to what I want. What's the stock number and the sticker price?

SALESMAN
Stock number 01665—it looks like it stickers for $23,565. But we can probably do a little better than that for you. When do you want to come in?

SMART CAR BUYER
I'll have to check my schedule and call you back. I'll be sure to ask for you when I come in. Thanks for your help.

you want to receive quotes from.

Most Internet managers will not want to e-mail you a price for the car you are searching for. However, the Dealer Locator will help you find out where the car is and who the Internet manager is. One phone call will probably be enough to make a deal with the Internet manager over the telephone.

Locating High-Demand Cars

In some cases, you might be trying to buy a car that is just appearing in dealerships and is in high demand. You will have to call many dealerships and be willing to pay a lot more—up to sticker and above. Keep in mind that once the excitement dies down, the prices will begin to fall and wider availability will give you a better selection. However, if you must buy while the fad is raging, keep these points in mind:

- Just because the car is in demand doesn't mean you can't try negotiating a lower price.

- If local prices are way over sticker, call other areas of your city or state.

- Consider paying a deposit and ordering the vehicle configured just the way you want it.

- Don't accept the first price quote from a dealer—initial quotes are often inflated just to see if you'll bite.

- Besides inquiring about cars that are on the lot, ask about cars that might be on their way to the dealership within the next week or two.

Final Thoughts

While trying to locate just the right car might seem like a giant hassle, it is worth the effort. Try looking at the search as an exciting treasure hunt that will be successfully completed with a mixture of determination, resourcefulness and luck. Then, when you've found your dream car, it's time to move on to the next critical phase in the process—making a deal.

Chapter 9

Negotiating Basics

"I really hate negotiating."

Just the word "negotiating" might make your stomach tighten. Negotiating is the very reason people dislike buying cars. Although they don't realize it, people negotiate everyday with family members, friends, bosses and co-workers. But people aren't familiar with how to negotiate to buy a car.

OK, so, how can you navigate your way safely through this process and get the car you want at a fair price? There are several styles of negotiating that are effective when buying a car.

Chandler Phillips Says:

Most people say they hate negotiating. But with a little preparation you might find it exciting.

One man we knew was very hard of hearing. When he went to buy a car, he would test-drive it and then go into the showroom with the salesman. He would sit and smile pleasantly, as the salesman talked on and on about what a great car it was and what an amazing price he was willing to sell the car for. Then, after a while, our friend would excuse himself, get up and leave. He would return several days later and repeat the process with the same salesman who had, by now, lowered the price substantially. Finally, on the third visit, he would buy the car for whatever price the salesman had arrived at—often thousands below the starting point.

This gentleman negotiated with his feet. He walked out twice, each time cutting the price by almost a thousand dollars. He hadn't said a word—he hadn't even heard a word the salesman had said.

We don't recommend this style; it doesn't have to take that long. Besides that, not everyone is hard of hearing. Instead, we recommend you negotiate using the most deadly of all weapons: knowledge.

The Ultimate Negotiating Weapon

Set aside your resistance to negotiating for a moment. Instead, consider this revised description of the car-buying process:

The dealer has a car they want to sell to you. They know, ahead of time, the lowest price at which they are willing to sell the car. Now, here you come into the dealership. You want to buy the car. You want to pay as little as possible. The problem is, you don't know the lowest price at which the dealer will sell the car. If the dealer's lowest price is within your budget, you will buy the car.

To put it in even simpler terms: you and the dealer are trying to find the price that is agreeable to both of you.

This all sounds pretty obvious to you. But what makes it complicated is that, while the dealer has a rock-bottom price, he will try like crazy to get you to pay more than that. This is known as maximizing profit. And the difference between a good deal and a bad deal can be thousands of dollars on even a modestly priced car. So there is a lot at stake: specifically, your hard-earned money.

In the old days, the only way to find the dealer's best price was to make a low-ball offer. The salesman would go into hysterics and make a counteroffer that was a bit lower. You would raise your price and he would lower his price. This process would be punctuated with threats to walk out or suggestions you would take your business elsewhere. It was a time-consuming and stressful process.

Now, however, there is another way to go.

Arming Yourself With Figures

Keeping in mind that the dealer already has a rock-bottom price in mind that he will sell the car for, this question is apt to spring to mind: Wouldn't it be great if you knew, ahead of time, what the dealer's lowest price would be? Well, at Edmunds.com we publish the TMV® figures on our Web site (remember, this represents the average price that other consumers paid for this vehicle in your area). If you want, you can make a lower offer to test the waters first. You will probably find that you wind up right at our TMV®.

Does this sound almost too easy to be true? Actually, it works for both the consumer and the dealer. We've gotten e-mails from buyers who said they printed out the TMV® from the Internet, presented it to the car salesman and concluded the transaction without any further negotiation.

In the following chapter, we will cover several other alternatives to negotiating. But there is still one important concept to cover at this point. Most consumers are familiar with the concept of "shopping around" for the item they want. This is more important in car shopping than in probably any other field. We believe that if you simultaneously solicit quotes from car dealers through our Web site, and let them know you are visiting other dealerships for competitive quotes, you will very quickly arrive at the lowest price.

Keep in mind that you will get some resistance from the car salesperson. They may be hesitant to give you a firm price if they know you are just going to go to another dealership. They believe the next place you visit will get your business by beating their price by a few hundred dollars. Still, since you are trying to save money, it is important for you to try to find the lowest possible price. Your final decision of where to buy might actually be decided by other factors—finding exactly the car you want, or a salesperson who was easy to work with—rather than getting a rock-bottom price for the car.

Tips for Haggling

Here is a summary of points to follow when negotiating:

- Keep negotiations relaxed and impersonal.

- Don't negotiate with someone who intimidates you or you think will try to cheat you.

- Get as much information as possible before entering into negotiations—incentives information is essential.

- Have a target transaction price, where you want to end up—this should be at about TMV®.

- Start as low as possible but still in the ballpark.

- Improve your offer slowly.

- Make them negotiate in relationship to *your* opening offer rather than you negotiating in relationship to *their* opening offer.

- Know what terms you're negotiating in—"out the door" or only the price of the car.

- Before you agree to a deal, find out if there are any extra fees or hidden costs.

- Use offers from other dealers as ammunition.

- Walk out if you are not making progress or you don't like how you're treated.

- Negotiate lowest price, then deduct the customer cash incentives.

- Use reasons to support your low offer "other dealers have offered it at this price but I like your color better," "I'm trying to decide between two cars and I'll buy the one that costs the least."

- Don't show enthusiasm for the car.

Final Thoughts

If this chapter about negotiating hasn't completely put your mind at ease on this subject, turn to Chapter 11 on page 78. We will tell you about three secret car-buying avenues that can speed up the process and beat down the price.

Negotiating Script: Presenting an Opening Offer

Let's assume you have found the car you want and test-driven it. You have researched the car ahead of time and know what Edmunds.com's TMV® price is. You set an opening offer several hundred dollars below TMV®. Here is an example of a way to present your price to the salesperson.

This is just an example of one way to present your offer to a dealer. The important thing is to let the salesperson know that your offer is based on information, not something you pulled out of thin air.

> SALESPERSON
> So, are you interested in buying this car today?
>
> SMART CAR BUYER
> If we can reach a good price.
>
> SALESPERSON
> Let's go inside and we'll work out the numbers.
>
> (The salesperson leads the way into the dealership and escorts the customer into a sales office. The salesperson pulls out a "four-square" worksheet and fills in the name of the customer and the sticker price of the car.)
>
> SALESPERSON
> Where do you want to be on your monthly payment?
>
> SMART CAR BUYER
> I'll be paying cash. So I just want to talk about the price of the car. I've shopped around and done some research so I know what these cars are going for and what a reasonable price is. So I'm willing to pay $18,500.
>
> SALESPERSON
> Plus fees?
>
> SMART CAR BUYER
> I'll pay tax, title and license.
>
> SALESPERSON
> $18,500...that sounds awfully low.
>
> SMART CAR BUYER
> Actually, it isn't. I've been to two other dealerships and that's what they offered to me for similar cars. I like this color better so that's why I'm here.
>
> SALESPERSON
> You need to do a little better with your opening offer. If I take this to my boss, I'll look like the backside of a horse going north.
>
> SMART CAR BUYER (Stands up)
> OK then, I guess I'll have to talk to one of the other dealers.
> I can live with a different color.
>
> SALESPERSON
> Tell you what, I'll run this by my manager, see what he says.
> Maybe he's in a good mood today.

Chapter 10

Primer for Young Car Buyers

"Dude, where's my deal?"

It's hard enough being a normal car buyer, heading into a dealership and bargaining with professionals. But as a young car buyer, you run the risk of being pegged as a novice who can be manipulated or taken lightly. And in the auto game, that means more money for the dealer.

Car salespeople are trained by experience to "qualify" customers the moment they walk in the door, to find the best angle to part them from their money. And, let's face it, young customers have a reputation preceding them. Here are a few of the preconceived notions that car salesmen have about young buyers:

- They are impressionable, gullible and easy to manipulate.

- They don't know how to choose the right car.

- They have poor credit or no credit.

- They have little knowledge of financing issues.

- Their negotiating skills are poor.

- A lack of experience means they can't make good decisions.

Interestingly, we've found that these stereotypes about young people are simple to overcome. If you're adequately prepared, you'll end up getting a good deal no matter who you are. But—as we found in our experience—it takes a lot less haggling if the salesman respects you and your car-buying abilities.

An Undercover Shopper Tests the Market

To get a feel of how young buyers are treated, we sent Edmunds.com's 20-something consumer advice editor, Mike Hudson, out to shop undercover. Through simple changes in his clothes, companions and attitude, he experienced everything from the red carpet treatment and decent starting offers to aloof salespeople, suspicious questions and horrible lease terms. Over the course of several days, he discovered some general guidelines that can make the buying process easier and likely save you some cash in the end.

Lesson #1: Know what you want before you go

Lesson #2: Arm yourself with pricing and model information

Lesson #3: Be confident, be yourself

Lesson #4: Negotiate your terms

Lesson #5: Be ready to walk away

If you follow these five tips, chances are you'll end up with the car you want for much less than what others have paid. And, not surprisingly, following these lessons led to more enjoyable experiences for our undercover editor at the dealerships. Ignoring them led to costly manipulation and general discomfort with the process.

Chandler Phillips Says:

As a young buyer, attitude is very important. And the right attitude comes from being prepared.

Lesson #1: Know What You Want Before You Go

Many dealers see young buyers as impressionable, gullible and relatively easy to manipulate. So when a first-time buyer walks onto a lot without a clue as to what they want, they'll walk out with whatever the dealer wanted to sell.

Case in point, Mike and his neighbor, Ben, walked into a reputable high-end German car dealership near Los Angeles and met a salesman. They had decided to seem indecisive and uninformed to see how the salesman reacted.

"Looking for a 2005 small car, like a convertible or something," Mike said.

"Right, OK, that's fine… you sure you want the convertible?" the salesman asked.

"Not really. Just thought I might like one."

"Well," the salesman said, scanning the cars in the lot. "Let's take a look around."

Before long, Mike and Ben were driving last year's hardtop sedan that the dealership was likely trying to clear out to make way for the new models. It had even been in an accident during a previous test-drive. Clearly, this vehicle was a dog that the dealership had been trying to sell for some time. To get rid of it, the dealer simply talked down what Mike wanted in order to push a car he needed to sell.

Take two: Mike and his wife, Rebecca, walked into a Dodge dealership where they were greeted by a salesman. In this encounter they had decided to be a little more direct in what they wanted. They were curious to see how actively the salesman would try to deflect their first choice.

"What are you looking for?" the salesman asked.

"Jeep Wrangler Rubicon for my wife," Mike replied.

"Those are nice, but I personally think you'd prefer something with more storage space."

"We like the Rubicon."

"Well we've got a special on these other models here," he said, leading them toward a line of cars, none of which were Jeeps.

Despite asking for a specific vehicle, Mike and Rebecca were being twisted to drive a different model—one that the dealership likely could make more money on. Car salesmen call this "switching" the customer.

This is fine in the test-driving stage, but could have been costly if Mike and Rebecca were ready to buy. All of a sudden, Mike went from talking about a car he wanted to buy to one the dealer wanted to sell—for any number of unknowable reasons.

It's a good idea to separate the test-driving from the buying process. If you're married, have your spouse agree on the model before you go to the car lot so you can present a unified front to the sales team. Get all doubts about storage, engine size, safety features, space, price and reliability out of your mind before you set off to make a purchase. This way, a salesman can't put his or her needs ahead of yours in the buying process.

Lesson #2: Arm Yourself with Pricing and Model Information

Once you've made up your mind on a car, make sure to get solid information on how much the car should cost to buy or lease. This should include all options you might want and the "destination charge" (an unavoidable fee charged by the manufacturer). First-time buyers are notoriously under-prepared when it comes to financial matters. Most haven't bought a house or started investing to any great extent and are somewhat naïve about money matters. Unscrupulous dealers will take full advantage of this inexperience by using every trick in the book against young buyers.

Some salespeople use language as a trap to put buyers at a disadvantage. It might help young buyers to know what these questions are—and give some thought to how to answer them. Here's a sampling of the questions you'll often hear from salesmen:

- "How much are you looking to spend?"

- "What kind of monthly payment can you afford?"

- "What do you do for a living?"

- "If I give you a good deal, will you buy today?"

- "Wouldn't your neighbors be jealous if they saw you pull up in this car?"

Each of these seemingly harmless questions is designed to gain a commitment from you or to feel out you and your budget. Mike was even asked by one car salesman, "If I gave you this car for free, would you take it?" The idea was to pose a question that Mike was certain to give a "yes" answer to. The salesman then gradually sharpened the questions trying to gain a sales commitment from him.

In many cases, the best response to salesmen's probing questions is to be vague. For example, if you are hit with the classic car salesman's query: "If I give you a good deal, will you buy today?" the best answer might be, "That depends on the car and the deal you offer me."

"So how much are you looking to pay a month?" said one salesman to Mike and his wife.

"About $600 or so," Mike said.

Sure enough, when it came time to talk numbers, the offers started at $680 a month. If Mike had said $700, the dealing would have started at $780 a month—for the same car. And—no surprise—the salesman will always seem to find a car that is just barely in your range. But these tricks won't affect you if you know what you want and how much it should cost. An old negotiating rule is: the person who speaks first, loses. Make sure you only divulge the information that helps you retain a strong position in negotiations.

A good place to start is by getting pricing information. The invoice price—the price the dealer pays—can be obtained from several Web sites for a small fee. However, you can get it for free by using Edmunds.com. On our site you also can get the True Market Value pricing tool for any new or used car. So you'll know how much the dealer paid for the car and what he will sell it for. Furthermore, you can find out the invoice and fair price for all available options. So if you're being offered a car with a navigation system, you'll know how much more it should tack on to your price.

If you are financing the car, make sure you know what interest rates are for car loans. It's strongly recommended that you arrange preapproved financing from a credit union, bank or on-line lender beforehand to use as a negotiation tool.

After you get the TMV® price of the car and you are confident you have the money to buy, contact the Internet departments of dealerships by phone or e-mail to see if they have what you're looking for. They'll often quote you a price over the phone. Take careful notes and say you'll come look at the car on a convenient day.

Lesson #3: Be Confident, Be Yourself

Most young people have been taught to respect their elders. But that doesn't mean you shouldn't take control of this significant financial transaction even if the salesman is older than you. When you arrive at the dealership, walk in with the intention of doing business. You already know exactly what you want and what you're willing to pay for it. And when you show up prepared, you're taking home court advantage away from the dealer. You know what a good price is and you already know what kind of offers they are giving over the phone.

When it comes to negotiating, a confident demeanor is a potent weapon.

Don't strut around like you own the place or you'll get tagged as a foolhardy kid with money to waste. At the same time, don't act like you feel out of place or uncomfortable. Know what you want when you walk in, shake hands like you want to do business and give the impression that you have made major decisions in your life prior to now.

An important part of your dealership demeanor is your appearance. In Mike's experiment, a simple change from khakis and button-down shirt to a T-shirt and ball cap elicited a marked change in how he and his companions were treated.

Generally, with decent apparel, Mike was able to get immediate help, avoid manipulative questions and bargain without promises of purchasing a car that day. And when dressed down, he often had to ask for assistance and was steered away from top products for test-driving without promising to buy.

It's hard to say clothes will make a definite difference in how you are treated. Dealers know rich clients often come in rough packages. But for a young buyer, the last thing you need is another obstacle keeping you from a firm bargaining position.

Chandler Phillips Says:

While car shopping, young buyers should dress like they would for work.

A good rule of thumb is to dress like you would for work or a casual social event. That way, you'll be comfortable and not making a major statement either way.

To illustrate, Mike and Ben confidently walked into a Lexus dealership one sunny day well dressed as described above:

"We're here to drive the convertible, a silver one," Mike said.

"You want to buy it today?" the salesman demanded.

"Not sure. But I want to drive it."

"Then we'll drive it! Come along, gentlemen!"

Soon enough, they were being hit with Danish and coffee and given four-star treatment. No questions of what they did for living. No attempt to sell another model or color. And the salesman even bargained with Mike with no promises of a sale.

At a Mercedes dealership just an hour later, Mike and Ben dressed down:

"Who do I talk to about buying a car?" Mike said to two gentlemen coolly staring at him from inside the dealership after waiting many long minutes for assistance.

Need we say more?

These were best- and worst-case scenarios, but if the sales staff isn't respecting your intentions to buy up front, they aren't going to respect them when it comes time to negotiate. So, as you see, your attitude actually makes a difference in the price you pay.

Lesson #4: Negotiating on Your Terms

After you reject attempts to switch you to a different car, you can make an opening offer to the salesman. When you present them with the TMV® price, they might ask why you think you can get such a great deal. Clearly, they weren't expecting such savvy behavior from a young buyer. That means you are bargaining from a strong position. Go ahead and support your offer with solid reasons: tell them how you looked up invoice prices and know how much people pay for the car you want. Show them your TMV® printouts from Edmunds.com.

Don't submit to the "How much do you want your payment to be?" bargaining tactic. Tell them you have preapproved financing and you are a "cash buyer." This means you only have to negotiate the total purchase price.

It's a hard position to argue with and they'll probably take your offer to the sales manager. Chances are they'll try to get you to move up in price. Generally, we recommend you make one offer—a price you'd be happy to get but not a low-ball to feel them out. If you're asking a reasonable price, they'll take it. And the negotiations may go a lot faster than you'll expect.

But that doesn't mean your deal is sealed. You still have to negotiate financing and the dealership will be looking to make more money off you there.

Chandler Phillips Says:

Many dealers assume young buyers don't have good credit. Know what your credit rating is—or get preapproved financing—before you go to the car lot.

As we said earlier, it's a good idea to get an offer for financing from a bank beforehand. The dealership will often offer rebates or low interest rates if you finance with them. Read our section on financing for more information.

You may find that you can make a deal over the phone or even e-mail and avoid the face-to-face negotiating. In this case, your job at the dealership is to verify that your agreement was accurately put into writing. Also, inspect the car carefully before you sign the contract to confirm that it has the options and is the trim level you agreed on.

Lesson #5: Be Ready to Walk Away

At any point during this process, from test-drive to price negotiation to financing, you are well within your rights to walk out. This is called "negotiating with your feet." Don't concern yourself with how much time the salesman or dealership has put into helping you. Your decision to leave is likely to save you a lot of money and heartache.

Many young people are very susceptible to being pressured to buy after being helped by a salesman. Often being on the lower rung of whatever company or business they are in, young folks are very sympathetic to a car salesman having to tap dance for customers who don't buy anything. Salesmen will talk about how they are fighting for you with their manager or how many hours they've put in that week in order to play this up.

Chandler Phillips Says:

Young buyers need to learn to walk out when they aren't treated with respect.

But behind the scenes, salespeople aggressively try to use any tactic to get as much money as they can from their customers. You should be just as aggressive in paying as little as you need. And the ultimate bargaining chip is walking out.

There's usually another local dealership that can help get you a car, so if you are uncomfortable for any reason, tell the salesman or saleswoman what you're thinking. If it doesn't improve, leave.

When bargaining for his first car, Mike overheard the salesman and the manager at a Saab dealership attempting to humble him after making a very low—but fair—offer on a car:

"He's asking this price, boss," the salesman said.

"But he's just a kid! What does he know?" the manager loudly shouted to the entire dealership.

At that point, Mike told the salesman he would be leaving if they couldn't get an answer. Suddenly, the theatrics ceased and the deal was done. When all else fails, remember that you, as the buyer, have the ace-in-the-hole as the buyer… even if it is your first time.

Young Car Buyer's Checklist

- ❏ Research the car you want to buy before you go to the car lot
- ❏ Know what kind of car fits your budget
- ❏ Test-drive and buy on different days
- ❏ Use Edmunds.com calculators to generate lease or buying payments
- ❏ Get preapproved financing from a bank, credit union or on-line lender
- ❏ Know your credit score and resolve any credit problems ahead of time
- ❏ Use the phone, e-mail and dealership Web sites to locate the car you want to buy
- ❏ Bring along True Market Value® printouts
- ❏ Act confident and businesslike when you're in the dealership
- ❏ Contact the Internet or fleet manager of a dealership
- ❏ Be respectful but demand respect in return
- ❏ Don't negotiate with salespeople who attempt to pressure you
- ❏ Watch how you dress—what message are you sending?
- ❏ Take a friend or family member along for moral support

Chapter 11
Alternative Buying Strategies

"I wish there was an easier way to buy a car."

There are many different approaches to car buying. And each different approach will probably suit the personality of the buyer who uses it. We've come across three different ways of car buying that we will outline here. Each one of these methods has been used by Edmunds.com editors to buy cars and avoid the ordeal of negotiating eye-to-eye with the salesman.

These alternative buying strategies fall into three categories:

1. **Internet:** You can locate and bid for cars on-line via e-mail.

2. **Telephone:** Fleet and Internet managers will sell cars over the phone.

3. **Fax:** You can fax offers to nearby dealerships and take the lowest bid.

Shopping On-line

Since you've already test-driven the car you want to buy, all you have to do is find the exact vehicle that suits your needs and reach an agreement about the price. All this can be done without visiting a dealership in person.

Go to Edmunds.com and configure the car the way you want it. Then, look for the links to find local dealers. You can, with very few clicks, solicit quotes for a number of different dealers. You receive prices either by return e-mail or over the telephone.

Here are a few additional tips to consider when buying your car on-line:

- Get bids from multiple dealerships using Edmunds.com.

- While many Internet managers will be reluctant to give

you a quote via e-mail, they will often quote you a price when you make a follow-up telephone call.

- Get the quote in writing via fax so you can lock it in and the price won't change on you later.

- When you get a quote, make sure it includes all related costs—tax, title and DMV fees.

- If you are getting a lease quote, get a list of all drive-off fees and taxes.

Traditional vs. Internet Car Shopping—Mystery Shopping Test Case

In an effort to find out exactly what the cost savings is by going through the Internet department, two Edmunds editors conducted two mystery shopper projects.

Scenario #1

The Edmunds.com editors located and test-drove a midsize family sedan before entering the dealership and negotiating for the car. After a drawn-out discussion in which the salesman's manager double-teamed the editors, a price was offered at about $500 below the sticker price. The editors then extricated themselves from the salesman's grasp, a difficult task in itself. They then called the Internet manager of the same dealership and asked for a price on the same car. The manager provided the price without further cajoling or hassle. He quoted them a price of $500 over invoice. The difference between the two figures—and the presumed savings—was at least $1,000. The time difference it took to get the price was almost two hours faster through the Internet.

Scenario #2

In a second test case, the Edmunds.com editors went shopping for a hard-to-find convertible that was selling for sticker price. They went to several dealerships and offered $500 over invoice for the convertible. Their offer was taken to the sales manager but then abruptly rejected. A counteroffer was not even made by the dealership. They then turned to the Internet, located the convertible at a local ible at a local car lot and called the Internet manager. After a short conversation, the manager offered to discount the car $800 off the sticker price. He even said he could do a little better because he was eager to make the sale. More significantly, he easily waived the sale of both paint protection and an additional alarm which was listed on a separate sticker on the window. Edmunds.com purchased the convertible for $1,000 below sticker.

Chandler Phillips Says:

Bottom line, car shopping through the Internet saves time and money.

Using the Telephone

The telephone can be used to speed up your search and cut through the haggling process. Here are things that can be accomplished by calling—rather than visiting—a dealership. You can:

- Locate the car you want without hiking across acres of inventory

- Qualify the salesperson—if you like who you talk to, make an appointment

- Ask about rebates, incentives and interest rates

- Begin to negotiate or even reach a deal to buy a car (if you talk to the fleet or Internet manager)

- More easily escape rude, aggressive or pushy salespeople

Be aware that some dealerships will be vague or uncooperative over the phone. They think you are trying to get a quote from them, so you can "shop" their rate with other dealers' rates. Of course, this is exactly what you are trying to do. But most dealerships understand how competitive the marketplace has become. They will give you enough information to make an informed decision.

When you make a deal over the phone, repeat the figures and say, "Let me write that down." Even better, have them fax you a worksheet with all the figures on it. Sign it and fax it back. Now you have proof of your agreement. Get the name of the person you talked to and set an appointment to see them at the dealership.

Once you arrive at the dealership, you will still have to test-drive the vehicle and go through the finance and insurance process. But you will have avoided the stress of negotiating face-to-face.

Using a Fax Machine—Get Bids for your Business

If you are looking for a type of car that is readily available, and there are a number of dealerships in the area, let them bid for your business.

1. Get the fax numbers of the fleet or Internet managers at as many dealerships as you can.

2. Fax them a description of the vehicle you want and request a price quote from them.

3. Make sure you include all options and a list of preferred colors. You can sweeten the offer by stating that you will also have the car serviced at the dealership where you purchase it.

4. Be sure to put a time limit on your offer.

5. Sit back and wait for the bids to roll in.

Since the dealerships know they are bidding against other dealerships, they will be very competitive.

Once you have all the bids, call the dealership with the best offer and confirm the price. Make sure there is a stock number for the car they are offering to sell you. If there is hesitation or a vague answer from your salesperson, ask them to fax you the car's invoice. Make sure

Chandler Phillips Says:

So-called "on-line car shopping" is really a mixture of using the Internet, fax and phone.

you are dealing on a specific car. Handwrite your acceptance of their offer and fax it back to them (don't worry, this isn't a binding agreement—if they change the terms of the sale, you can still back out). Then set an appointment to take delivery of the vehicle.

Putting the Deal in Writing

The critical step in buying a car is making sure that the agreement you have reached with the car salesman is accurately stated in the contract. You will be ushered into the "F&I Room" (finance and insurance room) of the dealership to review and sign the sales or lease contract. We have devoted an entire section to the financing of cars. However, we have summarized the process in the "10 Steps to Buying a New Car."

Final Thoughts

The world of car buying is changing rapidly. Some people have even predicted that car salespeople will be eliminated as Internet buying becomes more popular. There are many different ways to go about buying a car. Pick the one that is best for you. Adapt these steps to your personal style. The important thing for you is to get a good car, at a fair price—and be treated with respect in the process.

Just keep in mind that the car buying process is highly competitive. If you get bad vibes from one dealership, or the prices seem too high—leave and go elsewhere. There are many dealers out there who want your business.

Getting a new car should be exciting. And it can be if it's done the right way. If you follow these steps, you'll soon be driving a great new car—and you'll also have the satisfaction of knowing that you got a good deal.

Chapter 12

10 Steps to Buying a New Car

The following steps will tell you how to locate, price and negotiate to buy the car you want. Remember to consult our glossary if you find words here you don't understand.

1. Starting out.

These steps will help you to find the exact car you want, and at a price that is fair to both you and the dealer. In the previous steps, you did plenty of research to find the best car for your needs, and you got a good idea of what you should expect to pay for it. Now you need to narrow the search even more. You will soon be finding the exact car you want to buy — with the options you have chosen — and you will be setting a target price to pay. If you have done your homework, this will be a fairly easy process with no unexpected surprises. Buying a car is a big investment, but it can be exciting and rewarding, especially if you feel like you got the right car at a fair price.

2. Using incentives and rebates.

Today's new car market is crowded and competitive. Many new cars are offered for sale with attractive incentives to make you choose a particular model. In some cases, the cars with the best incentives are those that aren't selling very well on their own.

An incentive is anything that gives you an added reason to buy a particular car. Often, however, it comes in the form of a cash rebate or low-interest financing. A car might be selling for $22,000 but the manufacturer is offering $3,000 in customer cash for a final price of $19,000. In another example, a $22,000 car financed for five years at six percent would have a monthly payment of about $550. But with zero-percent financing, the payment is roughly $480. That's a huge savings to you.

Check the Edmunds.com Web site for the latest incentives. You can also watch for TV and newspaper promotions but, remember, the incentives don't apply to all models and are not offered in all regions of the country. Furthermore, your credit must be very good to get the low-interest financing. And finally, keep in mind that there are some hidden incentives paid directly to dealers to push certain cars. Edmunds.com tracks many of these as well and posts them on the Web site.

Research what incentives are offered for the car you want to buy. Write down this information and keep it in your car buying folder as you move to the next step.

3. Pricing the car.

Car salesmen will usually point to a car's "sticker price" as the correct amount to pay. However, the price the dealership is willing to sell a car for is often well below the sticker price. How do you know what to pay? Edmunds.com has created a valuable tool for car buyers called True Market Value (TMV®) pricing. Based on actual sales figures, TMV® is the average price buyers are *paying* (also known as the "transaction price") for a certain type of car in your area. The TMV® figures, found on Edmunds.com, are adjusted for many factors including options, color and geographic region.

To calculate TMV®, begin by looking up the car you want to buy in the Edmunds.com new vehicles section. Follow the prompts to arrive at a final TMV® price for the exact car you are buying. Keep in mind that this price includes the destination charge, which is levied by all manufacturers. (However, the invoice price might vary in certain regions where advertising costs and other fees are included. Edmunds recommends paying the fees listed on the invoice, but questioning any advertising fees that appear on the purchase contract.)

Now it's time to factor in the incentives you researched and wrote down in the previous step. Take the final TMV® price and deduct the amount of the cash rebate. In other words, you create your best deal based on TMV®, and then lower it by whatever the rebate is. If you are going to use low-interest financing, calculate your final buying price, then use the payment calculator on Edmunds.com to find your monthly payment.

Write down these figures—the TMV®, the incentives and the monthly payment—and carry them with you for reference as you continue the car buying process.

4. Finding the exact car you want to buy.

You should now have a very specific idea of the car you want to buy. This means you know the make, model, trim level, options and color. The more flexible you can be about these specifics, the wider the range of the cars you'll find available for sale. Ultimately, the ability to consider several versions of the same model can give you additional bargaining power. For example, a shopper might be very firm about the make, model and trim level, but could accept a variety of options and colors. If you're a shopper who definitely wants hard-to-find options and a specific color, it will be more difficult to make a great deal. Why? You have no leverage as a negotiator. You have to pay the dealer's price or try to locate another identical vehicle. Obviously, if you do find the exact car you're looking for, there's no need to volunteer this information to the salesperson.

In any case, locate the exact car you want by sending e-mails to the Internet managers of dealers in your area. Using Edmunds.com's Dealer Locator feature, you can simultaneously solicit quotes from multiple dealers. In many cases, you will have to follow up with a phone call. Say something like: "I'm looking for a 2003 Matsura Accell. I'm not too fussy about the color but I don't want black or white. I want ABS and side airbags. What do you have on your lot?" Often the salesperson will have to check his inventory and call you back. After a few phone calls, you will have a good idea of how widely available the car is. If there are several dealerships offering the same car, you will be in a better position to make a good deal.

As you make phone calls and exchange e-mails, take careful notes. You should record information about each car you locate, including the color and options, and the dealership name. This will save time as you continue through the shopping process.

5. Test-driving the car salesman.

As you make follow-up phone calls to dealerships to locate the exact car you want to buy, you can also test-drive the car salesman. In other words, you can determine if this is a person you want to do business with. It's a good idea to consider this issue ahead of time, before you get to the deal-making phase of the process.

The first way to evaluate a good salesperson is to ask yourself if you feel comfortable dealing with them. Are they impatient and pushy? Are they relaxed and open? If you asked them about a specific car's availability did they respond to your needs? Did they try to steer you toward another car simply because they have too many of that model in stock? Do they return your phone calls? Do they answer your questions in a straightforward manner? Are they evasive and confusing?

By considering these issues, you should have a sense of whether or not you want to buy from this salesperson. If you feel comfortable talking with the individual over the phone, and if the dealership does indeed have the car you're interested in, set up a time to test-drive the car, preferably when the dealership will not be very busy, such as a weekday morning. Before heading to the car lot, review all your notes and make sure you bring your car buying folder. This might include your checkbook, registration and proof of insurance. Keep in mind that you're bringing these items so you'll be ready to buy a car *if you get a fair deal*. Don't feel obligated to purchase a car simply because you have all the necessary paperwork with you.

6. If you are trading in your old car...

If you are trading in your old car to a dealer, you will probably not get as much money toward the price of a new car as you would have if you'd sold it yourself to a private party. However, trading in offers some advantages. You can solve all of your car buying problems in one visit to the dealer. You can unload a hard-to-sell car with no newspaper ads, DMV lines or tire-kicking buyers involved. In some states, you will even pay less sales tax on a deal that involves a trade-in.

Begin the process by looking up your car's trade-in TMV® on Edmunds.com. After you plug in all of the vehicle's information (mileage, options and colors) you will get a specific trade-in price. This figure will often be slightly different from the offers you get once you are on the car lot. At a dealership, the value assigned to your trade-in varies based on the time of the month, the dealer's specific inventory and the used car manager's mood, but at least TMV® will give you a rough idea of what your trade-in is worth.

If it's important to you to get the maximum value for your trade-in, you should visit several dealerships and solicit bids. Tell the salesperson that the sale of a new car will be contingent on the amount he or she will give you for your trade-in. Also, tell them you are visiting several dealerships. With a little legwork, you may be able to boost the price you get for your old car by several hundred dollars or more. Remember, the extra effort you spend in getting competitive bids is far less than what it would take to advertise, show and sell the car yourself.

7. Negotiating for your lowest price.

Many buyers like to handle the question of price before they even go to the dealer. Internet salespeople are willing to discuss price over the phone —sometimes even by e-mail. This wasn't the case a few years ago when the salesperson wanted you in his office before he would get down to brass tacks and talk price.

It's quite possible that, in your calls to various Internet departments, the selling price of the car has already come up. Often, Internet salespeople will volunteer the selling price of their car since they know this is the make-or-break factor in most buyers' decision-making process. If the price they've quoted is at or below Edmunds.com's TMV®, then you are already in the right range to buy the car. If you want to try to improve the deal, you have a few options.

Everyone has his own idea of what makes a good deal, but most people just want to know they got a fair price. Here, TMV® will be your best guide. If you want to try for a rock-bottom price, start by getting bids from three local dealers. Follow this up by taking the lowest price, calling the two other dealerships and saying, "I've been offered this car at this price. If you beat it, I'll buy it from you." They almost certainly will. However, keep in mind that you can't play this game forever. Eventually, they will give you a take-it-or-leave-it price.

Also, be warned that if you ask the dealer to cut their profit, they might try to take it back somewhere else. Remember, a good deal isn't just the lowest selling price. It's the lowest total out-the-door cost on a car that meets your needs.

8. Closing the deal.

If you feel good about the price you have been quoted, it's time to take a look at the big picture. Many buyers focus on the cost of the car and ignore the related expenses. Besides the cost, you will have to pay sales tax and various fees which vary from state to state.

The simplest way to estimate total cost is to ask the salesperson to fax you a worksheet and invoice before you go to the dealership. This way you'll be able to review the figures in a relaxed environment. Compare the numbers from the dealership to those you have calculated and the TMV® prices on Edmunds.com.

In some areas of the country, dealers have costs that don't show up on Edmunds.com invoice prices. This means the Edmunds.com invoice price of the car you are researching might not exactly match the dealer's invoice. Don't panic -- and don't begin making accusations. Edmunds.com can't track all regional fees, such as advertising costs. So, as a rule of thumb, consider the charges on the dealer's invoice to be nonnegotiable. However, if extra fees are written into the contract (such as "D&H" or "Administrative Costs") which seem bogus or redundant, ask to have them removed, or tell they you will take your business to another dealership.

9. Reviewing and signing the paperwork.

At the dealership, you will be presented with the contract for your new car and a dizzying array of forms to sign. This might be done by the Internet salesperson you have been dealing with, or it could be done in a separate office by the finance and insurance (F&I) manager. If this happens, the F&I manager might try to sell you additional items such as extended service contracts, fabric protection, alarms or a LoJack vehicle locator. In most cases, we recommend turning down these extras.

If you have already seen a worksheet for the deal you've made, the contract should be a formality. Make sure the numbers match the worksheet and no additional charges or fees have been inserted. You will also be asked to sign various forms that register your new car and transfer ownership of your trade-in. Understand what you are signing and what it means. Ask questions if you don't understand, and don't ever feel like you have to hurry. Buying a car is a serious commitment, and it's the F&I manager's job to ensure you are comfortable with every document involved. Remember, once you have signed, there is no going back.

10. Inspecting and taking possession of your new car.

Most dealerships detail the car and provide a full tank of gas. You will have one more chance to inspect the car before you take possession of it. Make sure you walk around the car and look for scratches in the paint and wheels or dents and dings on the body. If you are paying for floor mats or other dealer-installed items make sure they are included. If anything is missing, or if any work needs to be done, ask for a "Due Bill" that puts it in writing. You will then be able to come back and get the work done later.

As you drive away inhaling that new-car smell, there is only one more thing to be done: enjoy your new car.

New Car Buying Checklist

❑ Decide how much you have to spend on your new car purchase.

❑ Check to see what incentives and rebates are available on the car you want to buy.

❑ Print out the Edmunds.com TMV price on the car you want to buy (adjusted for options, color and region).

❑ If you are financing the car, use the payment calculators to determine the monthly payment for the car you want to buy (and remember to apply the incentives to the purchase price).

❑ Contact the Internet department and simultaneously solicit quotes from multiple dealers.

❑ If you are trading in your old car, check its Edmunds.com True Market Value and print out this information.

❑ Call the Internet manager to negotiate the best price of the car you want to buy.

❑ Once you've reached a good price, ask the salesperson to fax you a worksheet showing all the prices, taxes and fees.

❑ Bring your worksheet with you to the dealership so you can compare these numbers to the figures on the contract.

❑ Inspect the car for dents, dings and scratches before taking final delivery.

Buying a Used Car

Buying a used car could well be the smartest economic decision you make. Consider this: if a car depreciates an average of 30 percent in the first year, that's the amount of money you stand to save by buying a car that's only one year old. You don't want to be saddled with a lemon. But we'll walk you through the process. And soon you'll be riding in style.

Chapter 13
Why Buy Used?

"I can't afford a new car, so I guess I'll have to buy a used one."

Many people feel that buying a used car is a compromise. Instead, think of shopping for a used car as a treasure hunt: you might find a gem at a bargain price—a low-mileage creampuff for hundreds under its value. You might stumble across a car being sold in a hurry or a loaded luxury car being sold at a fire-sale price because of some minor damage.

Hey, hey…now, you might be feeling pretty excited about buying a used car. You should. Buying a used car is one of the smartest things you can do with your money. Why?

New cars lose between 20 and 30 percent of their value the moment you drive them off the car lot. It's better to let someone else take that hit and then buy the same car a year or two later. That's a big savings, and you still wind up with a nice set of wheels.

At this point you might be thinking:

"OK, how do I find these great used cars you're talking about?"

Well, that's the catch. Buying a used car will take more effort. That's because new cars come from one source: a dealership. Used cars can be bought from a dealership, a used car lot, at an auction or through a private party. In a later chapter, we will cover the search process completely. For now, let's just say the search is part of the fun.

Now, let's move on to your next objection:

"How do I know whether a car will be reliable?"

This is a valid concern. But keep in mind that cars are more reliable and last longer than ever before. Furthermore, with vehicle history reports available on the Internet, you can learn everything important about the car's history. Finally, if you don't like uncertainty, buy a certified used car that comes with a factory warranty.

So get ready to discover the wonderful world of used cars.

Chapter 14

Used Car Markets

"Where is the best place for me to buy a used car?"

Used cars are all over the place. One way to look for a used car to buy is to wait for the right car to roll past, with a "For Sale" sign in the window. This might take a while.

However, many of us don't have the luxury of time. There are many convenient places to buy used cars. We will cover them—and the pros and cons of each one—in the rest of this chapter.

New Car Dealerships

Driving around any American city, you see streets lined with new car dealerships. Usually, these dealerships are grouped together in a certain area or located in "auto malls." While new car dealerships usually carry no more than a couple brands of new cars, they carry a wide variety of used cars for sale.

Typically, the lot is divided in two with new cars on one side, used on the other. The sales staff is divided into new and used car salespeople, too. Now comes a little bit of surprising news: *the used car side of the dealership is more profitable than the new car side.* The proof of this: the veteran salespeople work on the used side of the lot, not the new side.

There is money in used cars—big money. Why? Because the profit margin—the amount the dealer stands to make—is higher with used cars.

How the Trade-in Process Works

Let's look at an example of how cars become trade-ins. A person drives into a Ford dealership in a Chrysler. He makes a deal on a new Ford and trades in the Chrysler. The Chrysler is worth about $12,000 if sold to a private party, about $13,000 if sold on the Ford used car lot.

However, our consumer isn't very savvy (he didn't read this book), and he doesn't know what his Chrysler is worth. Besides, he *really* wants the new Ford.

It's clean and shiny and smells good inside, not like his car which has gotten a little funky over the years. So, our consumer trades in the Chrysler for $8,000.

Now, the Ford dealer has a Chrysler to put on his lot. He details the car, puts on tire black, sprays the interior with air freshener and paints, "Super Clean! Low Miles!" in the windshield. Under that he paints the price: $13,999. Yes, this is a little higher than what the car is worth, even being sold through a dealer. But he figures, why not? Maybe someone will walk in, like the Chrysler and *lie down* (that's car salesman talk for when a person buys a car without bargaining).

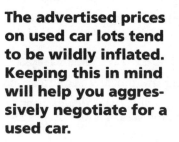

Chandler Phillips Says:

The advertised prices on used car lots tend to be wildly inflated. Keeping this in mind will help you aggressively negotiate for a used car.

Or, let's say that someone seems interested in the Chrysler, but they are hesitating. The car salesman (we say car sales*man* since most are men) can say, "Look, the car is priced at $13,999, but we're having a sale this week—all used cars are being discounted $500. We'll sell you the car for only $13,499. How's that sound?"

OK, you get the picture. The dealer bought low and sold high. Furthermore, he created a lot of "wiggle room" in the transaction by setting a high asking price. However, even if the dealer came down $1,000 on the price, he would still be making nearly $4,000 in profit. On new cars, the profit is only about $500.

From this scenario we can see that the new car dealership becomes an attractive source of used cars. Assuming you are willing to negotiate, there may be some bargains to be had here. However, you have to play the game against skilled professionals in an environment that some might find intimidating.

Used Car Lots

The used car lot may appear similar to a new car dealership, but there is a difference. The cars here have either come from auctions or were purchased from people who drove in off the street, needing quick cash. Think of the used car lot as the pawnshop of cars. As such, the cars tend to be older and somewhat less reliable than their counterparts on the new car lot. But the "buy low and sell high" rule still applies.

One difference between the used car section of a new car dealership and the independent car lot is that the used car lot has probably paid more for their cars since they didn't get them as trade-ins. Another difference is that used car lots usually offer no warranty or guarantee. Some car lots will offer what they call "certified" used cars—but read the fine print carefully. These are not the same as cars that have been certified by the manufacturer and come with a factory warranty.

Chandler Phillips Says:

Don't be fooled by the "certified" sticker in the window of cars on independent lots. This isn't the same as a "factory certified" used cars sold on dealership lots and backed by the original manufacturer.

In general we don't recommend independent car lots unless you are searching for a hard-to-find model that just isn't available elsewhere. While there may be some reputable car lots, the majority is on the shady side and should be avoided, particularly since there are plenty of other places to find the car you need.

Buying Used Cars From Private Parties

Buying a used car from a private party is a very different experience from purchasing through a dealership or a used car lot.

Buying a used car from a private party offers these advantages:

- A dealership marks up used cars to recoup its overhead, while private parties don't have these costs.

- Negotiations are low-key since you are dealing with an amateur, not a pro.

- The previous owner usually has the car's service records, so the history of the car is documented.

- A private owner probably won't cover up mechanical problems.

While the Internet has come of age, you should still check the newspaper. When shopping for a used car, take advantage of every source in finding the right car for you.

Certified Used Cars

You might consider buying a factory-certified car that has been inspected and is in good running order. When we say "factory certified" we mean that the manufacturer has warrantied it, not the dealership. You should always check to find out who is certifying (guaranteeing) the condition of the car. If the certification is only from the used car lot, it is likely to be of little value. If it comes from the manufacturer, it is the equivalent of a valuable warranty.

The beauty of buying a factory-certified used car is that, if anything does go wrong with the car during the warranty, it will be fixed for free. This means that if you are considering a certified used car, and it appears to be in good condition, you don't have to do any further checking to make sure it will be reliable.

Chandler Phillips Says:

Certified used buying tries to provide much of the peace of mind that new car buying offers.

Certified used cars are found on new car lots. Take Volkswagen, for example. Its certified used cars are subject to a 112-point inspection. VW then certifies the car with a two-year/24,000-mile limited warranty that even includes a roadside assistance program. At Edmunds, we bought a certified used 1999 Passat GLS. Four months later, it overheated. The repairs (not extensive) were covered by the warranty.

While buying a certified used car removes a lot of the guesswork about the vehicle's mechanical condition, you pay for this service. Certified used cars that sell in the $10,000 to $20,000 range are estimated to be $500 to $1,000 more expensive.

Auctions and On-line Auctions

Really looking for some bargains? You may have seen ads for car auctions in your area. These auctions are often for repossessed cars, cars that didn't sell at dealers' auctions or for cars seized in crimes. The auctions promise that you'll be able to buy cars for thousands less than their value. That may be true. But there are substantial risks, too. In many cases, the cars being sold at these auctions can't be taken for a test-drive. You can start the car and inspect it, but you can't drive it. At some auctions, the cars are sold at breakneck speed—two cars a minute. Needless to say, these cars are not under warranty. Unless you have extensive knowledge of mechanics and like to gamble, we don't recommend these auctions.

A higher breed of cars is sold at auto dealers' auctions. Unfortunately, these auctions are not open to the public and you need a car dealer's license to make a purchase. However, if you know someone who has a dealer's license, who will act as your agent, this might be a way to get a good used car at a wholesale price.

For the average consumer, however, auctions have blossomed on the Internet, especially through eBay (www.ebay. com). Pictures of the car, and the car's

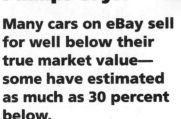

Chandler Phillips Says:

Many cars on eBay sell for well below their true market value—some have estimated as much as 30 percent below.

interior, are posted on the Internet so buyers can place bids. The seller can be e-mailed with additional questions. Some of these cars may still be under warranty.

If you are uncertain about the car's condition, you can hire a local mechanic to inspect the car and issue a report. On-line auctions can, in many cases, turn up bargains. But not always. The process pits buyers against each other and it's easy to focus on trying to win the auction rather than getting the best price. But if you know the value of the car you are bidding on, and promise yourself not to exceed that amount, the on-line auction can be a good way to go.

If you decide to go the on-line auction route, here are a few tips from an expert:

- **Narrow the search:** Choose a make, model and year. It's easier to perform frequent checks on the auction market by using an exact model in the search field.

- **Don't get an itchy finger:** Watch the auctions for a while before bidding. Or, use a "sniping" service to enter bids for you at the last second.

- **Search for completed items:** This will give you some idea of where the auction price will wind up.

- **Check the buyer:** Be sure to check the feedback from other buyers regarding the seller. Make sure the individual is rated as a seller, not a buyer. Read the auction description carefully and request more photos by e-mail if necessary.

- **Call the seller:** It can be reassuring to develop a rapport with the seller, and sale terms may be more flexible than you think.

- **Look for no-reserve auctions:** Find the seller who doesn't set a minimum winning bid amount, which often is as high as the car's retail value.

- **Make sure you have an out:** Bid only on auctions in which sellers allow you to cancel after you inspect the car.

- **Cash is king:** While the banking industry is getting more creative about financing on-line purchases, most interstate transactions are cash sales.

- **Have the car inspected by a mechanic:** Contact a mechanic in the city where the car is being sold and arrange for an inspection when you arrive. The eBay site offers inspection services in 50 major metro markets, as well as a free limited warranty for the drive home on many cars.

- **Use Carfax (www.carfax.com):** This company's on-line vehicle history report can tell you where the car has been, its accurate mileage and whether it has been damaged in a crash or flood.

- **Price the car with True Market Value (TMV®):** Visit our Web site at Edmunds.com and get a realistic idea of the value of used cars.

- **Bid and walk away:** Decide on a fair price for a car, then bid and walk away. Don't get caught up in a bidding war and end up paying too much.

- **Factor in travel or delivery costs:** Remember you have to pick up the vehicle or have it shipped when you win the auction. Include gas, hotels, food, lost work time and plane tickets in the total cost. And buy a round-trip plane ticket—it's often cheaper than a one-way ticket, and gives you flexibility if you decide you don't want the car when you see it.

The used car market is not limited to the sources we have covered in this chapter. However, these places are the most common and reputable sources of used cars. In the next chapter we will cover more ways to find bargains in the nooks and crannies of the auto market.

Chapter 15

Used Car Bargains: Demos, Rentals and Salvage Cars

In our eternal quest for deals on wheels, we decided to take a closer look at three types of used cars:

- "Program cars"—also known as finance, factory or executive cars

- Used cars from rental car lots

- Used cars with salvage titles

Can you get a good deal from these sources? Will they make solid, dependable transportation? Let's look at them one at a time.

Program Cars

Program cars have been owned by the manufacturer and given to employees for a short time to use for company business. The idea is to have a Ford employee, for example, drive a late-model Ford to advertise the company's product. These cars are maintained by the factory and usually sent to auction before the odometer turns 10,000 miles. The cars are sold to Ford dealers at closed auctions and then put up for sale on the car lot.

"Dealers like these cars because they can get them at low prices and then sell them at a good profit," one insider told us. "Besides that, program cars always get the service they need because dealers can work on them in their own shops."

These cars can be a great deal for the average buyer. They have been well maintained, and you are buying a nearly new car with no worries about mechani-

Chandler Phillips Says:

Buying a program car can save you money—but knowing what price to offer can be difficult. Do a thorough inspection and deduct for excessive miles.

cal problems. Furthermore, dealers may extend the warranty for the full term, or let you drive it for the balance of the factory warranty.

So how would the average consumer go about buying a program car? Just call used car dealers or check the ads. "Dealers are proud to advertise program cars," one expert said, adding, "The deals are there."

Knowing what to pay for the car can be a problem because you have no idea what the dealer paid for it. As a rule, you shouldn't pay more than the invoice price for a comparable new car. We recommend assigning a per mile charge for the distance the car was driven and deducting that amount from the invoice price. For example, lease cars that are over mileage are charged 15 cents a mile—a reasonable rate for your offer, as well.

Used Rental Car Lots

Former rental cars sometimes turn up on used car lots labeled as "program cars." This will be revealed if you run a Carfax report on the vehicle (www.carfax.com). For a modest monthly fee, you can run the VIN numbers of cars you are considering buying. The Carfax report will tell you who the previous owner was, whether the car has a salvage title and if there are any outstanding recalls on the vehicle.

Some rental car companies have their own used car lots where they sell cars they have taken out of their fleets. The cars are reasonably priced and usually offered at no-haggle prices. There are a good variety of cars, too, ranging from sedans to SUVs. In the past, buyers were warned to steer clear of former rental cars because drivers who rent them "beat the heck out of the cars." That might be true in a few cases, experts say. But there are other benefits to offset that argument.

"Rental companies take good care of the cars," one insider said. "And the rental car agencies buy them right to begin with—at net, net, net numbers (invoice price minus the holdback, minus the advertising costs and the like). But for peace of mind, you would probably like to have a third-party inspection because not all rental cars are alike—there are some plums and some peaches."

Used rental car lots offer benefits for shoppers in search of reliable, reasonably priced transportation. It's worth a look in your quest for a good used car.

Salvage Title Cars

Mention to a prospective buyer that the car has a salvage title, and they run in terror. Still, others have owned these cars and driven them for years. What is a salvage title and can these cars ever be a smart buy?

When a car has been severely damaged (either in an accident, or because of a flood or theft), the insurance company estimates how much it will cost to fix. At some point, the cost of repairs is more than the car is worth. Therefore, the car is often sold to a salvage company and used for parts. To alert future buyers to the car's history, it is given a salvage title.

In some cases, the salvage company, or an enterprising body shop, might fix up the car and try to sell it. Naturally, the price of the car will be below that of similar models because it has a salvage title. The danger is that the car might have been improperly repaired. The biggest problem in these instances is with the alignment of the wheels—if the frame has been bent, it is difficult and expensive to straighten. A bent frame will cause abnormal tire wear and improper handling characteristics.

"Some states require (totaled) vehicles to be branded as salvage cars," an expert told us. "But if it is sold in another state, and retitled, it can be sold to Mrs. Jones as a straight-up used car. She doesn't know it has been cut together from pieces of different cars."

Extreme caution is recommended when considering the purchase of a car with a salvage title. "I know of some cars that have gone through body shops and been made into drivable cars," said another expert. "But keep in mind that if you buy a salvage title car, the chances of selling it to someone else and recouping your money are very slim. If you buy a salvage title car, you might want to count on keeping it until the wheels fall off."

A body shop owner we spoke to also advised buyers to be cautious. However, he added, "Sometimes it works when you're dealing with a theft recovery where

Chandler Phillips Says:

You might be tempted to buy a salvage title car to save money. But that salvage title will cut the resale value by nearly 50 percent.

there was little damage. You might save $3,000, $4,000, $5,000. But you will lose that right off the top when you go to resell it."

Other Used Car Markets

A sales veteran we know, who is always on the lookout for cars he can "flip" (buy and quickly resell) says that his best used buys have come from spotting cars with "For Sale" signs in the window. "I like cars that people are trying to get out of," he told us. "Like if a kid is going off to college, I might be able to get that car cheap. And chances are, it's a little Toyota Corolla or something. People are always looking for a car in that price range."

When buying an older used car, this salesman always takes the car to a mechanic for an inspection. "I still spend the $50 to take it to a mechanic. Not because this person might be trying to trick me. He might say it's in great shape but he might not know that something's wrong with it."

As a closing note, the experts we spoke to steered us back to the old favorite: buying from a private party. When you buy a very old car, the most important factor is how it has been serviced. Only the previous owner can tell you the car's complete history.

Chandler Phillips Says:

When buying a used car, rule number one is: take it to a mechanic for an inspection.

Chapter 16
Locating Good Used Cars

You should consider trying to locate three cars that fit the criteria you are searching for (remember the research you did in the first part to determine what was the best car for you?). Why three cars? If you have a number of cars to choose from, you are in a stronger position when it comes time to bargain. If your top choice falls through, you have a fallback position. You won't be emotionally tied to one car.

Your search should be conducted using a number of different sources:

- On-line classified ads such as those that can be reached through Edmunds.com

- On-line searches of used cars at new car dealership Web sites

- Daily newspaper classified ads

- Weekly shoppers and giveaway papers

- Listings on college and business bulletin boards

- Word of mouth—ask all your friends if they know of any good used cars for sale

The Internet is a powerful tool for finding a good used car. Once you have configured the car you want through the Edmunds.com used vehicle section, you can type in your ZIP code and view a list of classified ads of cars for sale in your area. Many of these ads are for cars on dealership lots. Or try using AutoTrader.com, which brings you a mixture of dealer and private party ads.

Once you've located a number of ads that look attractive, it's time to work the phones.

Use the Phone to Pre-Qualify Prospective Used Cars

There are a number of questions you should ask about a car before you take the time to test-drive it. Some information may already be listed in the ads, but it is important to verify the facts. You might consider creating a form for yourself to keep track of the different cars you call about. Or, use the form we've included below. But be sure to take notes as you make calls. Different cars tend to blur together after a few days of shopping.

Once you have found three cars that seem to match your needs, it's time to test-drive them. For more information about test-driving, please refer back to Chapter 2 in Part 1.

Chandler Phillips Says:

Using the Internet and telephone will cut the legwork in used car shopping. Narrow the search with smart questions before going to physically inspect the car.

Used Car Question Sheet

Dealership/Name of Owner:_____ _____

Phone #:_____

Make/Model:_____ Year:_____

Mileage:_____ Why Low? High?_____

Exterior color:_____

Interior color:_____ Leather:_____ Cloth:_____

Number of doors:_____ Engine:_____

Transmission: Auto:_____ Manual:_____

Is car still under warranty?_____

Is there a salvage title?_____

Is it a trade-in? _____ Lease return? _____

Have any major parts been replaced? _____

Are any repairs needed? _____

Options/Add-ons: _____

Asking price:_____

Chapter 17

Inspecting Used Cars: Avoiding Lemons, Buying Creampuffs

"I don't know anything about mechanics. How can I tell if a used car is a lemon?"

Some people say that buying a used car is just inheriting someone else's problems. But if you choose the car carefully, you can avoid buying a lemon and get a creampuff instead.

Does this mean you have to put on a jumpsuit and climb under the car with a flashlight? Not exactly. For around $50, you can get a mechanic to put the car up on a lift and go over it with a fine-tooth comb. But even that doesn't tell the full story.

In recent years, largely because of increased record keeping and Internet access, companies have sprung up that sell vehicle history reports. This, and the report from a trusted mechanic, is the best way to reveal a car's potentially checkered past. Here's how it works.

The VIN Number Is the DNA of a Used Car

You're shopping for a used car when you think you've hit pay dirt. It's a 2001 import with low miles. It drives great, and the price is right. When you question the owner about the car's history, he says he bought it from a used car lot only two years ago.

You're about to write a check when you have a troubling thought: This deal seems too good to be true. Maybe something's wrong with the car that they are keeping hidden. Who owned the car before? Is there any damage or problems you should know about?

At one time there was no way to check a vehicle's history. Buyers could only go on the evidence in front of them, basing their decision on the mechanical condition of the car and the current owner's service records. But computer technology has made it possible to use the Vehicle Identification Number (VIN) to reveal a car's past.

Vehicle history reports can be ordered from a number of Internet companies. The first company to offer this service was Carfax (www.carfax.com) which, as the name suggests, began faxing used car reports as early as 1986. Now, the Fairfax, Virginia-based company accesses 450 different information sources to compile reports that are e-mailed almost instantaneously to customers.

Carfax has almost every car on the road in its database going back to 1981, a company spokesman told us. He notes that 1981 was when the U.S. government accepted the VIN as a standard tracking code for a vehicle's history.

Chandler Phillips Says:

Before you begin your used car search, order a 30-day Carfax vehicle history subscription. Run the VIN of every car before you take the time to go see the car.

Vehicle History Reports—A Growing Field

Many of these on-line vehicle history report companies draw on similar sources for their information and present the data in a compiled report at competitive prices. Carfax charges $14.99 for a single report and $19.99 for an unlimited number of reports for one month.

Recently, Carfax has added vehicle reliability information along with specific information about a car. Another company, *Consumer Guide* (www.consumerguide.com), draws from the monster database of Experian (with 1.7 billion records) and issues reports that include *Consumer Guide's* repair information.

Odometer Rollbacks

Another feature offered by vehicle history reports is their ability to spot odometer rollbacks. While the odometer of a used car might show that it has only 55,000 miles, the Carfax report might indicate that the odometer readings at key events in the car's history—emissions tests or title changes—don't match up.

For example, the report might show that a certain vehicle was inspected in December 2000 at 55,000 miles. But then, when a change of title was issued two months later, the odometer reading was recorded as being 45,000 miles. Obviously, there was some kind of foul play here.

The number of miles a car is driven directly affects the price of the car. Therefore, a seller has a strong incentive to rollback the odometer. Each excess mile a car is driven—over the expected yearly average of from 12,000 to 15,000—reduces its value. Therefore, turning back an odometer 10,000 miles can increase the sale price of the car by $600.

Title Washing and Curbstoning

Another scam detected by vehicle history reports is called *title washing*. This occurs when one state doesn't recognize titles from another state. However, Carfax reports track a vehicle as it crosses state lines. If a car has been "branded" in another state—with a salvage title, for example—this will be revealed on the report. Salvage titles are assigned to cars that have been declared a total loss by insurance companies. The car might still run and be drivable, but having a salvage title significantly reduces its value.

Curbstoning occurs when a dealer has an inferior or damaged car he can't sell on his lot. He gives the car to a salesperson to sell through the classifieds, as if it were a private party sale. However, a Carfax report will show that the title recently changed hands and may reveal that it is a lemon or an otherwise branded car. You should be suspicious of curbstoning if the seller's name is different from the name on the title.

Chandler Phillips Says:

Be wary of anyone selling several cars at once. This person is probably a pro.

Inspecting a Used Car Yourself

Earlier we mentioned that you should take any car you are *seriously* considering for an inspection by a trusted mechanic. What can a mechanic find that you can't spot on your own? For one thing, the mechanic will put the car up on a lift. Oil or fluid leaks are easier to spot. The mechanic might also do a compression check that would show engine wear. And finally, the mechanic's expert eye might spot a problem you overlooked.

However, you don't want to drop 50 bucks each time you look at a used car. So you need to prequalify a used car with an inspection of your own. Here's what you can do.

Look at the Big Picture First

Before you drive the car, do a "walk-around." Look at the car to make sure it has not been hit (a vehicle history report might also turn up a record of an accident). Crouch next to the front bumper and sight along the side of the car. Make sure there are no ripples in the door panels and that the gaps between the doors and along the hood are even.

Open all the doors and the trunk. Test all the lights, controls, heater and air conditioner. Open the hood and make sure there are no leaks or sprays on the underside of the hood lining that would indicate a burst hose or fluid leak. With the engine running, listen for noises that might indicate a mechanical problem.

Look at the transmission fluid (does it smell burned and look brown rather than pink?), the engine oil (beware of a car that has oil with metallic flakes), the antifreeze (it should be green) and the fan and timing belt. Finally, check to see how much soot is built up on the inside of the exhaust pipe—a heavy deposit might indicate worn valves or piston rings.

The checklist on the next page is designed to help you more thoroughly inspect a used car before you decide whether it is worth buying.

What to look for while test-driving a used car:

Handling:
- City street handling
- Highway handling
- Two-lane road handling

Suspension:
- Excessive body lean
- Body motion control
- Shock absorber dampening

Engine:
- Noise
- Acceleration
- Idle smoothness

Steering:
- Ease of operation
- Vibration through steering wheel
- Road feel

Transmission (automatic):
- Smooth shifts
- Noise
- Cruise control

Transmission (manual):
- Clutch feel
- Smooth gear changes
- Cruise control

Four-wheel drive:
- Easy to engage

Brakes:
- Parking brake
- Brake pedal pressure
- Stopping gradually
- Stopping suddenly
- Antilock brakes

What to look for in the Interior:

From the driver seat:
- Seat comfort
- Headroom
- Instrument panel clarity
- Road visibility
- Steering wheel position
- Legroom
- Ease of control use
- Armrest height
- Headrest comfort
- Power accessories
- Mirror controls
- Radio, cassette or CD player and speakers
- Heater, air conditioner and ventilation
- Remote trunk or fuel-door releases
- Horn operation
- Interior dome light
- Wiper/washer system
- Glovebox
- Cupholders

From the passenger seats:
- Ease of entry and exit
- Legroom
- Headroom
- Shoulder room
- Seat comfort
- Armrest height
- Headrest height
- Strap handles
- Reading lights
- Seatbelt operation
- Passenger airbag availability
- Folding rear seats
- Trunk pass-through
- Rear defogger
- Visor vanity lights

Look for quality of:
- Upholstery
- Headliner
- Fit of interior panels
- Trim and moldings
- Dashboard
- Carpet and mats

What to look for on the Exterior:

Visual inspection:
- Paint
- Rust spots
- Tire tread wear
- Smoke from the tailpipe
- Body-panel dents

Use keys to check the following locks and latches:
- Doors
- Glovebox
- Anti-theft system
- Gas cap
- Trunk

Check the trunk for:
- Spare tire
- Jack
- Lug wrench
- Carpeting and trim
- Trunk light
- Secure latching

Try these:
- Trunk release/catch
- Hood release/catch
- Childproof locks
- Headlights
- Parking lights
- Reverse lights
- Brake lights
- Taillights
- Hazard lights
- Turn signal lights
- License plate

Chapter 18

Closing the Deal: Paperwork and the DMV

"Do I need to get a bill of sale or something? And what about my plates?"

So you've got the car you want to buy and you've got the money to close the deal. (For information on used car loans, see the section on financing later on in this book.) The laws governing the sale of motor vehicles are regulated by the state's department of motor vehicles. These rules will vary somewhat from state to state. Make sure you check with the DMV in your state, and keep in mind that much of the information is now available on government Web sites. In some states, automotive transactions can be completed at auto club offices. If your state's auto club provides this service, it is highly recommended you go there rather than the DMV, since it is so much faster.

Although the registration process will involve talking to the DMV, here are a few general guidelines to help you through this process.

After you buy a used car, you have to transfer ownership of the car from the seller to yourself. If you bought the car from a dealership, they will file all the necessary documents (another advantage of buying from a dealer). If you buy from a private party you must do this yourself.

You will need to prove to the DMV that you have bought the car and are now the new legal owner. In some states, you might need a signed bill of sale. In other states, you must get the previous owner to "sign off"—release their ownership in the car—by signing the car's title. The title is sometimes called the "pink slip."

This sounds simple enough but there are things that make the process complicated. For example, there is the constant question of liability. The seller will want to limit their liability by filing a "release of liability" form with the DMV (if allowed by your state). Such a form records the date of the sale and the number of miles on the odometer at the time of the transaction. This means if you get in an accident while driving the car before a new title is issued, you are still liable for damages.

Once you have paid for the car you are buying (it's customary for the buyer to request a cashier's check or cash), the seller will sign the title over to you. A new title will be issued and mailed to you.

But what if the seller still owes money on the car, and the bank is holding the title? One way to deal with this is to conclude the sale at the bank where the title is held. The seller should call ahead and ask them to have the title ready. Then, once money has changed hands and the bank has been paid the balance of the loan, the seller will sign the title to you.

In some cases, however, an out-of-state bank might hold the title. In this instance, check with the DMV (or the auto club) and see if you can file what will likely be called a "transfer of ownership" form. This takes the place of the bill of sale. Then, after the seller has paid off the balance of the loan with the proceeds from the car sale, the title will be sent to the seller. They will sign it over to you and the transaction is complete.

In some states, an inspection or smog test is required when a vehicle is sold. Find out from the DMV whether the buyer or the seller is responsible for paying for this test. A "passed" inspection report may be required when you register the car.

Finally, remember to contact your insurance agent to start a policy on the vehicle you have just bought. If you are buying a used car from a dealership, proof of insurance will be required before you can drive the new car off the lot.

Who gets the license plates when a car changes owners? In some states, the license plates go with the car; in others, the seller retains the plates and the new owner must apply for his own set. Regardless, if a car has personalized plates, the previous owner will want to keep them.

Chandler Phillips Says:

Before you close the deal, ask the seller if he holds the title. Having to make a payoff to the bank to get the title delays and complicates the deal.

Negotiating Script: How to Negotiate With Private Parties

Negotiating with a private party is different than haggling at the dealership – you're talking directly with the owner of the car. To present a drastically lower offer than the asking price might insult them. Still, you want to arrive at a fair price. Here is a way to depersonalize the exchange.

> SELLER
> My price is $4,500—firm.
>
> SMART CAR BUYER
> Yes, but I've done some research. Your price is way above the market.
>
> SELLER
> What do you mean?
>
> SMART CAR BUYER
> I looked up the price of your car on Edmunds.com. I adjusted the price for mileage and condition. I'm getting a price of $3,960. How did you set your price?
>
> SELLER
> It seemed right to me—it's a good car.
>
> SMART CAR BUYER
> It sure is. And I want to buy it. But I can probably find another one at the going rate. So, would you accept my offer of $3,960?
>
> SELLER
> Well… Do you have cash?
>
> SMART CAR BUYER
> I'll give you a cashier's check.
>
> SELLER
> OK. You've got a deal.

The seller's "firm" price didn't turn out to be quite as immovable as he first indicated. It's always a good idea to back up your offer with evidence—Edmunds.com pricing—rather than subjective observations.

Chapter 19

10 Steps to Buying a Used Car

The following steps will tell you how to locate, price and negotiate to buy the used car you want.

1. Starting out.

If you've decided to buy a used car, you've already made a smart decision. You can get a car that's almost as good as a brand-new one, without suffering the depreciation that wallops new car buyers as soon as they drive the car off the lot. Used cars—even those that are only one year old—are 20 to 30 percent cheaper than new cars.

2. How much can you afford?

The smart shopper will consider how to finance the car at the beginning of the shopping process. This will avoid unpleasant surprises later in the game and help you make an unemotional decision that fits your budget.

You will need to estimate three figures that will guide you as you go shopping:

- **Monthly payment.** If you are going to take out a loan, how much can you afford to pay each month?

- **Down payment.** How much cash can you put down to reduce your monthly payments?

- **Purchase price of the car.** Answering the first two questions will provide the answer to this final question.

Once you've determined how much you can spend for a down payment, a monthly payment and the purchase price of the car, print out these figures. Later, in the heat of the moment, when you are negotiating for a used car and need to stay within your budget, you might need to check your printout to keep yourself from overspending.

3. Consider competing vehicles.

At the beginning of the car-buying process, many people already have in mind the car they want. But it's a good idea to stop right now and ask yourself: Will this car fit into my monthly budget? Does it meet my needs? For now, make sure your choice doesn't blatantly exceed your budget and will fulfill your needs.

It's possible that you need to expand your horizons when considering what to buy. You might want to think of other vehicles in the same class. For example, if you are considering an obvious choice like the Toyota Camry or Honda Accord, you should also look at the Nissan Altima, Mitsubishi Galant or Subaru Legacy. These cars were built for the same market, but they often have different features at lower prices.

4. Considering used car bargains.

The cost of a used car is based on its condition, mileage, reliability, performance and popularity. Of course, you want a car that is reliable and performs well. But do you want the same used car everyone else wants? If so, you will pay a premium for it. In some cases, the only difference is the nameplate.

Some shoppers believe they can get a killer deal by going to police auctions or buying a car with a salvage title (one that has been declared a total loss by an insurance company). True, the initial cost is much lower, but you know little about what you are getting. It could have frame damage, a safety problem or a faulty transmission. For most people, it's better to stick to the more common used car sources: private parties and the used car department of the local dealership. You might even consider buying a certified used car that comes with a factory warranty.

5. Research your prospective used car.

If you can visit Edmunds.com, you can broaden your base of knowledge by reading the editorial reviews and by checking out what current owners have to say in our Town Hall section. With over half a million registered users in Town Hall, you are almost guaranteed to find someone who has experience with the car (or cars) you are considering.

And remember that no matter how good a used car seems, you still have to run a vehicle history report on any used car you are considering. Several companies sell these reports, which are based on the vehicle identification number (VIN), but Carfax (www.carfax.com) seems to be the most comprehensive. With these reports, you will find out the vital information about a used car, including whether it has a salvage title or its odometer has been rolled back.

6. Set up financing for your used car.

There are three ways to pay for your used car:

- **Cash.** Need we say more? Money talks—you-know-what walks.

- **Financing through a bank, on-line lender or credit union.** Assuming you can't pay in cash, we highly recommend this route because it will usually save money and give you the most control over the transaction.

- **Financing through the dealer.** This can work for some people, depending on their credit scores and the current interest rates offered. Also, if you prearrange financing through an independent source, the dealer may sometimes offer to beat the rate with a low-interest loan.

7. Reviewing used car markets.

The three most common places to buy a used car are:

- Private parties

- New car dealerships

- Used car lots

A lot of time can be saved by calling the selling party before you go see the vehicle. In this way, you can eliminate cars that have problems such as excessive mileage or a salvage title. Here are a few key questions to ask over the phone:

- What is the mileage? Why is it low? High? (12,000 to 15,000 miles a year is average)

- What color is the exterior? Interior? Does it have leather or cloth seats?

- How many doors?

- Is the engine a four-cylinder, V6 or V8?

- Is the transmission auto? Manual?

- Is the car still under warranty?

- Is there a salvage title?

- What options/add-ons does it have?

- What is the asking price?

If, after talking to the seller, the car still meets your needs, set up an appointment for a test-drive. If possible, make this appointment during the day so you can more accurately determine the car's condition. Also, ask for the VIN number so you can run a Carfax report. Every time you get a line on a used car, run the VIN. This will tell you if the car is clean.

8. Inspecting and test-driving a used car.

Used car shopping will involve inspecting the vehicle to determine its condition. This process is simplified if you buy a certified used car that has passed a thorough inspection and is backed by a manufacturer's warranty. But while buying a certified used car removes a lot of the guesswork about the vehicle's mechanical condition, you pay for this service in the form of a higher purchase price.

If you are serious about buying a used car but have doubts about its condition, take it to a mechanic you trust. A private party will probably allow you to do this without much resistance. But at a dealership, it might be more difficult. If it is a factory-certified used car, you don't have to take it to a mechanic.

Now it's time to test-drive the car.

On the test-drive, evaluate these additional points:

- Acceleration from a stop

- Braking

- Cargo space

- Cornering (Do you feel in control when making turns?)

- Engine noise

- Hill-climbing power

- Passing acceleration (Does it downshift quickly and smoothly?)

- Rattles and squeaks

- Seat comfort/support

- Suspension (How does it ride?)

- Visibility (Check for blind spots)

- Wear and tear (Are interior components mostly intact considering the car's age or does it feel like it's falling apart?)

9. Negotiating for a used car.

Whether you are buying a used car from a dealer or a private party, let them know you have the cash in hand (or financing arranged) to make a deal on the spot. Preface your offer with a statement like, "I'm ready to make a deal now. I can give you cash (or a cashier's check) now. But we need to talk about the price."

At this point, you need to have a persuasive argument for why the price is too high. So let's talk about pricing. The foundation of successful negotiation is information. This is particularly true when buying a used car. Yet, the variable condition of used cars means prices will vary widely as well.

Edmunds.com has removed much of the guesswork in used car pricing by developing True Market Value pricing. After you have gathered information about a car you are considering, visit www.edmunds.com, click on the "Used" icon and follow the link that gives you a "Customized Appraisal." When you're finished, print out the three TMV® prices: Trade-In, Private Party and Dealer Retail.

10. Closing the deal.

If you are at a dealership, you still have to go through the finance and insurance (F&I) process. If you are buying a car from a private party, you have to make sure that payment is made and the title and registration are properly transferred.

In both cases, you also need to make sure you have insurance for the car you just bought before you drive it away. Also, at a dealership, the F&I person will probably try to sell you a number of additional items: an extended warranty, alarms or anti-theft services such as LoJack, prepaid service plans, fabric protection, rust-proofing and emergency roadside kits. Some people swear by extended warranties, so this is something you might want to consider (unless your used car is certified or still under the manufacturer's warranty). However, the other items typically sold in the F&I room are expensive and hold little value for you.

When you buy a car from a private party, you will probably be asked to pay with a cashier's check or in cash. But before money changes hands, request the title (sometimes called the "pink slip") and have it signed over to you. Rules governing vehicle registration and licensing vary from state to state. Check with the department of motor vehicles (DMV) in your state (much of this information is now available on DMV Web sites).

Once all of the paperwork is complete, it is finally time to relax and begin enjoying your new purchase: a good used car.

Used Car Buying Checklist

❏ Choose the right vehicle for you by making sure the car suits your needs.

❏ Consider all cars in the class you have chosen (compact sedan, large SUV, midsize wagon, etc.)

❏ Look up the vehicle on Edmunds.com and check its reliability, editorial reviews and consumer commentary.

❏ Check the Edmunds.com TMV price by visiting www.edmunds.com to get the most accurate price on the car you want to buy (adjusted for mileage, options, color, condition and region).

❏ Decide how much you have to spend on your new car purchase: down payment, monthly payment and purchase price.

❏ Decide how you are going to finance your car. If you are going through a bank, on-line lender or credit union, obtain loan approval before you start shopping.

❏ Using the Internet, including Edmunds.com's Used Vehicle listings, search for the used car you've decided to buy.

❏ Call the seller and verify the pertinent information. Get the VIN. Run a Carfax report on the car.

❏ Test-drive the car under your normal driving conditions. Take the car to a mechanic if it is not certified by the manufacturer or covered by a comprehensive warranty.

❏ Negotiate your best deal.

❏ Read the contract carefully before signing and always make sure you get a clean title.

❏ Inspect the car for dents, dings and scratches before taking final delivery.

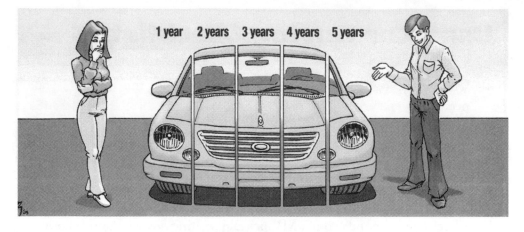

Leasing a Car

Leasing might seem confusing to some people. It's really just another way of financing a car that better suits some people's financial situation. If you take the time to understand it you can better decide if it works for you—and how to get the best deal on a leased car. We've demystified the process for you in the following chapters including our 10-Steps method that will quickly guide you through the process.

Chapter 27

How Leasing Works

"I just don't get it—is leasing a good deal or not?"

Leasing is, well, renting. As the cost of cars climbs, leasing offers a way for consumers to drive cars that are really too expensive for them to own. As such, leasing is just a way of financing a car, of fitting the expense conveniently into the average person's budget.

There are a few differences, however, between renting a car and leasing a car. When you rent a car, you pay more for an expensive car than for a cheesy little compact. But when you lease, you can sometimes get a *better* car for *less* money (we'll explain how and why later).

Another difference between *renting* a car and *leasing* a car is that when you lease a car it is for a very specific amount of time: usually three, four or five years (although lease contracts can be just about any length you want). Also, when you lease a car, you are paying interest, which is a substantial part of the payment (although it is tax deductible if you use the car for business purposes).

Simple Leasing Example

Say you want to lease a $20,000 car for three years. At the end of the lease, the car will have depreciated (decreased in value) to about $10,000. This is the car's "residual value"—how much it is still worth. OK, so you've used up $10,000 of its value. Divide this $10,000 by 36 to get your monthly payments which, in this example, would be about $277. Pretty simple, huh?

But wait a second. Remember that when you lease you pay interest on the transaction, plus, there are taxes, license fees, security deposits and other costs. Furthermore, all cars don't depreciate evenly so the residual value will be different. But still, the basic concept of leasing is that you pay for the depreciation of the car. In the above example, the taxes, interest and other charges would bring the total payment to about $400 (on a 36-month lease with $1,000 in drive-off fees).

So you see that there are some economic advantages to leasing. For one thing, you pay less in tax. For another, your initial outlay of money, the down payment (if you're paying one) and "drive-off fees," are much lower. We'll be going into the pros and cons in more detail later. For now, just know that when you lease, *you pay for the amount of the car's value that you use.*

Is leasing right for you? This question is hard to answer. It really depends on your lifestyle and your preferences. We have summarized some of the key points below.

Chandler Phillips Says:

Leasing is particularly attractive for people who have good credit but lack the ready cash to start a traditional car loan.

Pros and Cons of Leasing

The lists below summarize the pros and cons of leasing vs. buying:

Advantages of Leasing

- Lower monthly payments

- Lower down payment

- You can drive a *better* car for *less* money each month

- Lower repair costs (with a three-year lease, the factory warranty covers most repairs)

- You can more easily drive a new car every two or three years

- No trade-in hassles at the end of the lease

- You pay sales tax only on the portion of the car you finance

Disadvantages of Leasing

- You don't own the car at the end of the lease

- Your mileage is limited to a set amount, typically 12,000–15,000 miles a year (excess miles are paid for at lease termination)

- Lease contracts are confusing

- Leasing is more expensive in the long run (as opposed to buying and driving until the wheels fall off)

- Wear-and-tear charges can add up (paid at lease termination)

- It's costly to terminate a lease early if your driving needs change

Advantages of Buying

- Pride of ownership—you can modify your car as you please

- Car buying is more economical in the long run unless you buy and trade-in regularly

- No penalty for driving excess mileage

- Increased flexibility—you can easily sell the car whenever you want

Disadvantages of Buying

- Higher down payment is generally required

- Higher monthly payments

- You're responsible for maintenance costs once the warranty expires

- Trade-in or selling hassles when you're ready to get rid of your car

- More of your ready cash is tied up in a car, which depreciates, rather than an investment which appreciates

Certain lifestyles may work better with leasing than others. For instance, if you entertain business clients, leasing allows you to drive a luxury vehicle for less money (and there may be a tax write-off for certain professions). Other people just like to drive a brand-new car every two or three years. So ultimately, leasing isn't only a dollars-and-cents question—it's about personal tastes and priorities.

However, for some people, everything is a dollars-and-cents issue. If you are one of these people, or would just like to see how leasing stacks up against buying, we suggest you visit our Web site and use our "Decision Calculator: Lease vs. Buy" (look for the link that says "Auto Loan Calculators"). After selecting a car, you can see an estimated leasing payment, an estimated loan payment and which financing method is recommended. Furthermore, you can see how your payment will change if, for example, the length of loan is extended or the down payment is increased.

Long-Range Impact of Leasing

There is one aspect of leasing, often cited as a criticism, which you should be aware of. Once you begin leasing, it becomes difficult to break the cycle. You may find yourself leasing for 10 or 15 years. A 15-year time span would constitute five leases of 36 months in duration. While you are making lower payments during this time, and driving newer cars, the economic requirement is constant. If your lease payment is an average of $350 during this 15-year span, you will spend $63,000.

Now consider the person who bought a car and made five years of loan payments, totaling, with interest, $30,000. At the end of the five years, she might have a car that isn't worth very much in a monetary sense. However, she still has a car she can drive to work. So, let's say she decides that she likes not having car payments. She can drive that car for the cost of gas, repairs and insurance until the wheels fall off. That could be another five or 10 years of driving for not much more than her initial investment.

The person who leases has little freedom at the end of the lease contract. You can turn the car in and lease again, buy the lease vehicle or try to extend the lease contract. However, you are being pushed into a decision—you have to act. The person who bought a car can procrastinate. And while she procrastinates, she is saving money.

So, you have to be careful about making statements such as, "My car isn't worth *anything*." This might be true if you are speaking in a monetary sense. Still, if it is running, and getting you where you need to go, then there is a very real value to it.

How Long Should Your Lease Be?

We are very specific on this point. We believe the three-year lease (plus or minus a few months) is the best choice for several reasons:

- Most carmakers offer three-year warranties—this means you will always be under warranty without paying for an extended service contract.

- Cars begin to show their age after three years—right at the time the lease is expiring.

- A three-year lease allows you to continually drive a new, or nearly new, vehicle.

- Cars need new tires and expensive maintenance after three years—you can avoid this expense with the three-year lease.

If the above doesn't convince you, then think of this: Why would you lease for five years and be forced to deal with extended warranty fees and higher maintenance costs? If paying for these items doesn't bother you, maybe you should consider buying the car.

Of course, everyone wants a low lease payment, and extending the length of the lease will drop the monthly cost. But extending the lease means you're investing more and more money into a vehicle that will never be yours. It's better to shop aggressively for a competitive lease deal and keep the length of the contract to three years.

Chandler Phillips Says:

People who lease for four and five years often get turned off by the concept. They feel like they've made all those payments and should have something to show for their money.

Chapter 28

What Goes Into Your Lease Payments

"How do I know what a good lease payment is?"

Most people are out of their element when negotiating for a lease contract. Many people can't spot a good deal when they see one. For years, car salesmen have used this confusion factor to their advantage. They could preface any quote by saying, "This is an incredible deal..." and you had no choice but to believe them. Furthermore, they could manipulate payments by changing factors that most consumers were completely unfamiliar with.

But now the Internet has made it easy to generate your own lease payments. Before you even go shopping, visit the Edmunds.com Web site and go to "Auto Loan Calculators." From there it is easy to find the lease calculator. You can select a car and get an estimate of how much the lease payments would be. You can even manipulate the factors, such as term length, interest rate and down payment, to see how the payment changes. These payments are *estimates*, not quotes.

If you want to continue one step further, you can use "Dealer Locator" on the Edmunds site and solicit quotes from actual dealers. But at this point, you probably aren't ready for that. You should, before you go any further, know a little more about what makes up a lease payment so you can be an informed buyer when you are ready to shop.

Leasing's Hot Buttons

In every financial deal there are the significant figures and there are the related fees that don't have much effect on the bottom line. When you shop for a lease, you need to understand the four important figures and watch them carefully (other leasing terms are found in the Glossary).

Capitalized Cost: Lease payments are based on the *capitalized cost*, which is the selling price of the car. The price of the car is negotiable, so you should negotiate this price first and then have the dealer write you a lease based on this agreed-upon selling price of the car.

Money Factor: This is lease-speak for "interest rate." It plays a big part in the calculation of a lease payment. If the money factor is expressed as a percentage, convert the percentage to the money factor by dividing the number by 2,400 (yes, it's 2,400 regardless of the term of the lease). For example, a 7.0-percent interest rate converts to a 0.0029 money factor.

Residual Value: This is the predicted value of the vehicle at the end of the lease term, and is expressed as a percentage of the MSRP (the sticker price). Typically, a car is worth a little more than half its value after three years. Sometimes dealers raise the residual value to lower monthly payments. This is OK, unless you plan to buy the car at the end of the lease.

Chandler Phillips Says:

If you are interested in buying the car after the lease is over, you should keep your eye on the residual value. But remember, you might still negotiate an even lower buyout at the end of the lease.

Term of the Lease: This is the length, in months, of the lease. Popular leases are 24, 36, 48 and 60 months. Some lease companies write leases for 38 or 42 months. The 36-month lease makes the most sense for the reasons described in previous chapters because most cars will be covered by the factory warranty for the entire time.

Later on we'll show you how to calculate an estimated lease payment. You'll see that these four figures will have the biggest effect on what you have to pay each month.

How to Read Lease Ads

You're reading the paper one Saturday morning when your eyes fall on an ad that reads: "VW JETTA, $199 a MONTH!" Is there any truth to this? Or is it just advertising hype? There are several things to look for:

- **Incentives and Rebates:** Auto manufacturers sometimes offer incentives to spur the lease of slow-selling vehicles. Car ads are an important way to learn about this financing method.

- **Remember the Sales Tax:** Another favorite in leasing ads is to quote low monthly payments that don't include sales tax. Usually, you will find small print lurking somewhere that says, "Plus tax and license fees." To compute the tax yourself, multiply the monthly payment by your state's sales tax. Add the sales tax to the quoted payment to get the total monthly payment.

- **Length of the Contract:** Some monthly payments look good until you see the length of the loan. While $299 a month might look good for 36 months, it will break the bank when stretched to 60 months.

- **Interest Rates:** Dealers will offer low-interest rates available through the manufacturer. Sometimes, these rates are way below the prime rate available through banks. This can save you hundreds of dollars over the term of the loan.

- **Available Models:** Some models of selected cars qualify for big savings. Others don't. Read the fine print, and you'll find out where the bargains are.

If a dealership advertises a car at a certain price, they are legally bound to sell it to you at that price. That's why "ad cars" are usually parked on the back lot—they really don't want you to see *that* car at the advertised price. But if you are insistent, you can sometimes convince them to show you the advertised car and get a screamin' deal on it. Just tell them it will be much easier to sell you the car now than it will be to deal with your attorney later.

Chapter 29

How to Calculate Your Lease Payment

Earlier we explained that you can estimate your lease payments on the Internet by using the calculators on Edmunds.com. You can also request actual lease quotes via e-mail from dealers using our Web site.

Still, there might be some of you who want to calculate your lease payment yourself, from scratch. To help you do this, we are including, and will explain how to use, the lease formula employed by most leasing companies. If you go this route, we highly recommend that you create a spreadsheet into which you can put the figures of specific cars to generate accurate lease estimates.

To calculate a lease payment, you will need several figures:

1. **MSRP of the vehicle.** Find this price on Edmunds.com.

2. **The money factor.** This is the interest rate the lease is based on. A common interest rate is 6 percent (as a money factor, this would be 0.0025). If you know your credit is good, check to see what the current interest rate is, convert this to a money factor and plug it into the formula.

3. **Lease term.** Again, we recommend a 36-month lease to ensure warranty coverage.

4. **Residual value of the car.** Call the bank or dealer to find the residual value of the car you are considering. If you can't find the residual value, or you just want an estimate, use a figure of between 50 and 58 percent for a 36-month lease.

Calculating a Sample Lease Payment

In the following example, we have chosen a vehicle that has a sticker price of $23,000. You have negotiated the price down to $20,000. We'll also assume that the interest rate is 8.8 percent and the residual value is 57 percent. What are the monthly payments on a three-year lease?

The first step is to find out how much of the car's value you will use. In other words, three years down the road, what will it be worth? In this example, the MSRP of $23,000 is multiplied by the residual value of 57 percent (expressed as a decimal).

$23,000 X 0.57 = $13,110

The car will be worth $13,110 at the end of the 36-month lease. Since the car was worth $20,000 (after you negotiated it down) and it will be worth $13,110, you will be using $6,890 of the car's value.

Chandler Phillips Says:

The Edmunds lease calculator automatically inserts the money factor (interest rate) and the current residual value.

$20,000 - $13,110 = $6,890

The $6,890 is then broken into 36 monthly payments of $191.39.

Before you get excited about how low this payment is, remember that this figure doesn't include interest or tax. Finding the interest amount is the second half of the calculation. Interest on a lease is computed in a weird way. You add the negotiated price of the car to the residual value and multiply this by the money factor. In this example we have used an interest rate of 8.8 percent, which converts to a money factor of 0.0037.

($20,000 + $13,110) X 0.0037 = $122.51

Finally, these two figures are added together to give you the estimated monthly lease payment.

$191.39 + $122.50 = $313.90

Remember, this figure does not include taxes or fees and doesn't take into consideration any down payment or upfront money such as rebates or incentives. The entire formula looks like this:

1. Sticker Price of the car + options	$23,000
2. **Times** the residual value percentage	X 0.57
3. **Equals** the residual value	= $13,110
4. Negotiated price of car minus incentives (net capitalized cost)	$20,000
5. **Minus** the residual (from line 3)	- $13,110
6. **Equals** the depreciation over 36 months	= $6,890
7. Depreciation (from line 6) divided by term in months	÷ 36
8. **Equals** the monthly depreciation payment	= $191.39
9. Net capitalized cost (from line 4)	$20,000
10. **Plus** the residual (from line 3)	+ $13,110
11. **Equals**	= $33,110
12. **Times** the money factor	X 0.0037
13. **Equals** money factor payment portion	= $122.51
14. Monthly depreciation payment (from line 8)	$191.39
15. **Plus** money factor payment portion (from line 12)	+ $122.51
16. **Equals** bottom-line monthly lease payment	= $313.90

Don't forget that you haven't paid tax yet, and this is significant. To find out how much tax you will pay, multiply the monthly lease payment by the state sales tax. For this example, we use a sales tax of 8.25 percent:

$313.90 X 0.0825 = $25.90

This has increased your monthly payment to $339.80.

In the above example, you will probably be asked for $1,000 in "drive-off fees" (for loan initiation, security deposit and related leasing fees.) If you want to make a down payment, to reduce your monthly payment further, it would be subtracted from line 4, the negotiated price of the car.

While this calculation looks a bit complicated, it actually only takes minutes to plug in the data and generate a lease payment. It's time well spent, since this will guide you through the process and help you get a good deal on a leased car.

Chapter 30

How to Negotiate Your Best Lease

At the end of this section we have created a chapter called "10 Steps to Leasing a Car" which takes the information presented here and gives you a specific set of action steps to accomplish this goal. The purpose of this chapter is to expand on one element of that process—negotiating the lease. Also, please see "Chapter 11: Alternative Buying Strategies," which can also be applied to leasing.

Negotiating Redefined

When most people think of negotiating, they imagine sitting in a cramped sales office in a dealership, staring into the cold eyes of a car salesman. That certainly was the way it used to be done—and you can still do it that way if you want. However, we have an easier method.

First of all, you should understand that the basis of good negotiation is knowledge. If you have estimated your lease payment for the car you want, you have taken a huge step toward becoming a good negotiator. Why?

Let's say you know that a fair monthly lease payment for your dream car is $425 a month for a three-year lease. However, the salesman tells you that the best he can do for you is $550 a month. Are you going to say yes to that? Of course not. So, at the very least, you will reject his offer. Saying "no" is actually a form of negotiation. So, you see, without meaning to, you have now negotiated successfully based on accurate information.

What we want you to understand is that, if you have done your research, and you know the figures, negotiating will come naturally.

Pushing for Low Payments

So now you might be wondering how you get to the point of matching the fair lease payment you have estimated with a real offer from a dealer? Simple. You solicit quotes for lease payments from local dealers by going to Edmunds.com.

Or, you can do this by fax or phone (ask for the fleet or Internet manager). But e-mailing through Edmunds.com is the fastest way to throw a wide net over the market and reel in the best quote.

When you request a quote from a dealer, you have to provide certain information so his response will be tailored to your financial needs. Therefore, you need to give the dealer the following information:

- Year, make, model and trim level of the car you want to lease

- Your three favorite colors in order of preference

- The options you would like on the car

- The length of time you want to lease for (we recommend 36 months)

- The amount of down payment you want to make (we recommend telling them you want to pay "drive-off fees only")

- The number of miles you expect to drive (12,000 a year is standard, but buy more if you think you need them)

As you call for quotes, don't tell them you already know what a fair lease deal is for this car. Why? Well, they might be able to go even lower than the numbers you generated. You want to see what they come up with on their own, before you throw out any figures. Remember, as the old negotiation rule says, "The person who speaks first, loses."

Once you have contacted a number of local dealers (we recommend you contact at least three) you will have a variety

Chandler Phillips Says:

Don't make a large down payment to lower your lease payments. If you have an accident or the car is stolen in the first months, you will lose all this money.

of quotes. If they are close to the estimated lease payment you have calculated, then you might want to accept the offer. However, you need to verify certain specific information. Confirm that the monthly lease payment is an "out the door" figure—it includes tax, title and license. Also, make absolutely certain that it is for the stated number of months and includes at least 12,000 miles per year.

Once you get a good offer for a lease, you can ask them to fax you a "lease worksheet" that will show you all the numbers they have based your lease on. If they look good, tell the salesperson you will accept the deal based on the numbers on the worksheet. You now have a record of your agreement, not just a verbal promise.

Other Negotiating Styles

In the past, books on leasing have recommended negotiating on the purchase price of the car, and then telling the dealer to write up a lease contract for the numbers you've agreed on. You can certainly do this. But if your intention is to lease all along, you might just irritate a busy fleet or Internet manager. Besides, if you have no intention of buying the car at the end of the lease, the only figure you are concerned with is your monthly payment (with a specific down payment, lease term and amount of miles).

Incentives and Rebates

Another way to get a great lease deal is by waiting for an aggressive incentives program. Lease payments will be lowered substantially if the manufacturer is offering low-interest financing, customer rebates or inflated residual values. Check the Edmunds.com Web site under "incentives and rebates" to see which manufacturers are offering the best deals. Plug this information into the monthly lease payment calculator to double-check the figures. Remember that these incentives may not be available on all makes and models or in certain sections of the country. Call the dealers to confirm that the offer is still good before you go too far in your deal making.

Turning Internet Leads Into Price Quotes

In this book, we often recommend that you solicit Internet quotes for cars you want to buy or lease. Requesting the quotes is easy, but your return message may not have a hard price for the car you want. But here's how to work the system to your advantage.

If you visit the "New Cars" section of Edmunds.com, and look up a specific car, a pop-up window will ask if you want free quotes from local dealers. If you are buying or leasing, we recommend getting quotes from multiple dealers.

Be specific about the car you want to buy and when you want to buy it. Your message could read something like this: "I need to buy a 2003 Matsura Accell, LX. My first color choice is silver but I also like gold. I won't buy black or white. I am flexible on options but it must have... (name the options you want). What is the availability of this car and what are you selling them for?"

The answer you receive may be a form e-mail reading: "Hello, I'm the Internet dealer and I will be calling you soon with a price quote." But if you send out six requests, you are likely to get one that names a hard price. That message might read: "I have a loaded '03 silver Accel LX. The MSRP is $20,460. Your Internet price is $18,829."

Compare this price to Edmunds.com TMV®. If the Internet price is at, or below, TMV®, you know you have a competitive, fair price. If not, or if you are looking for a car with different options or in a different color, it's time to contact the dealers who didn't give you a firm price. Here's how to get a price.

Let them know you are "for real."

Most of the e-mails you have received, even the form letters, will have the telephone contact numbers of Internet managers. Call the office number first and you might catch them at their desks. If not, call the cell phone number.

You can tell the Internet manager: "I've gotten several quotes from other dealers and I was wondering what your price would be for the '03 Accell LX. I'm looking for either silver or gold." The price for different cars will depend on the options and color, so they will look through their inventory and find a car on which they can give you a "for instance" quote. Either that or they might say, "We sell the Accell for $500 over invoice."

Now, to get a lease quote, give them the terms: length of the lease, amount of miles you will drive (either 10,000, 12,000 or 15,000 miles) and the amount you want to pay in drive-off fees (we recommend putting $1,000 or less down). The Internet manager will crunch the numbers and give you a monthly payment quote. If you are serious about accepting this offer, ask them to fax you a worksheet listing all the numbers, so you can review it before making a final decision.

Chapter 31

Dissecting a Lease Deal—How to Spot a Good Lease

Every month lease specials are advertised with eye-popping low payments to entice the buying public to add that brand's car keys to their pockets. Sometimes these advertised specials represent a genuinely good deal. In other cases, as we shall see, they are just designed to get the customer into the showroom so the sales staff can practice their up-selling skills.

We will examine the actual lease offer made by a German car manufacturer which is highly sought after both for its luxury and performance attributes. While this car starts under $30K, adding in a few desirable options can raise the price considerably. A typical 60-month loan brings monthly payments soaring over $500 per month.

So this German carmaker has offered what appears to be an amazing lease deal; a 24-month lease on the sport sedan for $289 per month, or a little more than half that $500 per month loan payment.

Sure, this is only a lease, so you never actually own the car. And we don't mean to single out this carmaker as creating misleading advertisements—they all have similar come-ons. Suffice it to say that many people find leasing desirable and it allows most manufacturers to advertise low monthly payments. But the question remains: Is this lease really the deal it appears to be? Let's find out.

The Lease Details

The German carmaker advertises a monthly payment of $289 per month, for 24 months for a sedan with automatic transmission, sunroof and heated seats. Not loaded, but not a stripper either. You have to cough up a down payment of $2,500, your first month's payment of $289 and a security deposit of $300 for a total out of pocket of $3,089 due at signing (plus the small print items, but we will get to that later).

So, is there a catch? And if so, what is it? Well, there is a catch. In fact, there are four catches. Let's examine each one and see how they change the scope of this deal.

Down Payment

The first catch is the amount you have to put down, $2,500. Now, for most people when they buy a car, putting $2,500 down does not seem like a big deal. Putting money down when you finance a car is commonplace so you will, at some point, have enough equity to recoup your down payment and lower your monthly payment. The latter is true with a lease, too, but the former does not apply. Putting money down on a lease simply means you are paying some of your rent (and leasing is essentially renting) upfront, thus making for a lower monthly payment.

To put this another way, let's say you were going to rent an apartment and that apartment had a monthly rent of $1,200. Now, suppose the landlord told you that if you paid $1,200 upfront your rent would only be $1,100 per month. How many of us would do that? Not many we would guess. Well, the same holds true when you lease a car. Whether you pay it upfront or during the course of the lease, the total outlay is the same, therefore there is no real advantage to making a down payment.

There is, however, a big disadvantage when you put money down on a lease. Let's say you have put $2,500 down on your lease and the car is either stolen or wrecked. Well, your insurance and the gap coverage will pay off the car. But your $2,500 will never be seen again since it was used at the beginning of your lease to reduce your monthly payment. So, why gamble with your money? The smarter move is to keep that money that you would have used as a down payment in an interest bearing account and make payments from it each month. You will accomplish nearly the same thing as putting the money down, while assuring that your money is safe in the event something unforeseen happens to the car.

Chandler Phillips Says:

Once you learn how to read lease ads, you can quickly tell if it really is a good deal.

So, if we take away the $2,500 down payment, our $289 monthly payment suddenly jumps to $396 per month, or over $107 per month more! Now you see why many advertised leases have a significant down payment, as it can dramatically reduce your monthly payment (but not the total you will pay for the entire lease).

Mileage Limits

What's the next catch? Well, how about the allotted mileage? This lease includes 10,000 miles per year, or a total of 20,000 miles. That sounds like a lot, right? Well, it really isn't. Even people who work from home have little trouble putting 10,000 miles (or more) per year on their cars. It's doubtful that most people can deal with that kind of mileage limitation. If we changed the lease to include 12K miles a year, the payment rises to $409 a month, or $13 a month more.

But even this higher mileage limit is hard to stay within. The fact is that most people tend to drive at least 15,000 miles per year. When you are leasing, you want to be sure you don't go over your allowed miles, as it can be costly. Most leases these days typically charge 20 to 30 cents per mile over your contract miles. The additional 5,000 miles per year, or a total of 10,000 miles over the course of our 24-month lease could cost an additional $2,000! Adjusting this lease example to include the more realistic 15,000 miles per year would increase the payment to nearly $435 per month, or $39 a month more than the 10,000-mile-per-year lease.

Don't Forget Sales Tax

There is still a third bump in the road…the sales tax. The government wants its piece of the action, too, and this is where the small print comes into play. The small print states that the payment excludes sales tax (along with registration and title fees). How much can that possibly be? It depends on where you live. Some states, like Texas, charge sales tax on the entire selling price of the vehicle (the capitalized cost, in leasespeak). Most states, however, only charge sales tax on the monthly payment. Let's take an average sales tax rate of 6 percent. If the sales tax were charged on the entire selling price of the vehicle, you would have to come up with an additional $1,876. If the sales tax were charged only on the monthly payment, the additional

Chandler Phillips Says:

Even though the sales tax raises your monthly payment, you still come out ahead. You only pay tax on the amount of the car's value that you use.

monthly amount would be $26. This brings our monthly payment up to $461 or $172 per month more than the advertised payment!

Negotiating the Cap Cost

Here is a catch that actually works in the buyer's favor. Most advertised leases are based on a selling price that is higher than what one could reasonably expect to pay. In this case, the lease is based upon paying $31,270 for the car. However, the Edmunds.com TMV® price for the same car in the Los Angeles area is $30,971. If this were the price paid for the car, the lease price would drop to $447 per month. You might be able to negotiate an even lower price on the car. Every $100 you negotiate off the price of the car saves you about $5 per month. The message here is that you should never let the manufacturer determine the price of its car for you. Chances are it doesn't have your best interest at heart.

Summary

So, our $289 per month sport sedan is in reality $447 per month. Is this an amazing deal? Well, that is for you to decide, but let's also put this into context. If you had purchased this same car and financed over five years at an available 4-percent interest, you would have to put down over $6,700 (plus sales tax) to get the same $447 per month payment. Putting no money down would net you a monthly payment of more than $570 for 60 months. Of course you would then own the car, but it is still interesting to compare the payments nonetheless.

What is the lesson here? It is essential to read the small print and make sure that the terms that are being advertised will fit into your lifestyle and budget. This German carmaker is not unique in the way it advertises its leases. Most luxury brands will advertise leases with only 10,000 miles per year, and almost no manufacturer advertises a lease with less than a $1,000 down payment.

Chapter 32

Successfully Managing Your Leased Vehicle

Studies show that consumers generally like leases—until they end. The reason for their apprehension is that people who lease are sometimes charged additional fees for wear and tear or excess mileage.

With today's *closed-end leases* (the only type of lease you should consider), the lease-end fees are generally reasonable, unless the car has 10,000 extra miles on it or melted chocolate smeared into the upholstery. Dealers and financial institutions want you to buy or lease another car from them, and might forgive excess mileage fees and abnormal wear. After all, if they hit you with a bunch of expenses, you're not going to remain a loyal customer, are you?

Additionally, closed-end leasing establishes a set, nonnegotiable residual value for the car in advance, at the beginning of the lease. And, any fees or charges you may incur at the lease-end are spelled out in detail before you sign the lease. All the worry is removed by the existence of concrete figures. But keep in mind that if you take your business elsewhere, you might be sent a bill for items like worn tires, paint chips or door dings.

Here are the choices you have at the end of the lease. Typically, they are:

1. Return the car to the dealer and walk away from it after paying any applicable charges like a termination fee, wear-and-tear repairs or excess mileage penalties. Before you throw yourself at the dealer's mercy, have any obvious problems fixed. Wash and detail the car—good curb appeal will work in your favor.

2. Buy the car for the residual value established at the beginning of the lease (see "When to Negotiate the Price of a Leased Car"). If the car is in good shape, the residual value is probably lower than the true value of the car, making it a bargain. Many leasing companies will provide financing

at the lowest interest rate available at the time your lease ends.

3. Sell the car yourself and pay off the residual value, pocketing whatever profit you make.

Buying Your Lease Vehicle

At the end of your lease, you might decide you want to buy your car and keep it. There may be many reasons for you to do this. For example:

- The buyout price in your contract makes buying the car a great deal.

- You know the car's mechanical history and know it's very reliable.

- You don't want the hassle of starting a new lease or shopping for a new car.

- You've exceeded the number of miles allowed and want to avoid a penalty.

- There is excess wear and tear on the car and you want to avoid extra fees.

The simplest way to buy your car is to check its residual value in the lease contract. Once you know what you can buy your car for, check the Edmunds.com TMV® price. Is the TMV® price the same as or higher than the residual value of your car? If so, this might make a good deal for you.

However, if the TMV® price is less than the residual figure in the contract, don't despair. You can always try to negotiate a lower price for your leased car (see sidebar). Here at Edmunds.com we have bought several vehicles at the end of their lease. Each leasing company had a slightly different process for doing this. But, in at least one case, we saved a lot of money this way.

Tips on Buying Out a Leased Car

Your first step is to call the number listed on your monthly payment slip. You will usually reach an automated phone menu. One of the choices is for "lease-end options." When you reach a human being, tell them you want the "buyout amount" for your leased vehicle. The buyout amount may be slightly different than the residual because they will deduct your security deposit. Also, bear in mind that if you call several months before the lease ends, they will give you a buyout amount for that date, not the end of the lease. It will be the residual value plus the total of all remaining payments.

Chandler Phillips Says:

Not all lease companies will allow you to negotiate the buyout cost of the car. But if they call you and offer you a lower price, negotiate aggressively.

If you want to negotiate a lower buyout amount, you need to make sure you are talking to someone with the authority to make a deal. Furthermore, if you are

---

When to Negotiate the Price of a Leased Car

You've come to the end of your lease and you decide you want to buy the car. But when you look at the residual value in your contract, it seems high. You check Edmunds.com's TMV® price and, sure enough, it really isn't much of a bargain. Still, you like the car....

Leased cars fall into two categories: cars leased through the "captive finance company" (for example, a Honda Accord leased through Honda Financial Corp.) or through a bank. If you are driving a car leased through a captive finance company, it probably will not negotiate the residual value in the lease contract. Since the captive financer is there to serve the dealership organization, it would be undermining the dealers if it lowered the price of the car.

However, if your lease was written by a bank, you might get it to lower the price of the car in a buyout. Tell a bank representative you would be interested in buying the car if the price is right. If they are open to negotiating, they will indicate a willingness to discuss the price. If not, they will clearly state that they will only accept the residual value in the contract. If you want to sweeten your offer, tell them you will finance the car through them. Then they will make a little extra money in interest.

going this route, you should have a figure in mind at which to start negotiations. Here's how to arrive at that figure.

You have to assume that, if your car is returned, the leasing company will either:

1. Let a dealer put the car up for sale as a used car, or

2. Ship the car to an auction and accept the wholesale price

If the car is shipped to an auction, the leasing company has to pay a transport company to move the vehicle, and accept whatever is bid for it. This is likely to be far below the residual value of the car. This puts you in a good position to negotiate. Furthermore, the popularity of leasing has created a glut of good used cars coming off lease. This has lowered the prices of used cars.

When you've set a starting point for negotiations, call the leasing company and make your offer. It will either counteroffer or ignore your offer. However, leave your phone number and give it time to call you back.

As you talk with the leasing company representative, don't tell them you are over the allowed mileage limit, or that there is excess wear and tear on the car. If they know this, they will realize they have you over a barrel and might demand a higher price for the car.

Allow several weeks to negotiate a buyout figure for your leased car. And assume that the negotiations will probably go right up to the return date for the car. If negotiations look like they will continue, you can always arrange an extension of the lease.

Buying your car at the end of a lease is usually a win-win situation for you and the leasing company. Just make sure you have reached a fair price for the buyout and know about any other related fees before you agree to the deal.

Avoid Extra Expenses at Lease End

Many consumers are anxious about leasing's Judgment Day—when you return the vehicle to the dealer and have them inspect its condition. Extra charges may be assessed in the case of excessive wear and tear or additional miles on the odometer above the agreed-upon figure in the contract. Since almost all cars will show some signs of wear after three years, there is an amount of uncertainty that accompanies this exchange.

Such anxiety is not unfounded, experts say. "As the leasing market tightens up, banks are looking for a way to make money from returned cars," one insider told us. "They will be more critical about wear and tear and any deviations from the lease contract." Bottom line: Keep the car at a condition above and beyond "average wear and tear" to avoid penalties.

Here are a few additional tips to prevent dings to your wallet as you say good-bye to your leased vehicle:

- Have the vehicle washed and detailed.

- Make sure you service the vehicle at the required intervals.

- Keep all maintenance records.

- Have the vehicle serviced just before you turn it in.

- Fix things such as windshield chips, which are usually covered under insurance and may cost you nothing to repair.

- Make any needed repairs yourself.

- Stay within your mileage limit.

- If you're over the mileage limit, consider selling the car yourself rather than paying the penalty.

- Any dents should be removed by a local body shop rather than turning it in with the damage.

Additional Leasing Tips

Many problems with leasing can be avoided by negotiating a good lease in the first place. However, here are a few final recommendations:

Put as little money down as possible. If the car is totaled soon after you lease it, this will minimize your loss.

Be cautious about subsidized leases with inflated residuals. You won't be able to afford the car at the end of the lease, because it won't be worth what the contract states. You will be stuck and will have to turn it in. A lower payment isn't always a better deal.

Don't go into a lease longer than you would normally keep a car. If you keep a car about three years, do a three-year lease. A four- or five-year lease will be harder to get out of and more difficult to turn in without extra fees. Don't lease longer than the warranty period that covers the car.

When selecting a vehicle, choose a car with a naturally higher residual. If the vehicle holds its value—or surpasses its expected value—there may be an option to buy it and make money at the end of the lease.

Chapter 33

10 Steps to Leasing a New Car

In this section, we've taken the information you've just read and put it together into 10 steps. The information may seem repetitive, but it will ensure that you cover all the bases and proceed with the steps to successfully leasing your car in the right order. Each step is easy to follow and easy to remember. So read on and get ready for the best leasing experience of your life.

The following steps will tell you how to locate, price and negotiate to lease the car you want. Remember to consult our glossary if you find words here you don't understand.

1. How leasing works.

Leasing a car is just like renting a car—but for a longer time period. Unlike buying, you never actually own the car and you have to give it back at the end of the lease. Leasing became popular in the 1990s, because cars became too expensive to buy for many people. Leasing allows a person to drive a brand-new car and make lower monthly payments, thus making the "new car experience" more accessible to a greater number of people. Finally, leasing can offer tax breaks for certain occupations.

In an earlier chapter, "How Leasing Works," we talked about the pros and cons of leasing. It might be a good idea to review those points now. Remember that while leasing may not save you money in the long run, it might fit more easily into your budget on a monthly basis. Also keep in mind that some people find leasing to be confusing since many of the terms are different. We'll do our best to quickly and clearly explain the process in the following steps.

2. Checking incentives and special lease deals.

Car manufacturers commonly offer lease specials. This is a good way to shop for a leased car because it can save you additional money. However, the specials might have hidden costs that make the offer not as beneficial as it appears. You should always check to see if the promised monthly payment includes sales tax and fees. Also, does the advertised lease require a large down payment (sometimes called a "cap reduction payment" or "cap cost reduction"), bank fees and a security deposit? What about the annual mileage limit? These are questions you want answered long before you close a lease deal.

Edmunds.com compiles and regularly updates a list of lease specials. Check the "Incentives and Rebates" section of our Web site to see what is being offered in any given month. Be sure to confirm the specific make, model and geographic region that the incentive applies to.

3. How long should your lease be?

Cars are usually leased for two, three, four and five years. However, the three-year lease is the best choice for most people. The majority of carmakers offer three-year warranties. If your lease is for three years, you will always be under warranty without paying extra for an extended service contract. Furthermore, a car really begins to show its age at about three years—right at the time the lease is expiring. Remember, one of the reasons for leasing is to drive a new, or nearly new, vehicle on a regular basis. Why would you lease for five years and be forced to deal with extended warranty fees and higher maintenance costs? If these items don't bother you, you should seriously consider buying the car.

Of course, everyone wants a low lease payment, and extending the length of the lease will drop the monthly cost. But extending the lease means you're investing more and more money into a vehicle that's not even yours. It's better to shop aggressively for a competitive lease deal and keep the length of the contract to three years.

4. Estimating your lease payments.

A lease payment is calculated from many figures and can be difficult to understand. However, you should attempt to estimate your own lease payment before you go shopping to avoid overpaying. In the old days (like, five years ago), this meant an hour or two with a calculator. Now, the process has been streamlined by the Internet.

Visit Edmunds.com and look for the section on the home page that says "Financial Calculators." These calculators allow you to generate your own lease payments based on purchase price, lease length, interest rate and more. You can even use the same figures to create a side-by-side comparison to see what it would cost to buy the car. When you are done, print out the results and keep them with you in your car-buying folder as you continue shopping.

5. Finding the exact car to lease.

If you followed the "10 Steps to Finding the Right Car for You," it should be obvious what car you want to lease. This means you know the make, model, trim level, options and color. The more flexible you can be, the better the lease deal you will be able to make. For example, a shopper might be very firm about the make, model and trim level, but could accept a variety of options and colors. If another shopper definitely wants hard-to-find options and a specific color, it will be harder to make a great deal. Why? You have no leverage as a negotiator. You have to pay the dealer's lease rate or continue the laborious process of trying to locate another identical vehicle.

As you make phone calls and exchange e-mails with the dealership's Internet manager, take careful notes. You should record information about each car you locate, including the color, options and the dealership name. This will save time as you continue through the shopping process.

6. Test-driving the car salesman.

As you call dealerships to locate the exact car you want to lease, you can also test-drive the car salesman. In other words, you can determine if this is a person you want to do business with. It's a good idea to consider this issue ahead of time, before you get to the deal-making phase of the process.

The first way to evaluate a good salesperson is to ask yourself if you feel comfortable dealing with them. Are they impatient and pushy? Or are they relaxed and open? If you asked them about a specific car's availability, did they respond to your needs? Or did they try to steer you toward another car simply because they have too many of that model in stock? Do they return your phone calls quickly? Do they answer your questions in a straightforward manner, or are they evasive and confusing?

By considering these issues, you should have a sense of whether you want to lease from this salesperson. If you feel comfortable with the individual when researching by phone, and if the dealership does indeed have the car you're interested in, set up a time to test-drive the car, preferably when the dealership will not be very busy, such as a weekday morning. Before heading to the car lot, review all your notes and make sure you bring your car-buying folder. This might include your checkbook, registration and proof of insurance. Keep in mind that you're bringing these items so you'll be ready to lease a car *if you get a fair deal*. Don't feel obligated to sign a lease simply because you have all the necessary paperwork with you.

7. The final test-drive.

When you arrive on the lot, you will want to take a careful look at the car you are considering. You should also drive the car one more time. You might have driven several other cars during the "10 Steps to Finding the Right Car for You" phase, and need to refresh your memory. If you specified several options—such as side airbags or ABS—check the window sticker to make absolutely sure they are on the car you are leasing.

If everything checks out, it's time to make a deal for your lowest lease payment.

8. How to negotiate a lease payment.

Negotiations can be handled several ways. If the car is widely available, you can use our Dealer Locator feature to solicit bids. Take the lowest bidder and call the other dealers. Can they beat that price? If not, you are at rock bottom.

If the car is harder to find, and you are on the lot, you can still refer to the lease payments you calculated at home. If the lease quote from your salesperson matches your estimate, you're probably getting a fair deal, but make sure the numbers and terms match your calculations. Check the down payment (we recommend a zero down payment), the term of the loan, the monthly payment and the annual mileage allowance.

It is a good idea to ask the salesperson to fax you a worksheet, detailing all the costs before you go to the dealership. This will allow you to review the figures in a relaxed environment. Compare the numbers to those you have calculated and the TMV® prices on Edmunds.com.

9. Reviewing and signing the paperwork.

At the dealership, you will be presented with the lease contract for your new car and a dizzying array of forms to sign. This might be done by the Internet salesperson you have been dealing with or it could be done in a separate office by the finance and insurance (F&I) manager. If this happens, the F&I manager might try to sell you additional items such as extended service contracts, fabric protection, alarms or a LoJack vehicle locator. In most cases, we recommend turning down these extras.

If you have already seen a worksheet for the deal you've made, the contract should be a formality. Make sure the numbers match the worksheet and that no additional charges or fees have been inserted. You will also be asked to sign various forms that register the new car and transfer ownership of your trade-in. Understand what you are signing and what it means. Ask questions if you don't understand, and don't ever feel like you have to hurry. Leasing a car is a serious commitment and it's the F&I manager's job to ensure you are comfortable with every document involved. Remember, once you have signed, there is no going back.

Most lease cars are based on the owner driving 12,000 miles a year. If you drive farther than this, you are charged from 10 to 15 cents for each mile over the limit. If you think you are going to drive farther than the allowed mileage, you may be able to buy extra miles up front. Usually, you can buy extra miles at five cents per mile and have this rolled into your lease payment. This pay-as-you-go approach prevents any unpleasant surprises at the end of the lease.

One last thing, check to make sure the contract you are buying includes "gap insurance," which is recommended (and often, required) when leasing. Gap insurance will cover you if the vehicle is involved in an accident and the insured value is below the car's market value. If not, you can easily buy it from your own insurance agent.

10. Successfully managing your leased vehicle.

As you drive your leased vehicle, you need to remember that the car will have to be returned in good condition. Have all the scheduled maintenance performed at an authorized dealer and keep your eye on the odometer to avoid exceeding the mileage limit.

When the time approaches to end the lease, you will have several alternatives. You can turn the car back in and lease a new vehicle. You can buy the car for the amount stated in your contract and continue driving it. You can renew the lease contract on the car. You can turn the lease car back in and buy, rather than lease, another car. Whatever you decide to do, take the time to consider each avenue carefully. Check current market values of the cars that interest you and shop for lease deals from manufacturers. Making the effort to research your decision will save you money and ensure that you wind up driving the right vehicle.

Leasing Checklist

❑ Decide how much you can afford to spend on your lease payment. Decide on the right length of a lease for you (Edmunds.com recommends leasing for three years).

❑ Check to see what special leasing deals are available on the car you want to lease.

❑ Print out the Edmunds.com TMV® price on the car you want to lease (adjusted for options, color and region).

❑ Use the leasing calculator to determine the monthly lease payment.

❑ Contact the Internet department and tell them the car you are looking for. Simultaneously solicit quotes from multiple dealers for the best monthly payment (make sure the quotes are for the same length lease and the same mileage).

❑ If you are trading in your old car, check its value on Edmunds.com True Market Value (TMV®) and print out this information.

❑ Call the Internet manager to negotiate the best lease for the car you want to buy.

❑ Once you've reached a good price, ask the salesperson to fax you a worksheet showing all the prices, taxes and fees.

❑ Bring your worksheet with you to the dealership so you can compare these numbers to the figures on the contract you will be signing. Make sure the contract includes gap insurance.

❑ Inspect the car for dents, dings and scratches before taking final delivery.

❑ As you drive your leased car, make sure you perform all the scheduled maintenance and do not exceed the mileage limit.

Financing and Closing the Deal

Correctly financing your car is one of the most important steps in the car buying process. You need to make sure that all your hard work in negotiating is put into a contract you can live with. Doing your homework in this area means saving money – lots of it. You don't even have to be a math whiz to make a huge difference to the bottom line. In the following chapters, and our 10-Step Strategy, we'll show you how to safely navigate this essential process.

Chapter 34
How to Get a Good Car Loan

If you can pay cash for your car, you can skip this chapter. If you are like most people and need to borrow money to buy a car, take the time to study this information. Because when the haggling over price is done, you can still get taken for a ride in the financing room. Negotiating the financing of your vehicle is as big an opportunity to save money as negotiating the price of your car.

Begin the finance process by considering what size *car payment* would comfortably fit into your monthly budget. Once you know this figure and how much you want to put as a down payment, you will know how much you need to borrow.

Take your estimated car payment and multiply it by the length of the loan (we recommend 36- or 48-month loans for used cars and up to 60 months for new). For example, you want to have a $250 monthly payment: $250 x 48 = $12,000.

Add to this the amount of your *down payment* and your *trade-in*. For example, you have a $2,000 down payment and a $3,000 trade-in. That would be $12,000 + $2,000 + $3,000 = $17,000. This is the amount you can afford before interest, taxes and fees.

Now, compare interest rates at lending institutions for loans. Given the amount of disclosure required of lenders, this can be a fairly easy process. A lower interest rate is going to mean savings in the long term. And any loan origination fees should be minimal if anything.

Using the payment calculator on the Edmunds.com Web site, plug in the estimated price of the car you can afford and the best interest rate you have found. Adjust the vehicle price, until you reach the monthly payment you want. In this example, with a monthly payment of $256, at 6 percent, you could afford to buy a car costing about $12,500. Keep in mind this figure does not include tax and fees, which will vary from state to state.

To find out what tax and fees cost, multiply the total by the amount of your sales tax plus 1 percent. In the above example, using the California tax rate of 8 percent, plus 1 percent for Department of Motor Vehicles (DMV) fees, the formula would be 12,500 x 0.09 = $1,125 for a grand total of $13,625. This is the amount of money you need to borrow.

Prearrange Your Financing

We recommend getting an independent financing option before you go to the dealership because it puts you in a much stronger position to negotiate. This way, you can *bargain on the price of your car, instead of on your payment*—a common tactic among car salespeople to get you to pay more than you otherwise might. Independent financing presents a number of advantages:

- Keeps negotiations simple at the dealership

- Allows you to shop competitive interest rates ahead of time

- Removes dependency on dealership financing

- Gives you a position to bargain from in terms of the dealership's financing offer

- Encourages you to stick to your budgeted amount

Many people feel comfortable getting auto loans from their credit union. Credit unions often have the lowest interest rates around. However, there are some excellent on-line lenders. On Bankrate.com, you can easily check interest rates in your area. Keep in mind that the interest rates for used cars will be slightly higher than those for new cars.

Some on-line lenders have tailored their business to car buyers. One such company, Capital One Auto Finance (capitaloneautofinance.com), takes an application over the Internet and then calls within 15 minutes to let you know if the loan is approved. If a loan is grant-

Chandler Phillips Says:

By getting preapproved financing, you can negotiate as a "cash buyer." This takes away the salesman's favorite negotiating weapon—treating you as a monthly payment buyer.

ed, a line of credit is created and a check is issued. If you don't end up using the check within 30 days, you don't owe them anything. If you do use the check, the loan is activated and you begin making payments. Since it's never quite clear exactly how much you will need at the dealership (because fees and licensing costs differ), this lender usually issues the check for an amount over the purchase price of the car.

Financing Through a Dealer

Dealerships will also loan customers money to buy their cars, but often their interest rates are higher. If you wish to finance a car through the dealership, you will be asked to fill out a credit application. The information is run through a credit bureau and a credit score is returned within a short time.

One problem with financing through a dealership is that it opens the door for the salesman or finance manager (often called the "F&I" manager for finance and insurance) to play games with you. You might be told that your credit is weak so you will have to finance at a higher rate. If you didn't check your credit before going to the dealership, you have to take their word for it.

However, if you have prearranged financing, you won't have to worry about this. You are in a position in which you can sit back and tell the F&I manager to try to beat the interest rate you already have. If he can, great. If not, you're all set.

Credit Scores Demystified

A credit score is a measure of your ability to pay your bills; it allows lenders to quickly measure your credit risk in an objective manner. Your credit score not only helps determine if you will get the loan, but how much interest you will pay. So, needless to say, it's pretty important. The most commonly used assessment is the Fair, Isaac & Co.—or FICO score.

For years, credit scores were secret from consumers, available only to prospective lenders. This has changed. Under pressure from consumer groups and the government, FICO has now given you access to your score. While an exact breakdown of the formula used has not been revealed, it's now possible for consumers to gain some insight into what factors impact their score.

Five factors play a part in FICO's score calculation:

- **Payment history.** Your bill payment history is about 35 percent of your FICO score. Details regarding payments made on credit cards, retail charge cards, installment loans and mortgages play a part here. How timely have your payments been? How much do you owe? If you've made late payments, how recently did these payments occur? If you've got few or no late payments, your score will be improved. Also, recent late payments will hurt your score more than those made years in the past.

- **Outstanding balances.** About 30 percent of your score is impacted by the amounts you've got outstanding to creditors. Owing a lot on many accounts won't necessarily hurt your score. If you're at or near your limit on your credit cards and other "revolving credit" accounts, though, your score will be compromised.

- **Length of credit history.** The length of your credit history determines about 15 percent of your score. If you're just starting to build your credit history, there's not much you can do to improve your standing in this area over the short term.

- **New credit.** New credit acquired determines about 10 percent of your score. Applying for a slew of new credit is one of the easiest ways for people to mar their rating. The FICO model evaluates how many new accounts you've established, how long it has been since you've opened a new account and how many recent credit inquiries have been made by credit reporting agencies. Self-initiated credit report requests will not impact your score. FICO considers inquiries made within a short period of time as one inquiry. It makes sense, therefore, to try to make all your loan inquiries within a limited time.

- **Credit type.** Ten percent of your score hinges on the types of credit you use. What matters here is your mix of installment loans, mortgages, retail accounts, credit card and finance company accounts. According to FICO, this factor is given less weight if it has full information on you regarding the other four factors.

Now that you understand something about what goes into calculating your credit score, let's take a look at what the numbers typically mean.

Credit scores range from 300 to 850 points, with a score of 300 representing the highest risk borrower and 850 representing perfect credit.

A score of 720 or above typically indicates a very good credit history; those who fall within this range are considered "prime" borrowers, and tend to have no difficulty obtaining credit on favorable terms. However, some banks and finance companies have established differing tiers within this category. Rates can vary even for prime borrowers, so it's a good idea to shop around.

Average FICO scores fluctuate but tend to fall between 700 and 720. Again, rates can vary within this range, so it's in your best interest to evaluate all your options.

If your score is below 690, you may not be able to get the best interest rate. It doesn't, however, mean that you won't be able to get a loan. People in this range need to be very careful to understand the terms of their loan so as not to be taken advantage of. If the only offer a lender will make is more interest than you care to pay, consider not taking the loan altogether.

It suits you to know where you stand scorewise, so that you can target appropriate grantors in your search for a loan. Your credit score may be accessed on-line by visiting the Web sites of the nation's three credit bureaus: Experian (www.experian.com), Equifax (www.equifax.com) and Trans Union (www.transunion.com).

Chapter 35

Putting the Deal in Writing: The "F&I Room"

So it's all done. You've got the price you want and the dealership has accepted your offer. But whether you buy the car on-line, over the phone or in person, you will have to sign the contract in the finance and insurance room, also called the "F&I Room."

It is important for you to understand that the men and women working in the F&I room are really car salespeople. They were once on the lot selling cars but were promoted to their position in F&I where they make much more money. Their duties are to draw up the contracts on your new car, make sure you are insured and give you temporary registration.

Consider Dealer Financing

Hopefully you have followed our advice and secured independent financing before going to the dealership. If so, the F&I person is likely to ask, "What bank are you using? Maybe we can beat their rates." Sure, let them try. Just verify that the term (the length of the loan) matches what you have already arranged. Get everything in writing, and do the math yourself.

If you're leasing, make sure you have "gap insurance." Gap insurance covers the difference between what the insurance company will pay for the car, and what you might have to pay the leasing company in the event of an accident or theft. We believe that gap insurance is a necessity—but many lease contracts already provide it. So check before you pay extra for this service.

The F&I person is also there to make money in commissions by selling extras to new car buyers: rustproofing, fabric protection, emergency road kits, extended warranties, etc. They will offer to

Chandler Phillips Says:

Even if you have preapproved financing you can invite the F&I guy to "beat your rate."

fold the extra costs into your car payments. "You'll hardly notice the difference," they'll promise you.

Sometimes, these charges are attached to the car in the form of a supplemental sticker near the manufacturer's sticker price. These prices are normally highly inflated, but the dealership will fight to get you to pay them. They are very negotiable, however, and you shouldn't hesitate to bargain for or refuse add-ons that you don't want.

Contract Extras and "Gotchas"

Many people look up the invoice price on Edmunds.com and compare it to the invoice at the dealership. When the two sets of figures don't match, they assume the dealer is lying. Often, the numbers are different because the dealer has been forced to pay "advertising fees" by a regional dealer group. Should this cost be passed along to the buyer? This has been a bone of contention for some time, and the issue is still not crystal clear.

Basically, we believe the ad fee should be paid if it appears on the invoice for the car you are buying. If the dealer has inserted the ad fee into the contract we feel the buyer should ask that it be removed. Further complicating the issue, the advertising fee is sometimes given other names.

Ask the F&I officer to explain the appearance of any last-minute fees. If they seem redundant or unjustified you can try protesting them. If the negotiated price is already providing the dealer with a fair profit, additional fees (including an advertising fee written on the dealer's contract) should probably not be paid. And remember, the TMV® price has already taken into account that many other buyers in your area have paid this fee. Pay attention to the TMV® price and you can't go wrong.

The following lists may help you sort out what other fees you may encounter in the F&I room.

Chandler Phillips Says:

Most of the things offered to you in the F&I room are high-profit items and services for the dealer. Carefully consider ahead of time whether you really want to spend the extra money.

What You Should Pay:

- Destination charge

- Sales tax

- License & Registration fees (DMV fees) vary from state to state. These fees are usually from 1% to 3% of the purchase price of the vehicle.

- Reasonable Documentation fee ($100 is reasonable; $500 is not)

Charges You Should Question:

- **Extended warranties.** Sometimes warranties are added without the customer's knowledge or consent.

- **Appearance or Protection Packages.** Paint protection and air fresheners are basically worthless and unnecessary.

- **Administrative costs.**

- **Dealer Flooring Charge.** Another cost of doing business, and one that is covered by holdbacks (payments that come directly from the manufacturer to the dealer).

- **Dealer-installed security system.** Most new cars have a factory-installed system of some type—the dealer-installed system is redundant.

- **Delivery & Handling (D&H).** Delivery is paid for by the "destination charge" and does not need to be paid again.

- **Fabric protection.** Do your own with a $5 bottle of Scotchgard.

- **Pin-striping,** the most expensive tape in the world.

- **Rustproofing.** It is unnecessary and can void your warranty in some cases.

- **Stolen car retrieval system.** Offered in many large metro regions, these devices track the car via homing signal to help authorities track your vehicle if it is stolen. The system is very effective and a blessing to many consumers, but the prices are usually quite high. Make sure you consider the cost before signing up for this as you have a right to refuse it.

- **Teflon coating.** No longer needed because of clear-coat paint used on cars today.

A Word on Warranties

One of the big decisions you will have to make in the F&I room is whether to buy an extended warranty. Here are a few thoughts on this controversial subject.

In the past, Edmunds.com has recommended that consumers turn down offers of extended warranties. If you buy one, the F&I person will receive a large commission. There is also a high profit for the dealership.

However...

Readers have e-mailed us saying that these warranties provide an important function. One F&I manager even said he has seen repossessions because customers didn't have the money to repair the car themselves. For a few extra dollars a month, they could have fixed the car and avoided a blemish on their credit record, the manager said.

Extended warranties bring peace of mind to some people. However, all new cars come with a factory warranty and some of these last for up to 10 years. In other cases, a factory warranty lasts as much as five years—as long as you will own the car.

Remember, while extended warranties are expensive, they are negotiable, and if you have the misfortune to need

Chandler Phillips Says:

Some people like the peace of mind that an extended service contract offers. But remember, just like the car, these contracts are negotiable.

an expensive repair, such as a transmission job, they are well worth it.

Closing the Deal

Finally, after you've haggled your way through the price, the financing, the extras and the warranties, you'll need to sign various papers, many of which are related to the titling and registering of the vehicle. Each document should be carefully reviewed. Once your signature is on the paperwork, the deal is done; this is your last chance to back out. NOTE: There is NO cooling-off period for the purchase of an automobile, so make sure you are comfortable with the purchase before you sign.

While it may be impractical to read all the fine print, you should check all the figures and question anything that looks inflated or out of place. If you are pressured to sign the contract quickly, or the F&I officer refuses to relinquish his grip on the contract, proceed with caution. There might be something new in the contract he doesn't want you to see.

The F&I person will collect any down payment that is due and the papers on the trade-in. They'll give you the new car owner's manual and manufacturer's warranties and two sets of keys. You will probably be handed back to your salesperson, who will escort you outside where your new car is waiting. The car should be cleaned, detailed and filled with gas.

By now, you probably really want to leave the dealership. But don't hurry. Carefully inspect your car to make sure there are no dents, scratches or tears in the fabric. If it is nighttime, make sure you are under good lighting. If you find anything wrong, get the salesperson to put it in writing so that the service department will repair it free of charge.

Chapter 36

Financing Pitfalls and Solutions

In this chapter we've assembled some common problems car buyers encounter when shopping. We've presented easy-to-follow solutions that should put you on solid financial ground.

Pitfall #1:

Many consumers don't know what their credit rating is when they apply for an auto loan. The strength of their credit score largely determines what kind of interest rate they will receive. Therefore, it's critical to make sure your credit report is in the best shape possible before shopping for a car.

Solution:

Order a copy of your credit report and look for items that may stand in the way of you getting a good rate. Correct any issues or errors promptly. Are all of your lines of credit in good standing? Are there any signs of identity theft? The credit bureaus will tell you how to correct errors when they send you the report. The following numbers and Web site addresses will assist you in checking your credit.

Chandler Phillips Says:

When you apply for independent financing, you will learn how strong your credit is. The lender will tell you what interest rate you qualify for.

Equifax: 800-685-1111, www.equifax.com
Experian: 888-397-3742, www.experian.com
TransUnion: 800-916-8800, www.transunion.com

Pitfall #2:

Many consumers are tempted to overspend once they get to the dealership.

Solution:

It's a good idea to set a sensible price range for the car you want to buy and stick with it. Experts suggest that monthly car payments and related expenses should not exceed about 20 percent of your monthly net income. You can even bring a printout of your budget to the dealership as a reminder. And we always recommend bringing printouts of True Market Value (TMV®) prices to use as a guide when negotiating.

Pitfall #3:

Most consumers arrive at the dealership without having researched the current interest rates being offered in the marketplace, so they have no idea if they're being offered a competitive rate.

Solution:

Use the Internet as a research tool to compare rates. Check out Web sites like bankrate.com for national averages, and the Web site of your own financial institution.

Pitfall #4:

Most consumers arrive at the dealership without approved financing in hand. This is either because they are not aware of all the financing options available, or they assume they will qualify for a low rate at the dealer. This approach deprives the consumer of bargaining power when it comes to negotiating the lowest possible interest rate.

Solution:

Become an "empowered buyer" by getting a no-obligation loan before visiting the dealership. Having your own loan could save you significant money. For example, a 60-month $26,000 loan at 4.49 percent can save the consumer about $1,500 over the life of the loan, compared to a loan at 6.56 percent.

Pitfall #5:

Many dealers offer a choice between discounted (or zero-percent) financing or a rebate—but not both. Consumers may erroneously assume that the zero-percent loan will deliver the most savings.

Solution:

Sometimes it's better to take the cash rebate and apply it against the purchase price of the vehicle—and then use your own preapproved loan to finance the vehicle. The savings chart below shows how a low-interest rate and a rebate can "beat" a zero-percent deal.

36-Month Car Loan Comparison

APR	0%	3.99%
Cost of car	$20,000.00	$20,000.00
Less equity in trade	$4,000.00	$4,000.00
Less rebate	$0.00	$2,000.00
Amount to finance	$16,000.00	$14,000.00
Monthly payment	$444.44	$413.27
Total cost	$16,000.00	$14,877.85
Savings	$0.00	**$1,122.15**

Pitfall #6:

The F&I officer may try to confuse you by "intertwining" different elements of your deal. For example, they may say "we'll give you an extra-low price on the vehicle, but this interest rate is the best we can do."

Solution:

Consumers should "unbundle the deal" and treat the car-buying process as three separate negotiations—vehicle price, financing and trade-in value. Avoid discussions that can take you off of this track, such as "how much can you afford to spend per month?" With financing, focus on the APR, not the monthly payment.

Pitfall #7:

By the time they get to the finance department, many consumers are mentally worn out and don't review the contract thoroughly before signing. As a result, they may agree to buy things they didn't plan on (such as an extended warranty, rustproofing, etc.).

Solution:

Before you sign any papers or hand over any money, check the figures in the contract and understand all the charges. The sudden appearance of extra fees should be questioned. Sometimes, dealers add extra fees—so-called "junk fees"—to re-take profit they have lost by selling cars at invoice.

Pitfall #8:

The consumer feels rushed, pressured and confused by the dealership's staff. In some cases these buyers have second thoughts about completing the deal—but sign the documents anyway.

Solution:

Consumers who feel out of their comfort zone should walk away. The buyer—not the seller—should be the one in control of the process. Remember, the federal "cooling off" law does not apply to cars.

Chandler Phillips Says:

Even if you're tired or hungry when you reach the F&I room, don't drop your guard. And definitely don't sign the contract "just to get it over with."

Chapter 37

10 Steps to Financing and Closing the Deal

The following steps will tell you how to locate, price and negotiate to buy the car you want. Remember to consult our glossary if you find words here you don't understand.

1. Figure out how much you need to finance.

If you can pay for your car in cash, then great. But for most folks, you'll need to borrow a substantial portion of the purchase price of your car. Figure out how much cash you have for a down payment and add that to the trade-in value of your current car. This is what you'll be paying up front. Then multiply your ideal payment by the number of months you like to stretch your loan. This is the amount you'll be getting financed. Added all together, this will be the maximum price you should pay for your car.

For example: A $2,000 down payment + a $3,000 trade-in means you will be paying $5,000 up front. If you want a $250 payment for 48 months, then you'll be able to borrow $12,000. You should spend around $17,000 on your car.

2. Hunt for your best financing deal before you buy.

While many shoppers simply go right to the dealership to buy, we recommend arranging independent financing beforehand. This will allow you to get a feel for what interest rates are for car loans and exactly what type of loan suits you best. Bankrate.com is a great place to find market rates for loans across the country. If you belong to a credit union, ask about their rates. And don't be afraid to bargain several lenders against each other to get the best deal.

It's a good idea to understand your credit score before you shop for loans, as well. This way, you'll know exactly where you stand as a borrower and can more effectively bargain with a lender for their best rates.

3. Use your prearranged financing as a bargaining tool.

Many loan companies will print you a check that you can either use to buy your car or tear up in case you go with dealer financing. Once you have this in hand, you can bargain on the price of your car—as illustrated in Sections 2 and 3 on new and used car buying. This way, they won't be able to get you to bargain on your payment as opposed to purchase price. This will enable you to simplify the process and get the best deal using Edmunds.com's TMV® and invoice price information as your guide.

4. Prepare for the F&I room.

After you've agreed on a price, you'll be closing the deal in the financing and insurance or F&I room. This is where very experienced salespeople put together your financing, take your payment and arrange for the prompt handover of your vehicle. They will also be looking to add profit to the sale of this vehicle through financing and other little extras like rustproofing, rims or other goodies added by the dealership. Make sure you are prepared for another round of negotiating because everything in a car deal is negotiable. The order in which these many items are addressed may vary, but be prepared to deal with all of them beforehand. And just because you've already been through a lot with these people negotiating the price, understand that the price can still go up with fees and extras. With this in mind, keep your ability to walk out on the deal as your ace in the hole if you aren't satisfied with something.

5. Look at the extras.

As competition has stiffened, dealerships have looked for new ways to increase profits. One of these ways are dealer add-ons, like paint protection or special chrome body parts. These are nice things to have, but you aren't required to take them. Furthermore, if you do want them, the price of these items is negotiable. Look at every item the dealership is charging you for. These items are often on an additional price sticker near the manufacturer's price sticker. If the dealership won't bargain with you on an item you don't want, then consider it a deal breaker.

6. Look at the fees and taxes.

For the most part, fees are just a fact of life. The dealership has a right to recoup its costs and the government has a right to its share of the deal as well. But don't hesitate to recalculate the figures on your deal sheet. Mistakes are made. And feel free to question any fees that look out of the ordinary based on the list of acceptable fees in the preceding section. Once again, if you feel you aren't being dealt with fairly, consider it a deal breaker.

7. Extended warranty offers.

Generally speaking, if the extended warranty was a good deal for consumers, the dealerships wouldn't be selling them. These are very profitable items for the car companies and this is why they are sold instead of given away as an incentive to buy their cars. That said, for many people, the extended warranty has saved people thousands of dollars in unforeseen repairs and thus makes sense for a good slice of buyers. Consider your needs, research the quality record of your vehicle on Edmunds.com and make an informed decision on whether you need to buy an extended warranty.

8. Consider dealer financing.

At some point, likely before this, someone is going to want to know how you intend to pay for the car. If you have independent financing, tell them about it and disclose the rate you have. But tell them you are open to any other offers and let them try to beat it with an in-house financing offer. Sometimes, you can get special incentives such as cash back if you use the company's financing program. Take advantage of any benefits you can.

Carefully examine the details of any offer they make to ensure it really is a better deal. Go with whichever offer you prefer.

9. Reviewing and signing the paperwork.

Once you've negotiated the price, the financing, the fees, the extras and the warranty and you're happy with the overall price—it's time to sign! If you have already seen a worksheet for the deal you've made, the contract should be a formality. Make sure the numbers match the worksheet and no additional charges or fees have been inserted. Understand what you are signing and what it means. Remember, once you have signed, there is no going back. But if you've followed our advice, you can sign your name with confidence knowing you've gotten a great deal.

10. Inspecting and taking possession of your new car.

Most dealerships detail the car and provide a full tank of gas. You will have one more chance to inspect the car before you take possession of it. Make sure you walk around the car and look for scratches in the paint and wheels or dents and dings on the body. If you are paying for floor mats or other dealer-installed items make sure they are included. If anything is missing, or if any work needs to be done, ask for a "Due Bill" that puts it in writing. You will then be able to come back and get the work done later.

Financing Checklist

❑ Make sure the car you are considering will fit in your budget. Your car payment should be no more than 20 percent of your take-home pay.

❑ Decide how you will finance the car. Will you pay cash? Will you take out a loan? Will you lease?

❑ Look for low-interest financing or lease specials on Edmunds.com Incentives and Rebates page.

❑ Consider checking your credit with the major credit bureaus. Repair any problems you discover before going to the dealership.

❑ Apply for preapproved financing through your credit union, bank or an on-line lender.

❑ If you plan to lease, calculate your monthly payment with zero down for our recommended term of 36 months. Print out your result.

❑ If you plan to finance the car, calculate your monthly payment with 20 percent down and a loan term of 36 to 60 months. Print out your result.

❑ After you locate the car you want to buy, contact Internet or fleet managers for quotes on the purchase price of the car.

❑ If you go to the dealership to finalize the deal, tell them you are a "cash buyer" and have preapproved independent financing. This will allow you to bargain on the actual price of the vehicle.

❑ In the Finance and Insurance office, tell them what interest rate you are approved at and invite them to beat your rate with a loan from the manufacturer.

❑ Review the contract carefully before you sign it. Make sure no additional services or products have been added and no unexplained fees.

Insuring Your Car

So now that you're set to buy, it's a good time to consider the thorny question of insurance. If you don't have insurance yet, you will need to take out a policy that meets your state's minimum requirements and adequately covers you. If you already have insurance, you can transfer your current policy to your new car.

Chapter 38

How Insurance Works

Insurance is something we don't think much about until we need it. So maybe you've never considered this question:

"What is car insurance, anyway?"

Insurance is protection against that moment of bad luck or carelessness—either ours, or another driver's—that results in a costly accident. When we say "costly," we are referring to the expense of repairing a damaged car (or buying a new one), paying medical bills due to injuries, settling lawsuits and replacing damaged property. Yes, hundreds of thousands of dollars could be at stake—if you cause an accident. But remember, that is a big "if." And that "if"—the uncertainty of future events—is what insurance is all about.

It's almost as if you're betting that you will get into an accident, while the insurance company is betting that you won't. Obviously, the insurance company is in business to make money. If too many claims were filed and paid, the company wouldn't be profitable. So, if an insurer has agreed to protect you, it has decided you are worth the risk.

What is Your Attitude Toward Insurance?

Maybe you are reading this and thinking, "I'm not betting I'm going to get in an accident—I'm buying insurance because I have to!" Good point. If that is your philosophy, then you will probably be one of those people who will want the bare minimum coverage. If, on the other hand, you own a company, a house, and have lots of assets, you will want to protect all this with plenty of insurance. How much? We'll cover that later.

For now, you should ask yourself if you are a conservative type of person who wants to plan ahead for any possible misfortune. Or, are you someone who is willing to take a risk in return for saving money. Being aware of your attitude, and working with it, will help you navigate through this murky subject of auto insurance.

We have broken this subject down into a number of insurance topics that bear closer examination. You can review those areas that pertain to you. Once you've acquainted yourself with the separate topics, you will want to read "10 Steps to Buying Auto Insurance" to learn the actions necessary to accomplish this goal.

Chapter 39

How Much Insurance Do You Need?

"Come on, why get more than the minimum?"

If you're like many people, your inclination is to get the bare minimum amount of insurance required by law. That's not a bad place to start and then work your way up to any additional insurance you might need.

In the chart below, minimum liability limits are read as follows (in thousands of dollars):

- Bodily injury liability for one person in an accident

- Bodily injury liability for all people injured in an accident

- Property damage liability for one accident

So, for Alabama, the minimum requirements are $20,000 of bodily injury liability for one person, $40,000 bodily injury liability for all people and $10,000 property damage liability.

Personal Injury Protection (PIP), or Medical Payments (MedPay) in some states, pays for your own medical expenses, lost wages and other costs that arise when you're injured in an accident. It usually pays about 80 percent of your losses, and it also pays a death benefit. PIP is required in Colorado, Delaware, Florida, Hawaii, Kansas, Kentucky, Maryland, Massachusetts, Michigan, Minnesota, New Jersey, New York, North Dakota, Oregon and Utah.

Some states also require you to purchase insurance that will cover your own medical expenses, pain and suffering losses and, in some states, vehicle damage in the event that the other motorist is at fault and is either uninsured or underinsured. See the chart on the next page to find out if this applies to you.

Even though each state has minimum (or no) requirements for bodily injury liability, it is probably in your best interest to purchase higher limits. If someone else is injured and you're at fault, the minimum liability coverage may not cover

How Much Insurance Does Your State Require?

State	Liability limits (in thousands of dollars)	Uninsured/ Under- insured motorist coverage required?	State	Liability limits (in thousands of dollars)	Uninsured/ Under- insured motorist coverage required?
Alabama	20/40/10	No	Montana	25/50/10	No
Alaska	50/100/25	No	Nebraska	25/50/25	No
Arizona	15/30/10	No	Nevada	15/30/10	No
Arkansas	25/50/15	No	New Hampshire	Not required* 25/50/25	Yes
California	Not required* 15/30/5	No	New Jersey	15/30/5	No
Colorado	25/50/15	No	New Mexico	25/50/10	No
Connecticut	20/40/10	Yes	New York	25/50/10	Yes
Delaware	15/30/5	No	North Carolina	30/60/25	No
D.C.	25/50/10	Yes	North Dakota	25/50/25	Yes
Florida	10/20/10 (Property damage only is mandatory)	No	Ohio	12.5/25/7.5	No
			Oklahoma	10/20/10	No
Georgia	25/50/25	No	Oregon	25/50/10	Yes
Hawaii	20/40/10	No	Pennsylvania	15/30/5	No
Idaho	25/50/15	No	Rhode Island	25/50/25	Yes
Illinois	20/40/15	Yes	South Carolina	Not required* 15/30/10	Yes
Indiana	25/50/10	No			
Iowa	20/40/15	No	South Dakota	25/50/25	Yes
Kansas	25/50/10	Yes	Tennessee	Not required* 25/50/10	No
Kentucky	25/50/10	No	Texas	20/40/15	No
Louisiana	10/20/10	No	Utah	25/50/15	No
Maine	50/100/25	Yes	Vermont	25/50/10	Yes
Maryland	20/40/10	Yes	Virginia	25/50/20	Yes
Massachusetts	20/40/5	Yes	Washington	25/50/10	No
Michigan	20/40/10	No	West Virginia	20/40/10	Yes
Minnesota	30/60/10	Yes	Wisconsin	Not required* 25/50/10	Yes
Mississippi	10/20/05	No	Wyoming	25/50/20	No
Missouri	25/50/10	Yes			

*Liability insurance is not required if user has a large fleet, other insurance arrangements or submits a large deposit with the state's bureau of motor vehicles.

their medical expenses, in which case their attorney will most likely come after your assets. It is generally recommended that you purchase 100/300 limits of bodily injury liability. On the other hand, if your personal assets don't amount to much, the minimum requirements might actually suit you, and will save some much needed cash.

Collision and Comprehensive Coverage

Besides various forms of liability insurance, there is collision and comprehensive auto insurance coverage to consider. Collision covers damage resulting from running into anything, be it another car, a fire hydrant or a light post. Comprehensive coverage takes care of your car in the case of theft, fire, falling objects, explosions or other unexpected problems.

Collision and comprehensive coverage are required in most lease contracts, and are essential if you own an expensive car. If you're driving an old rattletrap, on the other hand, and the sum of your premium and your deductible nearly or in fact exceed the worth of your vehicle, you might want to consider doing without this coverage.

So, to summarize, experts' recommendation for liability limits are $100,000 bodily injury liability for one person injured in an accident, $300,000 for all people injured in an accident and $25,000 property damage liability. This would be expressed as 100/300/25. The property damage figure is based on the fact that half of the cars on the road are worth more than $20,000. Here again, though, let your financial situation be your guide. If you have no assets, don't buy excess coverage.

Other Forms of Coverage

Before you purchase any type of auto insurance coverage, be sure to study your other insurance policies so you don't end up paying for something you don't need. If you have a decent health insurance plan, you can get away with purchasing the bare minimum personal injury protection coverage—or none at all if your state doesn't require it. However, you might end up paying a co-pay and deductible under your health plan that wouldn't apply with PIP or MedPay. Uninsured or underinsured motorist coverage might also be a wise buy, even if you have full medical coverage, as it can pay for your pain and suffering damages. If you belong to an organization that offers roadside assistance, you don't need to purchase that through your insurer. The same thing applies for mechanical breakdown insurance if you own a newly financed or leased vehicle which is still covered under the basic warranty.

It's easy to be resentful of the money spent on insurance. But just keep in mind that auto insurance will most likely come to your rescue at some point, so it's imperative to purchase a worthwhile policy. Know what coverage you must have and know what additional coverage fits your lifestyle. Then, when trouble strikes, you will be ready.

Chapter 40

How to Save Money on Auto Insurance

There is a very good chance that you are—this very moment—paying too much for your car insurance. There is an even better chance that you could get a better rate from another insurance company than you could from your existing insurer.

So why not take an hour or so and review your policy for potential savings? Or, if you're fed up with the high premiums from your current insurer, shop around for a new company.

The competition between insurance companies has increased in recent years. If you haven't assessed your insurance lately, it's a good time to do so. It is easier than ever for consumers to shop for low insurance rates, analyze coverage and compare premiums.

You can save on auto insurance in five ways:

1) Make sure you get all discounts you qualify for.

2) Keep your driver's record clean and up-to-date.

3) Adjust your coverage to assume more risk.

4) Drive a "low profile" car equipped with certain money-saving safety features.

5) Shop around for a good, low-cost insurance provider.

First, let's look at the discounts you might qualify for. Discounts fall into a number of categories:

- Low-risk occupations

- Professional organizations

- Combined coverage and renewal discounts

- Discounts for safety features

- More risk assumed by driver

- Discounts for senior citizens

- Good student discount

Low-Risk Occupations

Insurance is a numbers game. Adjusters collect information about what types of people get into accidents. Over the years, they see a trend. For example, drivers who work as engineers tend to get into fewer accidents. While it might be fun to speculate about the reasons, insurance companies don't really care about that. All they know is that, in fact, engineers are a low risk. Since there is less chance that they will wrap their cars around a tree trunk, engineers get charged less for insurance. Simple.

But you say you are a teacher instead of an engineer? You might still be in luck. There may be discounts for teachers. You never know unless you ask—and unless you shop around. Not all insurance companies are the same.

Professional Organizations and Auto Clubs

Have you ever been about to pay $100 for a hotel room, only to discover that a AAA discount saves you 15 percent? Now you're paying $85 and feeling proud of yourself. It's similar in the insurance business. Affiliation with AAA—and certain other professional organizations—will lower your rates. You should check with your employer to see if there are any group insurance rates. At the same time, try checking directly with the insurance company representative when you inquire about the cost of policies.

Combined Coverage and Renewal Discounts

A big source of savings is to insure your cars with the same company that insures your house. Make sure you ask if combined coverage is available. This will lower your payments on your car insurance and make your homeowner's policy cheaper, too.

It's also important to make sure you are getting a "renewal" discount that many insurance companies offer. This is a discount given to people who have been with the same insurance company for an extended period of time. If you have carried insurance with a company for several years, and not had an accident, your insurance company likes you. Think about it. You paid them a lot of money and they didn't have to do anything except send you bills and cash your checks. True, they were ready to do something if you got into an accident. But you didn't get into an accident so they're happy and want to continue their relationship with you. A renewal discount is a good incentive to urge you to return. And it's a good reason for you to stay with them.

Discounts for Auto Safety Features

Auto safety features will also lower your payments. Heading the list of money saving safety features is antilock brakes. Certain states—such as Florida, New Jersey and New York—encourage drivers to buy cars with antilock brakes by requiring insurers to give discounts. Check to see if you live in such a state, or if the insurance company you are considering gives a discount for this feature. Automatic seatbelts and airbags are also frequently rewarded with insurance discounts.

Assume More Risk

One powerful way to bring your insurance premium down is to assume a higher risk. This is done in two ways. The most dramatic reduction can be realized by dropping your collision and comprehensive coverage on an older car. If the car is worth less than $2,000, you'll probably spend more insuring it than it is worth. The whole idea of driving an older car is to save money, so why not get what is coming to you?

Another way to redesign your policy—and save money in the process—is to ask for a higher deductible. The deductible is the amount of money you have to pay before your insurance company begins paying the rest. In other words, you pay for the little dings and bumps and let your insurance company pay for the heavy hits.

For example, a common deductible amount is $500. This means if you're in an accident that causes $1,500 worth of damage, you pay $500 and the insurance company pays $1,000. You could, however, set your deductible at $1,000. This still covers you against heavy losses, but it may decrease your monthly premium by as much as 30 percent.

Final Thoughts

As a final note, if you are being strangled by high insurance costs, keep this in mind when you go car shopping next time. The more expensive and higher-performance a car is, the higher your premium will be. This is particularly true of cars that are frequently stolen or are expensive to repair. Insurance companies keep this in mind when setting their insurance rates for this vehicle. Shop for a low-profile car and get your kicks in other ways. You'll love the savings.

Chapter 41

What to Do After an Accident

Each year, hundreds of thousands of people across the country are involved in traffic accidents. If you are one of these unfortunate people, will you know what to do in the aftermath of a collision? How you react can prevent further injuries, reduce costs and accelerate the clean-up and repair process. Here are some steps to help you deal with the aftermath of a traffic collision.

Action Plan to Deal with Accidents:

1. Keep an emergency kit in your glove compartment.

Drivers should carry a cell phone, as well as pen and paper for taking notes, a disposable camera to take photos of the vehicles at the scene and a card with information about medical allergies or conditions that may require special attention if serious injuries are involved. Also, keep a list of contact numbers for law enforcement agencies handy. Drivers can keep this fill-in-the-blank accident information form in their glove compartment. A set of cones, warning triangles or emergency flares should be kept in the trunk.

2. Keep safety first.

Drivers involved in minor accidents with no serious injuries should move cars to the side of the road and out of the way of oncoming traffic. Leaving cars parked in the middle of the road or a busy intersection can result in additional accidents and injuries. If a car cannot be moved, drivers and passengers should remain in the cars with seatbelts fastened for everyone's safety until help arrives. Make sure to turn on hazard lights and set out cones, flares or warning triangles if possible.

3. Exchange information.

After the accident, exchange the following information: name, address, phone number, insurance company, policy number, driver license number and license plate number for the driver and the owner of each vehicle. If the driver's name is different from the name of the insured, establish what the relationship is and take down the name and address for each individual. Also make a written description of each car, including year, make, model and color—and the exact location of the collision and how it happened. Finally, be polite but don't tell the other drivers or the police that the accident was your fault, even if you think it was.

4. Photograph and document the accident.

Use your camera to document the damage to all the vehicles. Keep in mind that you want your photos to show the overall context of the accident so that you can make your case to a claims adjuster. If there were witnesses, try to get their contact information; they may be able to help you if the other drivers dispute your version of what happened.

5. File an accident report.

Although law enforcement officers in many locations may not respond to accidents unless there are injuries, drivers should file a state vehicle accident report, which is available at police stations and often on the Department of Motor Vehicles Web site as a downloadable file. A police report often helps insurance companies speed up the claims process.

6. Know what your insurance covers.

Dealing with the whole insurance process after an accident will be easier if you know the details of your coverage. For example, don't wait until it's too late to find out that your policy doesn't automatically cover costs for towing or a rental car. Generally, for only a dollar or two extra each month, you can add coverage for rental car reimbursement, which provides a rental car for little or no money while your car is in the repair shop or if it is stolen. Check your policy for specifics.

7. Who will pay for the damages?

If the accident was minor, you and the other drivers may decide to handle the damages yourselves without the involvement of an insurance company. But this isn't always the best idea, for several reasons.

While the other driver may agree to pay for the damage to your car on the day of the accident, he may see the repair bill and decide it's too high. At this point, time has passed and your insurance company will have more difficulty piecing together the evidence if you file a claim.

Also, keep in mind that you have no way of knowing whether another driver will change his mind and report the accident to his insurance company. He may even claim injuries that weren't apparent at the scene of the accident. This means that your insurance company could end up paying him a hefty settlement, or worse yet, you could be dragged into a lawsuit. So make sure that your company has your version of what happened. And check your policy—if the damages paid out by your insurance company are below a certain amount, the accident may not be considered chargeable and you will avoid the penalty of a premium hike.

Final Thoughts

Auto accidents take a tremendous toll on everyone involved, both financially and emotionally. If you're one of the lucky ones who have thus far avoided a serious accident, hopefully the tips on prevention will help keep it that way. The chances are high, though, that at some point you will be involved in a minor accident. Just keep a cool head and make safety your primary concern. You'll have plenty of time to deal with the consequences later.

10 Ways to Prevent Accidents

It's much easier to prevent accidents and injuries in the first place than to deal with the painful aftereffects. Here are 10 ways to keep you safe and reduce accidents:

1. Carefully look both ways—twice—before crossing an intersection. An oncoming car might be hidden by your car's windshield frame.

2. Don't speed into an intersection the instant the light turns green. This is a good way to get rammed by someone running the red light in the other direction.

3. Try to anticipate unexpected changes in traffic.

4. Always check your blind spot before changing lanes—don't just rely on your rearview mirrors.

5. Use extra caution when passing large vehicles, such as semi trucks, which have even larger blind spots.

6. Closely observe posted speed limits around schools and in residential areas; children and pets may unexpectedly run into the street.

7. Leave enough space between yourself and the car ahead of you.

8. Go to a high-performance driving school. Understanding more about high-speed maneuvers could save your life.

9. Don't put off performing safety maintenance and repairs on your car. Have your brakes checked and wheels aligned as soon as it's needed.

10. Use seatbelts. While seatbelts don't prevent accidents, they greatly reduce injuries and fatalities.

Accident Information Forms

You may make copies of the forms on the next few pages to document accidents. Keep a set in your car at all times.

Basic Accident Information	
Date:	Time:
Location:	
Weather Conditions::	

Your Car	
License Plate #:	VIN:
Year/Make/Model:	
Driver:	
Passenger 1:	
Passenger 2:	
Additional Passengers:	

Driver #1		
Name:		
License #:	Issuing State:	Exp. Date:

Insurance Card Information	
Name:	
Relationship:	
Company:	Policy #:
Agent:	

Other Car

License Plate #:	VIN:
Year/Make/Model:	
Driver:	
Passenger 1:	
Passenger 2:	
Additional Passengers:	

Driver #2

Name:		
License #:	Issuing State:	Exp. Date:

Insurance Card Information

Name:	
Relationship:	
Company:	Policy #:
Agent:	

Other Car

License Plate #:	VIN:
Year/Make/Model:	
Driver:	
Passenger 1:	
Passenger 2:	
Additional Passengers:	

Driver #3

Name:		
License #:	Issuing State:	Exp. Date:

Insurance Card Information

Name:	
Relationship:	
Company:	Policy #:
Agent:	

Police Report

Responding Department:	
Officer's Name:	
Badge #:	

Accident Description:

Witnesses:

Name:	Phone #:
Name:	Phone #:
Name:	Phone #:
Name:	Phone #:
Name:	Phone #:
Name:	Phone #:
Name:	Phone #:
Name:	Phone #:

Chapter 42

10 Steps to Buying Auto Insurance

1. Starting out.

When it comes to auto insurance, you want to be adequately covered if you get in an accident but you don't want to pay any more than you have to. Keep telling yourself there is money to be saved. Compare rates from many different companies. Make sure you keep your driving record and your credit rating clean. Beyond that, remember that shopping your policy against others may be well worth the effort.

2. How much coverage do you need?

To find the right auto insurance, start by figuring out the amount of coverage you need. This varies from state to state. So take a moment to find out what coverage is required where you live. General recommendations for liability limits are $100,000 bodily injury liability for one person injured in an accident, $300,000 for all people injured in an accident and $25,000 property damage liability (that is, 100/300/25) given that half of the cars on the road are worth more than $20,000. Here again, though, let your financial situation be your guide. If you have no assets, don't buy excess coverage.

3. Review your driving record and current insurance policy.

Before you begin shopping for insurance you should check the following: the status of your driving record, your current coverage and the premiums you are paying.

You should know how many tickets you have had recently. Nothing drives up the price of insurance like a bad driving record. Also, pull out a recent insurance bill and jot down the amount of coverage you currently have and what you are paying for it. Take note of the yearly, also semiannual—a lot of policies bill you every six months—and monthly cost of your insurance since many of your quotes will be given both ways (but keep in mind that paying monthly will include higher interest rates and cost you more). Now you have a figure in mind to try to beat.

4. Solicit competitive quotes.

Now that you have made several practical and philosophical decisions, it's time to start shopping. Begin by setting aside about an hour for this task. Bring your current insurance policy, your driver license, your vehicle registration and all your records to the table.

You can try getting quotes on-line from some of the insurance companies listed on the Edmunds.com Web site—Esurance (http://www.esurance.com/), Geico (http://www.geico.com/), GMAC Insurance (http://www.gmac123.com/) or Progressive (http://www.progressive.com/). These forms will take about 10 minutes each to complete.

5. Record and compare quotes.

While you're researching companies, make notes in a separate computer file or on a piece of paper divided into categories. This will keep you from duplicating your efforts. When you visit the different on-line insurance sites, you should take note of several things:

- Annual, six-month and monthly rates for the different types of coverage; make sure to keep the coverage limits the same so that you can make "apples-to-apples" comparisons.

- An 800 number to call for questions you can't get answered on-line.

- The insurance company's payment policy (when is your payment due? What happens if you're late in making a payment?).

- Discounts offered by the insurance company that pertain to you.

- The insurance company's consumer complaint ratio from your state's department of insurance Web site.

6. Work the phones.

Once you have exhausted your on-line options, it's time to work the phones. Those companies you haven't been able to get an on-line quote from should be contacted. Sometimes, doing this process over the phone can actually go faster, providing you have all the information regarding your driver license and vehicle registration close at hand. When you get a quote, be sure to confirm the price. Also, ask the representative to fax or e-mail the quote to you so you have a record of the price.

7. Look for discounts.

While talking to the insurance companies' telephone salespeople, make sure you explore all options relating to discounts. Insurance companies give discounts for a good driving record, safety equipment (antilock brakes, for example), certain occupations or professional affiliations and more. For more in this area, make sure you read the previous chapter: "How to Save Money on Auto Insurance."

8. Choosing the right insurance company.

You now have most of the information in front of you that you need to make a decision. However, there is something more to consider. You know which companies are offering the least expensive policies, but which is the most reliable insurance company?

Below, we offer a number of issues to consider.

1) Visit your state's department of insurance (http://www.ican2000.com/state.html) and check consumer

complaint ratios and basic rate comparison surveys.

2) Consider contacting an insurance agent for additional information about a particular company. Some companies have their own local agents and others sell policies through independent agents. Companies without agents often offer lower rates.

3) Look over J.D. Power and Associates' (http://www.jd-power.com) consumer satisfaction surveys reviewing auto insurance companies.

9. Review the policy before you sign.

So, you've done your research, and you've decided on a company. Before you sign, though, read the policy. In addition to verifying that it contains the coverage you want, there are two clauses that you should look for in the contract:

A) Retain your right to sue.

Find out if you are giving up your right to go to court and will be forced into arbitration if there is a disagreement between you and the insurance company, experts advise. You're better off if you don't give up this right. In some cases you might be able to cross out that line in the policy and still obtain coverage from the company.

B) Avoid aftermarket parts requirements.

If an insurance company has written in the policy that "new factory," "like kind and quality" or "aftermarket parts" may be used for body shop repairs, consider going to another company, experts advise. If you own a relatively new car that you plan to keep for a while, you will probably be much happier if you spend a little more time researching companies on the front end rather than try to fight the company when you have a claim.

10. Cancel your old policy.

After you lock in the insurance policy you want, you have two more things to do. The first is to cancel coverage with your existing insurance company. Second, if your state requires you to carry proof of insurance, make sure you either have it in your wallet or the glove compartment of your car.

Now, there's one last thing to do: reward yourself for saving so much money.

Insuring Your Car Checklist

❑ Determine your state's insurance requirements.

❑ Consider your own financial situation in relation to the required insurance and consider buying more to protect your assets.

❑ Review the status of your driving record—do you have any outstanding tickets or points on your driver license?

❑ Check your current coverage to find out how much in premiums you are paying.

❑ Get competing quotes from an Internet insurance Web site such as InsWeb.com (www.insweb.com), YouDecide.com (atl.youdecide.com) or InsureOne.com (www.insureone.com).

❑ Make follow-up phone calls to insurance companies to get additional information about coverage.

❑ Inquire about discounts you might qualify for such as a multiple policy discount.

❑ Evaluate the reliability of the insurance company you're considering by visiting your state's insurance Web site.

❑ If you have chosen a new insurance company, remember to cancel your old policy.

How to Sell Your Car

Selling your old car is easier and cheaper than ever before thanks to the internet. But you still have to give your car "curb appeal" before it goes on the auction block. And make sure you've priced it to move. We'll walk you through the whole process in this section – and even show you some sales tools you didn't know existed.

Chapter 43

Your Car Might Be Worth More Than You Think

"Selling my old car is going to be such a hassle."

To you, your old car looks like an eyesore. Every ding, dent and scratch screams out for attention. The inside looks like an unmade bed and it creaks and groans when it's on a bumpy road. You're sick of the darn thing and wish it would just go away.

But wait! While it might seem worthless to you, it is actually a hidden treasure. With a little bit of elbow grease, some creativity and a few hours' effort, you can turn your old car into a stack of hundred dollar bills. Exactly how tall a stack of bills, you may ask? Well, that depends on your resourcefulness.

The point is that people tend to overlook the value of their used car. There is always someone who needs reliable transportation. And, if your car is running, it has value.

Chandler Phillips Says:

When pricing your used car for sale, make Edmunds TMV® your first stop. It takes the guesswork out of determining a car's value.

One Man's Used Car Story

A friend of ours called us one day with a problem. He had a 1970 MGB in his garage that didn't run. Well, actually, it was running when he drove it into the garage 10 years ago but he never drove it out again. He needed the space. He was thinking of paying someone to tow it away. He thought no one would pay a dime for it.

A neighbor came over with his teenage son and together the three of them pushed the old sports car out into the sunlight for the first time in 10 years. They hosed it off. They inflated the tires. They vacuumed the interior. The teenager fell in love with it. "It would be so cool to fix it up and get it running again," he said. The father was hesitant: "Let's post an ad and see what happens."

They advertised the car on the Internet and a strange thing happened. They began getting calls from all over the world. The MGB, which didn't even run, was sold for $1,600 to a man who lived in the Netherlands. The man pushed the car onto a trailer and paid in cash.

So, instead of paying someone to tow the car away, this man made $1,600 in cash. Had he researched the market a little more aggressively, he probably could have sold the car for even more money.

The moral of the story: one man's trash is another man's treasure. Welcome to the world of used cars.

Get Ready to Cash In

We hope you are encouraged by the above story. And it's not the only one of its kind. It happens all the time, all across the country. Keep in mind that beauty (and value) is in the eye of the beholder. Now that you have upgraded to a new (or newer) car, your old car looks shabby by comparison. But imagine the teenager who can only scrape together a few weeks' pay for a used car. He's not looking at your car as a discarded junker. He's looking at it as his first set of wheels, his ticket to freedom.

Before we begin down this road to used car selling, there is a final point to keep in mind. While you are, at this moment, without a single lead to accomplish your goal, you have to trust in the serendipity of sales. Unexpected things happen that bring strangers together to solve problems. Open yourself up to the mystery of the sales process. And let's begin.

Chapter 44

Get Your Car Ready to Sell

"What can I do to make my car sell quickly?"

Getting your car ready to sell breaks down into three steps:

1. **Washing, detailing and fixing** your car to give it "curb appeal."

2. **Pricing:** finding out what your car is worth.

3. **Advertising:** creating and printing ads that draw buyers.

Notice that we have put the washing, detailing and fixing *before* the pricing and advertising. Actually, these steps can be done in any order. However, if you do the cosmetic work first, you will have a more accurate idea of what to ask for the car. Also, the car will have more value for you if it looks sharp. You will be a better salesperson and you'll get a better price. Here's what we mean.

Uncovering Your Car's Value

At this point your car might be in pretty rough shape. The interior looks like the aftermath of a wild party. The paint is covered with dust and mud and the air conditioner doesn't work. Can you still sell your car? You bet you can. But it will take a little work.

Start by washing the car. When we say washing we mean to clean all the exterior surfaces and dry it so that there are no chalky white water marks. Pay particular attention to the glass surfaces so that no streaks are left. Step back and assess the car's look from the point of view of a buyer. If you were driving by and saw your car with a "For Sale" sign

Chandler Phillips Says:

Car salesmen know the importance of giving a car "curb appeal." You want the buyer to fall in love at first sight.

in the window, would you stop and take a closer look? And how much would you pay for it?

So, with a minimum amount of effort, your car looks 50 percent better, right?

Checklist for Cleaning and Detailing

Here is a to-do list that will help you turn your heap into a creampuff:

- Have your car washed, waxed and detailed.

- Make sure your car is both mechanically sound and free from dents, dings and scrapes.

- Consider making low-cost repairs yourself rather than selling it "as is."

- Shovel out all the junk from the inside of the car. You don't want prospects to feel like they've walked into your messy bedroom. Let them visualize the car as theirs.

- Use touch-up paint on scratches and pitted areas.

- Wipe the brake dust off the wheel covers and apply a product such as Armor All to the tires.

- Thoroughly clean the windows (inside and out) and all mirrors.

- Wipe down the dashboard and empty the ashtrays.

- Eliminate stale odors with an air freshener.

- Shampoo or vacuum carpets and floor mats.

- Use engine degreaser at a car wash to clean engine.

- Organize your maintenance records and your car's title and have all the documents neatly arranged in a folder, ready to show prospective buyers.

- If the car needs routine maintenance, such as an oil and filter change, take care of that before putting the car up for sale.

- Have your mechanic check out your car and issue a report about its condition. You can use this to reassure a doubting buyer.

- Obtain a Carfax report (www.carfax.com) to show the prospective buyer that the title is clear, no salvage title exists and the odometer has not been rolled back.

And you're just getting started!

Now turn to the interior. Cars are a little like houses: we buy them for their exterior style, but we live in the interior. Aside from the few moments it takes to walk up to the car, you spend most of your time seated behind the wheel. So make the area around the driver seat sparkle—it's the first place prospective buyers will sit as they contemplate whether to buy your car.

At this point we should say that all this washing, waxing and detailing could easily be done by a professional. You could just have your car professionally washed, waxed and detailed. While this is expensive—it could easily cost more than $100—it might substantially increase the selling price of the car. So, here you are faced with a typical problem: should you lay out additional money up front so you can get a higher price on the sale?

Chandler Phillips Says:

While washing your car you will see all the dings and dents on the body. Fix anything major before putting it up for sale.

And what about the broken air conditioner? Should you have that fixed, or sell the car "as is"?

As you prepare your car for sale, you may ask yourself these types of questions several times. Answering each one becomes a judgment call that only you can make. But here are a few thoughts to consider as you ponder this subject.

To Fix or Not to Fix

The essential question when pondering repairs and other out-of-pocket expenses is this: will you get your money back when you sell the car? Certain expenses are unavoidable; others are like elective surgery. However, you can usually make a decision if you ask three questions:

1. Is this repair necessary to the operation of the car?

2. How much will the repair cost?

3. Can I increase the selling price of the car by the amount of the repair?

The broken air conditioner is a good example of the kinds of questions you might face. Sure, you can still sell the car and it has good transportation value. But a broken air conditioner might make some people lose interest in the car altogether. Others might not consider this very important, especially if you live in an area where the temperatures are mild.

Visiting the Edmunds Maintenance Guide can give you an idea what repairs will cost. It will also show what maintenance should be done at different mileages.

Handling Problems

You've decided to sell the car "as is" and let the next person either deal with it or live with the broken air conditioner rather than spend the $500. Still, how do you present the car in less-than-perfect condition?

We don't recommend that you put "broken air conditioner" in your ad. However, before someone takes the time to come and see your car, probably assuming that the car is in good shape, you should alert them to the problem. Say something like, "I should let you know that the air conditioner isn't working right now. I took it to a shop and they estimated the repair will cost $500. So I've reduced my price by $500."

At this point, some people will drop out of consideration. But bargain hunters may be attracted to the car for the very reason that they feel they are getting a special price. At least you have been honest about the whole issue and not tried to hide it.

Chandler Phillips Says:

Price the car a little higher than you expect to sell it for. This leaves you wiggle room to negotiate and still get a good price for your car.

Setting Your Price

By now you are probably experiencing a renewed appreciation of your old car. It is washed, detailed and ready for sale. Now you are in a good frame of mind to set a price for it. While Edmunds.com, and the Edmunds Used Car Book, can help you get an exact figure, every used car is a little different. Furthermore, the older a car gets the more subjective the price becomes.

We recommend that, when setting the price, you start with the hard data and then work toward the soft issues. In other words, look up the TMV® price on Edmunds.com and adjust that figure for options, condition, color and mileage. Look at the classifieds and see what others are asking for the same car as yours. Then, begin considering how to handle problems such as the broken air conditioner. Finally, use your intuition. Take one last look at the car and say, "What would I pay for it if I needed a car?"

Also, you have to keep in mind that most buyers will test your "asking price." They will want to know if it is "firm" or open to negotiation. If you are eager to sell the car, you should indicate this by a few well-chosen words: "Must sell!" or the ever-popular "OBO" (or best offer).

For now, just know that the price you put in your ad should be a little higher than what you actually plan to sell the car for. This is known as creating "wiggle room." With this in mind, consider your "transaction price"—the price you will actually sell it at—and the "asking price." Working backward will give you the best idea of where to set your price.

Writing an Ad for Your Car

What is the most important factor in selling your car? Is it the car itself? Is it the price? The condition of the car? The color of the car? Is it the wording of the ad?

Actually, it is a combination of all these things. Also, different aspects are important to different buyers. So you need to prepare for anything. Keep these thoughts in mind as you prepare an ad for your car.

If you are going to advertise your car in the classified section of a newspaper, your space will be limited so little room is left for creativity. In fact, you will probably find yourself following the prompts of the classified advertising representa-

Chandler Phillips Says:

Little words in your ad like "firm" or "must sell" can send a signal to buyers. It tells them how eager you are to move the car.

tive who answers your phone call. They will want to know the make, model and year of the car. They may ask for the current Vehicle Identification Number (VIN) and the license plate number. Beyond this skeletal information, you will want to provide the car's trim level, color, current mileage, condition and price.

If you advertise on the Internet, you will have room to describe the car in more detail. But this doesn't mean you should go on and on about the virtues of the spoiler you installed or the aftermarket mood lighting in the backseat. The purpose of the ad is to take prospective buyers to the next step in the process. And that next step is to give you a call. With this in mind, you are making people curious enough to want to call you.

Moving to the Next Step

By now, we hope you have at least rekindled your appreciation for your old car. We hope you have, in a sense, seen the prince, rather than the frog. If so, then you will do a good job when it comes time to take calls from prospective buyers, show the car and close the deal.

Places to Advertise

Creativity is needed when selling a used car. However, there are tried-and-true ways to find buyers. Here are the main avenues for advertising used cars:

- On-line classified ads such as those on Edmunds.com

- eBay or other on-line auctions

- Daily newspaper classified ads

- Weekly "shoppers" and giveaway newspapers

- Bulletin boards at your job, a local supermarket or on a college campus

- Word of mouth—tell your friends and family you have a car for sale

- Put a "For Sale" sign in the car window or use white shoe polish on the back window to make an eye-catching sign

- Create a flyer with tear-off strips containing your telephone number

Chapter 45

Showing Your Car to Buyers

"Should I trust strangers when selling my car?"

It is tough to sell a used car without taking phone calls from strangers and eventually meeting people you don't know. Maybe you can sell it by word of mouth to a friend or family member. But most of us will eventually have to sell our used car to someone we don't know. This will take some trust in your fellow human beings. However, if you are careful and use common sense, it can be a pleasant process that brings you some much needed cash. Furthermore, you are helping other people, too—providing transportation to a college student or young working person struggling to make ends meet.

Still, there are ways to protect yourself during what could be a sticky process. The first step deals with how to take phone calls from prospective buyers when they call.

Taking Calls From Buyers

People who call you after seeing your used car ad will want a little information before they take the time to come and see the car in person. Your job, then, is to give them the information they need to make this decision, while presenting your car in the best light. However, you don't want to waste their time. So be honest and let them make the final decision on whether to come see the car.

It's better to think of yourself as an information provider than a salesman. However, it's not a bad idea to let your enthusiasm for your car come through by volunteering: "You know, it's been a great car." Or, "I'm sorry to be selling it but I got a new car I like even better."

Some people who call you may be a little tongue-tied; they don't really know

Chandler Phillips Says:

It's best not to try too hard to "sell" the car or you'll turn buyers off. Be friendly, open and let the car sell itself.

what to ask. So be ready to give them the vital statistics on your car even if these were already listed in your ad (see sidebar on handling calls). If they are focused on their own list of questions, then fine, let them run the show. If not, take charge and give them the information you know they need.

Handling Calls From Prospective Buyers

Some callers don't really know where to start when inquiring about the car you have for sale. Here is how to handle a shy or hesitant shopper:

(Phone rings; you answer it.)

CALLER
Er, yeah. Um... You have a car for sale?

YOU
Yes, it's a 2000 Matsura Accell—the EX model.

CALLER
Oh. OK... Thanks. So....?

YOU
It's in good running condition and it has 67,500 miles on it.

CALLER
So, 67,500 miles, huh? Cool. Yeah, so anyways...

YOU
It's a black four-door with gray interior. It has the cloth interior, not leather.

CALLER
How much ya want for it?

YOU
My asking price is $4,500. If that's the range you're shopping in, you're welcome to come take a look at it.

CALLER
Look at it? Good idea. Cool. OK.

Remember, the basics that most people are interested in are as follows:

1. Make, model, year and trim level
2. Mileage
3. Color
4. Price
5. Options
6. Condition

Once you have covered the basics, an interested caller might want more details before they decide whether to come and look at the car. You can now move to another level of detail by making the following points:

1. **Options:** "It's got a lot of options on it for the price. It has the CD changer, leather seats and a power moonroof. Not only that but…" Don't go on and on, but let the caller know what they are getting for their money.

2. **Condition:** "The car has been garaged so the paint job is in great shape. I'm not a smoker, so the interior is clean and doesn't smell. The car has never been in an accident and doesn't have any scrapes or dents."

3. **Why you're selling it:** "I really like the car, but I changed jobs and need a bigger trunk to carry sales samples with me."

Now the caller is definitely interested. So it's a good idea to divulge any obvious problems that might impact the sale.

1. **Complications:** "Before you come, I just want you to know that the air conditioner isn't working. My mechanic said it would cost $500 to fix so I deducted that from my selling price."

2. **Additional incentives:** "I should mention that the car is still under the factory warranty. It's in great shape but if something were to go wrong with it, you'd be covered."

Handling Callers' Questions

In some cases, you might get a caller who asks a few questions and then blurts out: "OK, what's your best price?" It's really too soon for such a question. After all, they haven't even seen the car yet. Still, you might want to indicate that you are flexible. An appropriate answer might be: "Why don't you come down and take a look at the car first? If you like it, I'd be willing to discuss the price."

Another question you might get is, "So, why are you selling the car?" Be ready for this question. Sometimes your only reason for selling the car is that you've gotten sick of it. This doesn't sound very good to a prospective buyer. So you need to flip it around. "I got a raise so I've decided to move up to a car with more features on it."

Other callers will think they are being very savvy by suddenly blindsiding you with a question such as: "OK, so what's wrong with the car?" Notice they don't ask, "Is there anything wrong with the car?" Instead, they ask the question in an assumptive form trying to flush out hidden problems. Be ready for this one by calmly answering, "Well, as I mentioned, it's in great shape. In fact, I have a report from my mechanic who inspected it thoroughly. I'll show it to you when you come to see the car. "

Setting Up an Appointment

If you are uncomfortable with prospective buyers coming to your house, you can always arrange a meeting at a shopping mall parking lot or at a city park. You could even volunteer to bring the car to the buyer. However, when documents are exchanged, they will see your address on motor vehicle transfer documents. And, if your conversation thus far has made you suspicious of a caller, then just end your interaction at this point.

A prospective buyer will want to look the car over and then take it for a test-drive. It's a good idea to stay with them during this process to answer any questions they have. While you want to be friendly and open in your attitude, you also need to allow them the chance to concentrate while they inspect the car. If you feel they have missed key features, point these out to them after they seem to have exhausted their own exploratory efforts.

It is a good idea to go with a prospective buyer on a test-drive because:

- The buyer is probably unfamiliar with the area and they might otherwise get lost.

- You can point out additional features and explain how to operate the controls.

- Any questions that arise are easily answered by you.

- Negotiations might begin as the test-drive is still in progress.

In some cases, a person who is interested in the car might want to take it to a mechanic. You should allow this as long as you make it clear that they have to pay for the inspection. If you would like to eliminate this, take the car to your mechanic first. Conversely, their request might be fulfilled by showing them service records of work you've had performed on the car. Finally, if the car is still under warranty, and the coverage is transferable, they might waive the inspection knowing that any repairs will be covered.

After the Test-drive

Your interested buyer has looked the car over, driven it and asked all sorts of questions. They are now standing beside the car, looking it over, forehead creased in deep thought. Then they say, "Would you consider…?" and you know you are about to get an opening offer. How you respond could make all the difference to getting a good price, and successfully selling the car. We'll examine your response—and other important issues—in the next chapter.

Chapter 46

Negotiating and Closing the Deal

"What do I do if someone starts pressuring me to drop the price?"

Negotiating makes some people nervous. But keep in mind that your prospective buyer is probably just as nervous as you are. However, it doesn't have to be unpleasant. And you can still wind up at an agreeable price—if you keep a few points in mind.

If you were paying attention earlier, you read that your asking price should leave you some "wiggle room." Well, now it's time to start wiggling. Let's say you have asked $5,000 for your car, but you would like to get $4,500. Your prospect is likely to approach you in one of several ways.

Opening Negotiations

"I like the car, but…" This is the softest way to negotiate on the price. They may not even state that the price seems too high. However, if they say, "I like the car, but…" and then lapse into uncomfortable silence, you might consider an appropriate response. If you really want to move the car, you could say, "How much would you be willing to pay?"

"What's your best price?" This is a more direct way to probe the seller to find how much he or she would come down. If you get this from a prospective buyer, don't seem too eager to reduce your price.

"Would you accept…?" Now we're getting somewhere. This buyer has thought it over and is making an offer. But the offer is being presented in a polite manner designed to allow for a counteroffer.

"Take it or leave it." This buyer is making an offer that supposedly leaves no room for a counteroffer. In reality, this buyer might be bluffing. Still, they are sending a message that they are close to their final price. The only way to know for sure whether it really is a "take it or leave it offer" is to leave it. They may be back tomorrow ready to pay your price.

"**All I can afford is…**" This one is a little tough to handle because they are making a pity plea. However, keep in mind that this is often a ruse. People feel they can't "afford" something even if they have the money to buy it.

Making a Counteroffer

Once an offer is on the table, it is up to you to accept it, reject it or make a counteroffer. Let's say they have offered you $4,500 for your car that you advertised at $5,000. In other words, they have undercut your offer by $500. That's quite a big drop in price. Still, $4,500 is your rock-bottom price.

First of all, don't answer right away. Take a moment to think it over. And as you think about it, restate your reasons for selling it at $5,000. You can try something like this, with a pained look on your face: "Four thousand five hundred dollars? I don't know…I mean, this has been a great car. I really didn't want to sell it at all but we needed a bigger car for my job. I checked Edmunds.com and $5,000 is what they are selling for so…."

Then, lapse into silence for a moment, pretending you are deeply thinking about this. But what you are actually doing is waiting for them to up their offer. It's best if they bargain against themselves because it leaves you more room to maneuver. Let's say that during your meditative silence they lose their nerve and suddenly blurt out, "Well, I guess I could go as high as $4,700."

Now it's time to wrap things up. You should probably say, "Tell you what, I'll let it go for $4,750. That's $250 off my asking price. But —" and then repeat any conditions that might be important to you, such as paying with a cashier's check or holding the car for a day while they get cash. You might also ask for a deposit on the car if they want a longer period to arrange financing.

Chandler Phillips Says:

Think through the negotiation beforehand and set your rock-bottom price. Then, drop the price slowly to make the buyer feel they are getting a great deal.

Now that wasn't too hard, was it? You don't have to get nasty about things, but you do want to get a good price for your used wheels. Now that you have a deal in hand, you want to quickly conclude the paperwork and transfer the title to the new owner.

Getting Paid

In most cases, buyers are prepared to pay either with cash or a cashier's check. Avoid taking a personal check unless you know them personally. If they only have a personal check, go with them to their bank and cash the check while they are present. In this way, you will avoid bouncing a bad check and losing your car.

If they are paying you in cash, and the selling price is in the thousands, you will have quite a wad of bills. Remind yourself to watch carefully as they count out the bills. Or, if they just hand you a fistful of money, count out loud as you sort the bills. You want to eliminate the possibility of any misunderstandings.

Filing the Paperwork

Once you've been paid for your car, you need to transfer ownership to the buyer. The rules governing the sale of motor vehicles vary somewhat from state to state. You should check with the department of motor vehicles in your state (much of this information is now available on-line—see Appendix A for a list of department of motor vehicle Web sites).

The forms listed in the sidebar on page 216 will fulfill the requirements of most states' department of motor vehicles. However, there are complications that arise when, for example, the title for a car has been lost and a new one has to be printed. These issues take time to resolve so try to anticipate complications and resolve them before trying to sell your car. If you get in a bind, remember that your state's AAA auto club will often perform most of the services of your state's department of motor vehicles—with half the wait.

Another complication that sometimes arises is that an out-of-state bank holds the title. In this case, it is recommended that you go with the buyer to the department of motor vehicles and get a temporary operating permit based on a bill of sale. Then, after you pay off the balance of the loan with the proceeds from the car sale you can sign the title over to the new owner. The new owner will then have to apply for a title in their own name.

Forms for Car Selling

Here are the forms you may need to complete when selling your car:

Bill of sale: Often, the title or "pink slip" acts as a bill of sale. Also, the department of motor vehicles can provide a transfer of ownership form when the title is not available.

License plate application: In some states the license plates go with the car. In other states they stay with the owner. If you have personalized plates, you will want to keep them. There are various forms to keep, or transfer, the license plates.

Odometer statement: Some states will require you to record the odometer reading when the car is sold.

Release of liability: A release of liability form is available in some states to eliminate your liability if the buyer is in an accident before the new title is issued.

Smog certificate: Some states require a smog inspection to be performed on a car when it changes hands. It is often considered the seller's responsibility to have this done.

Transfer of ownership: In some states, this form takes the place of a bill of sale.

Title: The title, also called the "pink slip," can be signed over to the new owner. The odometer reading will also be required. If there is a loan on the car, the loan must be paid off before the title is released.

Finally, remember to contact your insurance agent to cancel your policy on the vehicle you have sold or transfer the coverage to your new car.

Before your car drives away for the final time, take a last look through the glove compartment, in the trunk and under the seats. You might find some long-forgotten treasures you misplaced years ago.

After the Sale

In most states, the condition of a used car for sale is considered "as is" and no warranty is provided or implied. Therefore, if the car breaks down after you have sold it you are under no obligation to refund the buyer's money or pay to have it repaired. If you have sold a car to someone who took it for inspection at a garage and the mechanic found nothing wrong with it, you have done all you can to protect yourself and the buyer.

The best way to feel peace of mind after selling your used car is to make sure you did everything correctly. This means being open about the condition of the car before the sale and timely when completing department of motor vehicles paperwork after the sale.

When done correctly, selling a used car can be a win-win situation. You have turned your used car into cash and provided reliable transportation for the next owner. Focus on the benefits to both parties and you are likely to have a smooth and successful experience.

Chapter 47
Selling Rare and Exotic Cars

The Internet has made it much easier to sell rare or exotic cars because buyers from all over the world will see your ad. Still, before you advertise your car you will need to arrive at the right asking price for it. This is one of the hardest parts of the selling process. If you price it too high you won't get any calls. If you price it too low you could be cutting yourself out of a lot of cash. So be patient and research your car's value thoroughly.

Here are some tips for finding out exactly how much your car is worth:

- Consult any pricing guides for the type of car you are selling

- Search on-line ads for similar cars— adjusting for condition, option and mileage

- Review finished auctions on eBay and other auction sites

- Contact collector clubs and ask their opinion

- Find mechanics who service your car and invite their input

- Ask car dealers (but take their opinion with a grain of salt—they might want to buy your car at a bargain price)

Once you have a rough idea of what the selling price of your car is, set the asking price to provide some wiggle room. Again, you want to make the price inviting, but high enough to let the buyer bargain you down a little. Think of the price at which you want to end negotiations and work up from there. And who knows? Maybe someone will come along and pay you your asking price.

Preparing Your Car for Sale

If you have owned your car for a long time you are, no doubt, intimately acquainted with all its lovable idiosyncrasies. While you may know how to work around these bugs, the next owner may not be as tolerant. So fix anything you can before listing the car for sale.

It's also a good idea to take your own car to a mechanic and have him draw up a service report. Then you will have a specific idea of the car's condition and can proceed with confidence. This places the responsibility on the mechanic rather than asking the buyer to trust your word—after all, you're likely not a mechanical expert. Furthermore, a problem may have materialized without your knowledge. When the mechanic puts the car on a rack it, will be easy to spot any leaks or rust.

Chandler Phillips Says:

Buyers of exotic cars have a much higher expectation for the cars they want, particularly when you ask top dollar. Be ready for detailed questions about your car's history.

Everything you can't fix will have to be disclosed before you can sell it. As mentioned earlier, you don't want to list every niggling detail in the ad. Then, a prospective buyer might get cold feet. A more general phrase might serve best: "Car is in average condition for a 10-year-old car." Or even, "Paint is in good condition but there are some dings and small scratches."

Providing good records is more important with a rare or exotic car. Make sure to have all service records neatly arranged in a file for review along with your mechanic's report. Run a Carfax report and have that ready to show a buyer, too. Your organization and attention to detail will go a long way to reassuring hesitant buyers.

Where to Advertise

Where you advertise your exotic car will determine what type of buyer you will deal with. The normal avenues (local newspaper ads, for sale signs in the window) might not work for a highly specialized car. Instead, you have to be more creative.

For starters, get in the habit of telling everyone you meet you have an unusual car for sale. For one thing, it's a heck of a conversation starter. For another, you might find a friend of a friend who is actually in the market for the car you're selling.

It is also good to cast a wide net (as in Internet) when selling an exotic or rare car. For one thing, you are appealing to a much smaller pool of buyers. However, if your ad is available on-line, people from all over the world will see it.

Here are a few places to advertise when you are selling a rare car:

- Classic car Web sites (AutoTrader has a special site devoted to classic cars)

- Collector club Web sites

- eBay Motors

- Newspapers in upscale areas

Selling Rare or Exotic Cars on eBay

eBay is the perfect place to sell hard-to-find cars. It allows buyers from all over the country to view your ad. eBay has become the place that collectors routinely check looking for their favorite types of cars. However, the very thing that makes eBay a valuable tool for you is also its biggest drawback: the price you can sell your car for is usually lower than you would get through other avenues. Even this should not discourage you though, since the eBay auction is quick and relatively easy, avoiding many of the pitfalls of the standard sales route.

Here are some simple rules to follow when selling cars on eBay:

- Do not inundate the auction with high-resolution pictures since many users are still using dial-up service.

- Good photos are essential. Additional photos can be posted on a separate site linked to the eBay auction. Photos should also show any significant damage on the car.

- Disclose the right amount of information about the car. It is a good idea to provide plenty of detail not only about the car's condition but the history of the car. Anything interesting about the car's past should certainly be highlighted. In most cases, the more information and photos you include in the auction, the better.

- Clearly state what service records are available.

- Be clear about whether required maintenance has been performed, how much tire tread remains, the condition of the paint and the number of owners.

- Get a CarFax and link to the CarFax site or even include the pertinent information in the auction. Bidders like this reassurance.

- Be sure to set a reserve, but set it at the lowest price you'd accept. Set the reserve to protect your bottom line. Search for your car and look for completed auctions to see how high the bidding went.

- Offer local buyers the chance to view the car before the auction closes.

- Offer transportation from the airport and help arranging shipping for non-local buyers.

- Ideally, arrange the auction to begin and end at 7 p.m. Pacific Standard Time (which will be 10 p.m. Eastern Standard Time).

- The auction should end on a weekday since people are busy on weekends.

- Run the auction for at least seven days for maximum exposure.

- Categorize your car carefully when setting up the auction. If you happen to miscategorize it, the auction could be a bust.

Chapter 48

10 Steps to Selling Your Car

Here are 10 simple steps to turn your used car into cash in the shortest amount of time.

1. Know the market.

Is your car going to be easy to sell? Is it a hot commodity? Or will you have to drop your price and search out additional avenues to sell it?

Here are a few general rules to answer these questions:

- Family sedans, while unexciting to many, are in constant demand by people needing basic, inexpensive transportation.

- SUVs are very popular right now and often move quickly, even older models.

- The sale of convertibles and sports cars is seasonal. Sunny weather brings out the buyers. Fall and winter months will be slow.

- Trucks and vans, used for work, are steady sellers and command competitive prices. Don't underestimate their value.

- Collector cars will take longer to sell and are often difficult to price. However, these cars can have unexpected value if you find the right buyer.

Your first step is to check the classified ads in your local newspaper and online. See what is for sale and at what price. Edmunds.com and other Internet sites allow you to search with specific criteria. For example, select the year and trim level of your car and see how many similar cars are currently on the market. Take note of their condition, mileage, geographic location and selling price.

2. Price your car competitively.

The best way to price your car is to use the information in this book. If you want a more up-to-date price, visit Edmunds.com and look up the car you are selling. You will see a link under the "Used Car Prices, Reviews & Info" heading near the top of the page labeled "What is your car worth?" Click on this and follow the prompts. This will give you an Edmunds.com True Market Value price that is adjusted for mileage, color, region, options and condition.

There are exceptions to the rules of pricing, so you should follow your intuition. And be sure to leave a little wiggle room in your asking price. You should always ask for more money than you are actually willing to accept. If you want to get $12,000 for the car, you should list the car at $12,500. That way, if you get $12,500—great! But if you have to go lower, it won't be a terrible loss.

You may have noticed how creative used car dealers get in pricing cars. Their prices usually end in "995," as in $12,995. Are we not supposed to notice that the car basically costs $13,000? There is a lot of psychology in setting prices. A product that doesn't sell well at $20 might jump off the shelf at $19.95.

On the other hand, as a private party you don't want to look like a car dealer. Therefore, you might want to take a simple approach and set your price at a round figure such as $12,750 or $12,500.

3. Give your car "curb appeal."

When people come to look at your car, they will probably make up their minds to buy it or not within the first few seconds. This is based on their first look at the car. So you want this first look to be positive. You want your car to have "curb appeal."

Before you advertise your car for sale, make sure it looks as clean and attractive as is realistic. This goes beyond just taking it to the car wash (see "Cleaning and Detailing" checklist in "Get Your Car Ready to Sell," page 203).

4. Where to advertise your car.

Now that your car is looking great and running well, it's time to advertise it for sale. Traditionally, people advertise in newspaper classified ads. These ads can be expensive, but they get results. However, on-line ads are becoming more popular, particularly with hard-to-find or collector cars.

Creativity is required when it comes to advertising. Think of unusual places to put ads (skywriting is probably too expensive), and you will get results (see "Places to Advertise" sidebar in "Get Your Car Ready to Sell", page 207).

One last word of advice about advertising: if you run an expensive classified ad, be sure you are available to take phone calls from possible buyers. Many people won't leave a message for a return call. So answer the phone—and be polite. This is the first hurdle to clear in getting buyers to come and see the car in person.

5. Create ads that sell.

When creating "For Sale" signs or putting a classified ad in the paper, you have an opportunity to show how eager you are to sell the car. This can be done by inserting the following abbreviations and phrases such as "Must sell!" or listing the price as "OBO" (or best offer). The important thing is to think about what you are telling people by the way you phrase your ad. Little words convey a lot.

6. Showing your car.

Keep in mind that when you sell your car, people will also be evaluating you. They will be thinking, "Here's the person who's owned this car for the past few years. Do I trust him/her?" Make the buyers feel comfortable. They will probably be uneasy about making a big decision and spending money. Put them at ease and answer their questions openly.

While showing your car, keep these key points in mind:

- Evaluate prospective callers before agreeing to show the car. If anyone seems difficult, pushy or suspicious, wait for another buyer.

- Ride along on the test-drive to answer questions about the car's history and performance and guide through an unknown area.

- Show the car in a neutral place (a shopping mall parking lot or public park) if you are uncomfortable with having buyers come to your house to see the car.

- Provide buyers with an inspection report from your mechanic. But if they still want to take the car to *their* mechanic, this is a reasonable request.

- Be ready for trick questions such as, "So, what's really wrong with the car?"

- Refer them to the mechanic's report or invite them to look over the car more carefully.

7. Negotiate your best price.

If a person comes to look at the car and it passes their approval after a test-drive, you can expect them to make an offer. Most people are uncomfortable negotiating, so their opening offer might take several forms. (See "Negotiating and Closing the Deal," page 213.)

Your prospective buyer is apt to approach you in one of several ways. Think of your response ahead of time so you won't be caught unprepared. And take your time. Some people don't visualize numbers very well—and this isn't a time you want to make a mistake. You can even write the numbers down if that helps you. In general, it's a good idea to hold to your price when your car first goes up for sale. If you don't get any buyers right away, you'll know you have to be flexible about the price.

8. Handling complications.

In some cases, you might reach an agreement with a buyer that is contingent on performing repair work on the car. This can lead to misunderstandings down the line, so avoid this if you can. The best thing to do is have your car in good running order while being fully aware of any necessary repairs. If you state clearly in your ads that the car is being sold "as is," you can refer to this statement when it's time to close the deal.

Still, a trip to the prospective buyer's mechanic might turn up a new question about the car's condition. Get a price for the repair and offer to pay for half of the total price. If your buyer is reasonable, you might still be able to make the sale.

9. Finalize the sale.

Rules governing the sale of motor vehicles vary somewhat from state to state. Make sure you check with the department of motor vehicles in your state, and keep in mind that much of the information is now available on department of motor vehicles' Web sites (See Appendix A).

Once you have the money from the sale (it's customary to request either cash or a cashier's check), record the odometer reading and sign the car's title over to the buyer. In some states, the license plates go along with the car. A new title will be issued and mailed to the new owner. Finally, remember to contact your insurance agent to cancel your policy on the vehicle you have sold (or transfer the coverage to your new car).

10. After the sale.

In most states, the condition of a used car for sale is considered "as is" and no warranty is provided or implied. Therefore, if the car breaks down after you have sold it you are under no obligation to refund the buyer's money or pay to have it repaired. If you have sold a car to someone who took it for inspection at a garage and the mechanic found nothing wrong with it, you have done all you can to protect yourself and the buyer.

The best way to feel peace of mind after selling your used car is to make sure you did everything correctly. This means being open about the condition of the car before the sale and timely and complete in transferring department of motor vehicles paperwork after the sale.

Selling Your Car Checklist

❏ Consider market factors affecting the sale of your car (don't try to sell a convertible in the winter).

❏ Check local classified ads to see what others in your area are asking for your type of vehicle.

❏ Determine a selling price for your car using Edmunds.com's True Market Value system.

❏ Give your car "curb appeal" by cleaning and detailing it. Fix any problems with your car or drop the price and sell it "as is."

❏ Consider buying a Carfax (vehicle history report), or getting a mechanic's inspection report to show prospective buyers.

❏ Create a "For Sale" sign for your car window.

❏ Post an eye-catching on-line or print classified advertisement.

❏ Make yourself available to answer calls from potential buyers.

❏ Arrange to show the car to prospective buyers.

❏ Get a smog inspection if required by your state department of motor vehicles.

❏ Negotiate your best selling price by knowing the market and not dropping your price too quickly. Be patient. Don't let yourself be pressured.

❏ Collect payment for the car by getting a cashier's check or cash.

❏ Finalize the sale by fulfilling all department of motor vehicles paperwork to transfer ownership and limit your liability.

❏ Get all personal items out of your car before it is driven away.

Appendix A:

Web Sites for State Motor Vehicle Departments

Except for Kansas, Nevada, South Carolina and West Virginia—all the authentic department of motor vehicles sites use the standard state government formats for Web addresses, ending with ".gov" or ".us."

ALABAMA Department of Public Safety: www.dps.state.al.us

ALASKA Division of Motor Vehicles:
www.state.ak.us/local/akpages/ADMIN/dmv/dmvhome.htm

ARIZONA Motor Vehicles Division: www.dot.state.az.us/MVD/mvd.htm

ARKANSAS DFA Motor Vehicle Division:
www.state.ar.us/dfa/motorvehicle/index.html

CALIFORNIA Department of Motor Vehicles: www.dmv.ca.gov

COLORADO Motor Vehicle Division: www.mv.state.co.us/mv.html

CONNECTICUT Department of Motor Vehicles:
www.ct.gov/dmv/site/default.asp

DISTRICT OF COLUMBIA Department of Motor Vehicles:
dmv.washingtondc.gov

DELAWARE Division of Motor Vehicles:
www.delaware.gov/yahoo/DMV

FLORIDA DHSMV, Department of Highway Safety
and Motor Vehicles: www.hsmv.state.fl.us

GEORGIA Department of Motor Vehicle Safety:
www.dmvs.ga.gov/index.asp

HAWAII Motor Vehicle Registration:
www.state.hi.us/dot/publicaffairs/motorvehicleregistration.htm

IDAHO Division of Motor Vehicles: www.state.id.us/itd/dmv

IOWA Motor Vehicle Division: www.dot.state.ia.us/mvd

ILLINOIS Services for Motorists:
www.sos.state.il.us/services/services_motorists.html

INDIANA Bureau of Motor Vehicles: www.state.in.us/bmv

KANSAS Department of Revenue: www.ksrevenue.org/vehicle.htm

KENTUCKY Department of Vehicle Regulation:
www.kytc.state.ky.us/motorcarriers/home_vr.htm

LOUISIANA Office of Motor Vehicles: omv.dps.state.la.us

MARYLAND Motor Vehicle Administration: mva.state.md.us

MASSACHUSETTS Registry of Motor Vehicles: www.state.ma.us/rmv

MAINE Bureau of Motor Vehicles: www.state.me.us/sos/bmv

MICHIGAN Secretary of State:
www.michigan.gov/sos/

MINNESOTA Driver and Vehicle Services:
www.dps.state.mn.us/dvs/index.html

MISSISSIPPI Motor Vehicle Licensing:
www.mstc.state.ms.us/mvl/main.htm

MISSOURI Motor Vehicle and Drivers Licensing:
www.dor.state.mo.us/dmv

MONTANA Department of Justice Driving:
doj.state.mt.us/driving/vehicletitleregistration.asp

NEBRASKA Department of Motor Vehicles: www.dmv.state.ne.us

NEW HAMPSHIRE Department of Safety: www.state.nh.us/dmv

NEW JERSEY Motor Vehicle Commission: www.state.nj.us/mvs

NEW MEXICO Motor Vehicle Division:
www.state.nm.us/tax/mvd/mvd_home.htm

NEW YORK State Department of Motor Vehicles:
www.nydmv.state.ny.us

NORTH CAROLINA Division of Motor Vehicles:
www.dmv.dot.state.nc.us

NORTH DAKOTA Department of Transportation: www.state.nd.us/dot

NEVADA Department of Motor Vehicles: www.dmvnv.com

OHIO Bureau of Motor Vehicles:
www.ohio.gov/odps/division/bmv/bmv.html

OKLAHOMA Tax Commission's Motor Vehicle Division:
www.oktax.state.ok.us/mvhome.html

OREGON Driver and Motor Vehicles Services: www.odot.state.or.us/dmv

PENNSYLVANIA Driver and Vehicle Services: www.dmv.state.pa.us

RHODE ISLAND Division of Motor Vehicles: www.dmv.state.ri.us

SOUTH CAROLINA Department of Motor Vehicles:
www.scdps.org/dmv

SOUTH DAKOTA Motor Vehicle Division:
www.state.sd.us/revenue/motorvcl.htm

TENNESSEE Department of Safety: www.state.tn.us/safety

TEXAS Motor Vehicle Registration and Titling:
www.dot.state.tx.us/VTR/vtrreginfo.htm

UTAH Division of Motor Vehicles: dmv.utah.gov/register.html

VERMONT Department of Motor Vehicles:
www.aot.state.vt.us/dmv/dmvhp.htm

VIRGINIA Department of Motor Vehicles: www.dmv.state.va.us

WASHINGTON DOL, Department of Licensing: www.dol.wa.gov

WISCONSIN DOT, Drivers and Vehicles: www.dot.wisconsin.gov/drivers

WEST VIRGINIA Division of Motor Vehicles:
www.wvdot.com/6_motorists/dmv/6G_DMV.HTM

WYOMING WYDOT Driver Services:
dot.state.wy.us/web/driver_services/index.html

Confessions of a Car Salesman

What happens when an auto journalist becomes an undercover car dealer? Chandler Phillips tells all about his time "on the lot."

Introduction

What really goes on in the back rooms of car dealerships across America? What does the car salesman do when he leaves you sitting in a sales office and goes to talk with his boss?

What are the tricks the salespeople use to increase their profit and how can consumers protect themselves from overpaying?

These were the questions we wanted to answer for the readers of our Web site. But how could we really know that our information was accurate and up to date? Finally, we came up with the idea of hiring an investigative reporter to work in the industry and experience, firsthand, the life of a car salesman.

We hired Chandler Phillips, a veteran journalist, to go undercover by working at two new car dealerships in the Los Angeles area. We asked him to start at a high-volume, high-pressure dealership selling Japanese cars. Then, he would work at a smaller car lot that sold domestic cars at "no haggle" prices.

We invite you to read the following account of Phillips' day-to-day experience on the car lot. Reading about his experiences will broaden your understanding of the dealership sales process. It will also cast new light on the role of the car salesman. And, finally, it will help you get a better deal—and avoid extra charges—the next time you go to buy or lease a new car.

Read, learn and enjoy.

— The editors at Edmunds.com

Chapter 49

Going Undercover

I had driven by the dealership a hundred times and never stopped. As I passed, I would look over at the row of salesmen standing in front of the showroom windows, white shirts gleaming in the sun. This phalanx of salesmen looked so predatory, it always made me think, "Who would ever stop there?"

But today, I knew I would be the one stopping there.

I turned my ancient Dodge Conquest into the dealership parking lot and immediately felt their eyes on me. As soon as I opened my car door a salesman was on me.

"Is that a Mitsubishi? Or a Dodge?" the salesman asked, seeking common ground, a way to relax me before getting down to business.

"It's a Mitsubishi imported by Dodge," I said, and quickly added, "Who do I see about applying for a job?"

His attitude changed in a heartbeat. Not only was I not going to buy a car, but I wanted to be his competition.

"See the receptionist," he muttered, and walked away.

Inside, the receptionist was fortified behind a semicircular counter.

"I'd like to apply for a job," I told her.

"What department?" she asked, yawning.

"Sales."

"New or used?"

"New."

She whipped out an application form and slapped it on the desk. "Fill out both sides and complete this, too." She slammed down another form. It looked like the SAT tests I took in high school.

I took a seat in a nearby sales cubicle. It was in a large room divided into glass-walled sales offices. In the corner was a large glassed-in office with a high counter in front of a raised platform. The salesmen in this room looked older, better dressed and had an air of power and authority. They sat behind computers and also seemed to be eyeing the salesmen out on the lot.

Looking down at the application, it blurred in front of my eyes. Could I really do this? Could I really become a—a car salesman? Me, a law-abiding middle-aged American. A—gasp—college graduate (well, barely). A writer. A person sometimes described as soft-spoken and reserved? Why was I applying for a job in one of the most loathed professions in our society? I'd seen rankings of the most hated people and they stacked up in this order: child molester, lawyer, car salesman.

Well, here's how a strange turn of events turned me into a car salesman.

About a month earlier I applied for a job at Edmunds.com, touting my experience as a How-To book writer. One book I ghostwrote was about buying used cars, the other was about leasing cars. The books were published under the name of a guy who had once been a car salesman. I assumed the books qualified me to work for the fast-growing consumer-based Web site. As I saw it, I would sit in the comfort of an office and, from this lofty perch, dispense advice on how to buy and sell cars.

The Edmunds.com editors had other plans.

After we finished lunch, one of the editors suddenly asked, "How would you feel about an undercover assignment?"

"What do you mean?" I asked, even though I suspected where this was going. His question had stirred something I had thought about for a long time.

"We would hire you here at Edmunds.com. Then you would go out and get a job as a car salesman and work for three months."

"Selling cars?" I asked unnecessarily.

"Right."

"Where would I work?"

"Wherever you can get hired. That would be up to you. We were thinking you should work at two dealerships. The first would be a high-volume, high-pressure store. Then you could quit and go to a no-haggle dealership. You could tell them you didn't like the pressure at the first place and you'd probably get a job on the spot."

The editor explained that they wanted me to write a series of articles describing the business from the inside. Of course I would learn the tricks of the trade, and that would better prepare me to write advice for Edmunds.com. But the benefits of the project would be greater than just information. I would live the life of a car salesman for three months. That would give me an insight and perspective that couldn't be gained by reading books or articles or interviewing former car salesmen.

"So what do you think?" the editor asked. "Interested?"

I have a history of acting before I think things through. I jump in with both feet and sometimes live to regret my decision. But here I was, in the middle of my life, long past the adventures of adolescence, past all the lousy summer jobs, past my early newspaper days on the police beat. It had been a long time since I'd had a good adventure. But selling cars?

"Sure, I'll do it," I said. A week later, they offered me the job.

It was several weeks before I started at Edmunds.com, and then several more weeks before I was to begin the undercover project. Plenty of time to wonder what the hell I'd gotten myself into. I began clipping newspaper ads for car sales positions. Just the language in the ads made me nervous: "Aggressive sales professionals wanted!" or "Selling hot cars at MSRP. Join the #1 Team. Xlnt pay & benef. App in person." I could almost sense the pressure of the car business coming through the newspaper.

A friend of mine used to have an office surrounded by car lots. He would eat lunch with car salesmen and listen to them brag about the tricks they used to move cars. Occasionally, another man would join them, a guy they called "Speedometer Shorty." He would go from one car lot to another winding the odometers back to show fewer miles.

"What do you think they would do to me at the dealership if they found I worked for Edmunds.com?" I asked my friend.

"They'd kill you," he said without hesitation. Then he began laughing. "What they'd do is put your body in the trunk of a competitor's car."

He was yanking my chain, of course. But the fact that he answered so quickly gave me pause. Still, I told myself nothing like that would happen to me. I wasn't there to hurt the dealership. I wasn't there to steal anything or to hurt their business. We weren't going for dirt. But if dirt was there we would report it. Basically, we just wanted to see what was happening at ground zero in the auto business.

The date finally arrived for me to leave the Edmunds.com offices and begin looking for a job selling cars. As I prepared to leave, my editor offered me this advice: "When you're interviewing, don't tell them you know a lot about cars. They don't care. If they ask why you want to work there, just tell them you want to make a lot of money."

He then flipped open his calendar and counted off the weeks. "You're due back in the office in 10 weeks. We won't expect to see you until then. Let us hear from you every 48 hours or so with a phone call or e-mail. And good luck."

That weekend I went to the store and bought three new white shirts and a pair of black shoes with soft soles. I figured I'd be on my feet a lot. Monday morning I put together a resumé. How should I present myself? Why would someone hire me to sell cars? I thought back to what my editor said, "Just tell them you want to make a lot of money." Good advice. But I needed more than that. There would be questions about who I was. Where I had worked. Requests for references maybe.

I decided that I would look over my recent past and select those things that could be viewed as being sales-related. In other words, I wanted to avoid lying. For the previous three years, I'd written video proposals for training films. A proposal is a form of selling—right? Maybe that would work. I called my friend and asked him to back me up in case the dealership called him. No problem, he said. I had also sold sporting goods at one time. And I had written proposals for grants for another company. I was beginning to see a biography that might work.

The following Monday morning rolled around and I realized that the time had arrived. It was time to get a job as a car salesman. I drove to an auto mall near my house. Acres of shining cars stretched out in front of me. One dealership had a large banner reading, "We're growing! Now hiring! Apply within."

That was when I pulled in and got the application.

"I understand you want to sell cars." The voice brought me back to the present. I looked up from the application. A man stood there smiling at me. He had carefully cut black hair. He wore a white shirt and a silk tie. As he extended his hand to shake, light flashed off a gold Rolex.

"I'm Dave. When you're done filling that out, have me paged and we'll talk."

He smiled again, evaluating me. Then he disappeared.

Nice guy, I thought. Maybe this won't be so bad. I was about to begin work on the application when I looked around. I glanced toward the glassed-in office in the corner of the building. The one with the raised platform and the senior sales guys watching over the car lot. Dave was in there speaking to several of the older men in white shirts and ties. They all turned and looked at me.

It was too late to turn back now. I bent over the application and began writing.

Chapter 50
Getting Hired

The application they gave me at the car dealership included a "personality test," a list of about 80 questions to which I had to answer yes or no. There were no right answers, the instructions told me. The questions gave me insight to the kind of people who typically apply for jobs at car dealerships.

The first few questions were innocent enough, something like: "I enjoy relaxing and listening to music: Yes or No?" But soon I noticed a trend developing. Question 7 was, "I enjoy going to bars: Yes or No?" A few more innocent questions followed, then, "After going to a bar, I feel good about myself: Yes or No?" Questions about bars continued throughout.

Then, at about number 73, was this loaded question: "I like guns: Yes or No?" I wondered how they would react if I crossed out the word "like" and put in "love." Better yet, I considered inserting the word "automatic" in front of "guns."

It was pretty obvious what they were looking for. So I recorded my answers and took the application back to the receptionist.

"Dave told me to page him when I was done with this," I said.

She stabbed a button on a phone panel and spoke into the receiver. "Dave, to the front desk. Dave, to the front desk." Her voice echoed down the hallways and boomed out onto the car lot. She turned back to me, "He'll be right with you."

I sat down and waited.

And waited. But he wasn't "right with me."

The thing about car dealers is they seem to like to keep you waiting. Later, I would find out how important it is for the salespeople to feel they are controlling the customer. If you are waiting for them, they must be controlling you. This obsession with control extended to job applicants, too.

As I waited, I tried to look like a promising candidate for a job selling cars—whatever that looked like. I tried to look eager and hungry. These are not traits that come easily to me, so I studied the other salespeople around me. They stood in poses of assertion and power: legs spread, hands on hips, arms folded across chests. All the men (99 percent of the sales force) wore white shirts and ties. Their hair was slicked back, and they favored jewelry.

Soon, I noticed that dealership people were walking past where I sat, and they were taking an unusual interest in me. A sandy-haired man strolled by several times. On the next pass he nodded and said, "Good morning."

"Good morning, how are you?" I returned. The man nodded and kept walking. I began to think the reason Dave kept me waiting so long was so they could eyeball me before I was interviewed.

I wondered if Dave was testing my assertiveness, so I returned to the receptionist and asked to have him paged again. She did, and Dave immediately reappeared and led me to a sales cubicle in the back.

Sitting across from Dave I saw that he had a wandering eye. I kept trying to figure out which eye to look at. Dave reviewed my application and frowned.

"You've never sold cars before. Is that right?"

"Right."

"Why do you want to work here?"

My first inclination was to say, hey, *I'm a car freak.* I could explain cars, how they work, get people excited about the performance and the different features. But then I remembered my editor's advice.

I smiled at Dave, trying to convey the feeling that the answer was obvious.

"I want to make a lot of money," I said.

The effect on Dave was amazing. He smiled and relaxed, as if I had said the password to enter an exclusive club. If this had been a cartoon, dollar signs would have appeared in his eyes accompanied by a loud *"Cha-ching!"*

Next, Dave asked me what the best part of my personality was, and what the weakest part of my personality was. After I was done answering, he said he didn't really care what I said, it was the fact that I replied immediately that he liked. He added, "Your answer could even be a lot of B.S., but in sales you have to always have an answer."

It was clear that Dave liked me. And I sure liked Dave. Still, I had never sold cars before. My application showed I had a background in video sales.

Suddenly, Dave extended a ballpoint pen to me, one of those 59-cent jobs made of clear plastic. "You want to be a car salesman. OK, sell me this pen."

Over the years, I've read a number of self-help books about positive thinking. It always seemed these books were written by salesmen. So I've absorbed a lot of information about selling without realizing it. Here was my chance to put all that into action.

I picked up the pen, paused dramatically and began speaking slowly and deliberately. "Dave, you've asked me to make a recommendation about a pen. You're in luck because I know a lot about pens and I'm in a good position to point out the features and benefits of this model of pen. The first thing you'll notice is the cap. This can easily be removed and stored on the other end of the pen so you don't lose it. The next thing you'll notice is how it feels in your hand. Also, you'll notice it's easy to see at a glance how much ink is left. This means you'll never run out of ink without..."

I continued in this ridiculous fashion for a few minutes. Then I set the pen back in front of Dave and stopped. I held his gaze firmly—hoping I had focused on his good eye.

He picked up his pen as he said, "Yes, well, that's very nice." He thought it over for a second and said, "I'll be right back."

But he wasn't right back. I sat there for at least 15 minutes. I had a good opportunity to look around. On the wall of the cubicle was a sign stating that in California there was no "cooling-off period." It said that once you sign a contract, it is binding even if you change your mind or decide that the car costs too much money.

Eventually, another man appeared around the corner of the cubicle and introduced himself. His name was Michael, and he was the sandy-haired man I had exchanged greetings with earlier. He had a very pleasant, confident manner. He didn't ask me anything about myself; instead, he talked about how the dealership worked. I would be on a team of six salesmen of which he was the assistant sales manager, or ASM. He told me that I would train for about a week, but then I would be selling cars.

"Selling cars isn't hard," Michael told me. "It's dead easy. You just got to get right up here." He tapped his forehead.

I used the same tactic I had with Dave, repeating that I wanted to make a lot of money. It seemed to be the magic word.

"Oh, you can make money here," Michael assured me, smiling. Then he lowered his voice as if telling me a secret. "You could make three or four grand here your first month. It's happened. Sometimes the green peas are the best salesmen."

Green peas. That's what they called the new guys. I had heard that nickname once before from a car salesman friend. I would be hearing it a lot in the coming weeks.

Michael stood up to leave, saying that other people would be in to meet me. But then he ducked back into the cubicle and said in a low voice, "Your driving record—is it clean?" I assured him it was.

I sat there for another 15 minutes before a young woman named Rosa, from human resources, arrived. She led me to a small room where I watched a videotape about the dealership—one of a chain of dealerships across the Southwest. The video also had interviews with people who worked in car sales telling how much money they made and how they loved their jobs. They didn't read very convincingly from the teleprompter.

When the tape was over, Rosa reappeared carrying the personality test that asked me how I felt about going to bars. She said the test showed I was, "dominant, competitive and impatient."

"Impatient? Is that bad?" I asked her.

"Oh no! No!" she assured me. "It means you want results now! Now! Now!" she said snapping her fingers. She then explained how the shifts were handled. I would work from 50 to 60 hours a week, with a lot of night and weekend shifts. She also said they use an "eight-step process" for selling cars. This probably worked well for applicants who spent a lot of time in bars.

Then she dropped a bomb on me.

"I was going to have the general manager interview you," she said. "But he listened in on your interview and he liked you."

Listened in on me? I realized she had just confirmed a rumor about dealerships: the selling rooms are bugged. Later I learned that they aren't actually bugged, it's just that the phones have intercoms that can be used easily for listening.

I had been in the dealership for three hours and I was eager to leave. Rosa told me I would need to take a drug test and that they would then do a background check on me. She then paused and looked at me as if waiting for an answer.

"Is there anything you want me to know about?"

"About what?" I asked.

"Sometimes, when I say I'm going to do a background check, people stop me right there."

"Oh," I said, catching on. "My background's clean. No felonies."

"No DUIs?"

"No. I've been a good boy."

"You never know," she said. "I'll call you in a few days and if everything looks good, we'll send you to get your sales license."

It was a relief to leave the dealership. As I drove home, I reflected on what I had learned so far: To be a car salesman you needed to be able to sell pens, have a clean driving record and be drug-free.

I expected to get a call the next day and begin work immediately. But Rosa didn't call—and she didn't return my calls.

Over the next few days I continued applying for sales jobs. At one dealership, which sold high-end Japanese cars, a manager named Sid reviewed my application.

"But you don't have any experience selling cars," he said, as if I had misrepresented myself.

I went back to the formula that had worked so well.

"No, but I want to make a lot of money."

"Really?" he said. "How much do you want to make in, say, a month?"

I remembered Michael saying they made three or four grand in the first month. So I repeated this figure.

Sid burst out laughing: "I got guys out there makin' 20, 25 grand a month."

"You're kidding."

"No," Sid said, "I'm telling you, man, this is the big leagues."

Sid continued reviewing the application as if he might have missed something. "So you've got no experience selling cars?" he repeated.

"No," I admitted for the second time. "No experience."

Regretfully, he said he couldn't hire me until I had experience. He added that treating their customers well was more important than selling them a car. I told him that was exactly why I was here. I knew I could treat his customers well. This didn't cut any ice with him. He'd seen guys like me before, trying to fast-talk their way into a job they weren't qualified for.

"I'm sorry, my friend, but you have to prove it first. We need quotas. It's not enough to talk the talk. You need to walk the walk before you can work here." He handed me back the application and I left.

The next day I had a chance to interview at a dealership that sold American cars. Right away I sensed these guys were different than the salesmen at the dealerships that sold Japanese cars. There, they were slick young guys with expensive silk ties and gold watches. Here they were down-home, average Joes selling pickups and American-built cars.

I shook hands with a man named Jim who had slicked-back hair and a goatee. We sat in a selling room, and he began telling me how great business was here. He said the dealership was perfectly situated on the Auto Mall, and the Auto Mall was the busiest in the area. And this area was the busiest place in the country. And America was the busiest place on the planet. So life was good and everyone was making lots and lots of money.

Jim asked me a number of questions about how I would handle situations on the car lot. He wanted to know how would I go about selling cars. I told him simply the best way to get a sale was to repeatedly ask for it. He liked this a lot. I could tell he was agreeing with all my answers, so I wasn't surprised when he told me he was going to have his manager speak with me.

Several moments later (no waiting around like at the other interviews), a new guy entered named Stan. He said he had just told the sales staff, "If you guys sell two more cars by 6 o'clock, we're all going out for pizza and beer."

I could tell that Stan couldn't figure out why I was there. I didn't make sense to him as a car salesman. But the more I talked, the more he warmed to me. Finally, he said, "You play any sports?" I told him I was a big golfer. He asked me what my handicap was. I told him I was down to a 12 but I knew that if I took this job my golf game would suffer.

"Oh no. You're gonna get to play a lot of golf on this job. You have your mornings free and you'll be working evenings." He snapped the folder shut and said, "I asked you about sports because I wanted to see your competitive side."

I knew these interviews came in threes, so I wasn't surprised when Craig walked into the room. He told me that he had been a schoolteacher before he got into the car business. I could see him as a teacher—he had a warm, intelligent manner. He said that being a car salesman was hard on your life. "Truth of the matter is, you lose all your friends. Not because you're a car salesman, but because when you're around, they're not. And when they're around, you're not. You wind up making all new friends." I thought of the guys getting pizza and beer after selling two more cars. Would they be my new friends?

Craig asked me questions about myself, but mainly he was there to tell me the realities of the job. He told me that I would be successful selling only 20 percent of the time. So about 80 percent of the time I would be failing. He asked me how I took rejection. I said, "If you knew my wife, you'd know I'm an expert on handling rejection." He laughed and said, "A good sense of humor is important."

I was left alone for a few moments, while my three interviewers held a pow-wow. I overheard one of them saying, "He seems like a nice guy." The other one said, "Yes, definitely." Craig returned and told me that I would be sent for a drug test and background check. If both of these were clear, they could start me in about 10 days.

As I left the dealership, I realized I was facing a dilemma: did I want to work with the slippery guys who first interviewed me? Or should I go with the good-ol' boys at the American dealership? At this point I was leaning toward the slippery guys. I knew I was going to leave in a month anyway. I wouldn't mind cutting and running from the Japanese dealership. The other American boys might shake their heads and say, "If only he'd hung in there, we could've helped him become a successful car salesman."

I called the first dealership back for about the 20th time. This time I didn't give my name, but I had Rosa paged. After a long wait, she came on the line.

"Oh yes," she answered cheerfully (no mention of why she hadn't called back). "Come down Monday morning and we'll send you off to get your car sales license. You can do that while we're finishing your background check."

Did that mean I was hired? On Monday I went to the dealership and Rosa gave me the forms to take to the DMV. But first, I had to have my fingerprints scanned. I went to a local university's security office where they had a special computer for this purpose. I waited three hours before being led into a small, hot room. A sweaty young technician rolled the pads of my fingerprints across a glass plate. He told me that my prints were being sent by modem to the justice department—a scary thought. I then went to the DMV where I had another long wait because the computers were down. Finally, I went to the window, paid $56 and had my picture taken. A few moments later I was handed my "Vehicle Salesman Temporary Permit" with my photo on it. I was now a car salesman. So I decided to play the part.

Speaking through the glass, I told the DMV clerk, "I just got my sales license. You'll have to come on down to the dealership. I'll sell you a car."

"Sorry," she said. "I just bought a new Toyota."

The rejection had already begun.

Chapter 51

Meeting, Greeting and Dealing

My first day on the job started with signing about 50 different forms. Most of these were for specific purposes—to show that I understood I wasn't supposed to take dealership car keys home, drive under the influence or sexually harass my co-workers. But one form was of particular interest. It showed the breakdown of the commission structure.

Commissions were based on the "payable gross" to the dealership and were applied in three tiers. If the payable gross was from $0 to $749, our commission was 20 percent of the profit; from $750 to $1,249 the commission was 25 percent of the profit. Above $1,250, the commission was 30 percent of the profit. In other words, the higher the profit for the dealership, the higher the commission I would earn. Obviously, this motivated salespeople to build profit into the deal so they could hit that magic mark and get into the 30 percent bracket.

When I was interviewed for the job, the dealership was vague about how I would be paid. On the one hand, they promised I could make serious money through commissions—maybe four or five grand my first month. On the other hand, they alluded to an hourly wage to begin with. Now I found that I was, in fact, working on straight commission. If I sold cars I made money. If I didn't sell, I didn't make a penny. Maybe that's why there were so many salespeople working here (about 85 in new and used cars). It didn't cost the dealership extra to have a big staff.

When I was done signing forms, I was turned over to Michael, my assistant sales manager (ASM). He told me I would be working with five other guys on the "A Team." They were just arriving for work—still straightening their ties, combing their hair—and he introduced me to them as they showed up. There was Oscar, a barrel-chested young guy with a tattoo on the back of his hand; Richard, a 6-foot-3-inch weightlifter from Hungary; Tino, who had a quiet dignity that made me think of him as a restaurant maitre d'; Jimmy, a mustachioed soccer fanatic; and Juan, six months out of the U.S. Marine Corps.

These were my team members, Michael said. They would be like family, like my brothers. If I couldn't make a deal with a customer, I was to turn them over to someone on my team. Then, if that customer bought the car, we'd split the commission. This practice of "turning" customers was stressed repeatedly. I was working in what is known in the business as a "turnover house."

We had a brief meeting in one of the sales cubicles, and then the rest of the team went out front to look for "ups." Ups are customers who walk onto the lot. This name comes from the way customers are handled by whichever salesman or woman is "up." The salespeople are always asking, "Who's up next?" The "up system," the order in which customers are taken by the sales staff, is very serious business.

Michael began explaining how the dealership was run. We sold new cars on our side of the building, and used cars were on the other side. In each of the front corners of the building were the new and used car "towers." These glassed-in offices were restricted to employees. Inside was a raised platform where the sales managers sat. When you went into one of the towers, you found yourself behind a high counter, looking up at your bosses, like being in a courtroom or a police station. The sales managers are sometimes referred to as "the desk." Salespeople would say, "You have to clear that deal with the desk." Or, "Who's on the desk today?"

The next step in my training involved the use of the "four-square work sheet." Michael told me the four-square was my friend, it was the salesman's tool for getting "maximum gross profit." As the name implies, the sheet is divided into four sections. When you have a prospect "in the box" (in the sales cubicle), you pull out a four-square and go to work.

The information about the customer is written along the top together with the make, model and serial number of the car they want to buy. Then the salesman writes the sticker price of the car in large numbers in the upper right square on the worksheet. Michael stressed that the price of the car should be written in large clear numbers to give it a feeling of authority. He added that we should always write "+ fees" next to the price of the car (to cover the costs of license fees and sales tax.).

"Good penmanship is essential," he said. "This makes it harder for them to negotiate. You're saying, 'Mr. Customer, if you want our beautiful new car, this is the price you're going to have to pay.'"

The other boxes on the four-square are for the price of the trade-in, the amount of the customer's down payment, and the amount of the customer's monthly payment.

"When you negotiate, this sheet should be covered with numbers," Michael said. "It should be like a battleground. And I don't want to see the price dropping $500 at a pop. Come down slowly, slowly. Here I'll show you how."

The process begins by asking the customer how much they want for a monthly payment. Usually, they say, about $300. "Then, you just say, '$300...up to?' And they'll say, 'Well, $350.' Now they've just bumped themselves up $50 a month. That's huge." You then fill in $350 under the monthly payment box.

Michael said you could use the "up to" trick with the down payment, too. "If Mr. Customer says he wants to put down $2,000, you say, 'Up to?' And he'll probably bump himself up to $2,500." Michael then wrote $2,500 in the down payment box of the four-square worksheet.

I later found out this little phrase "Up to?" was a joke around the dealership. When salesmen or women passed each other in the hallways, they would say, "Up to?" and break out laughing.

The final box on the four-square was for the trade-in. This was where the most profit could be made. Buyers are so eager to get out of their old car and into a new one, they overlook the true value of the trade-in. The dealership is well aware of this weakness and exploits it.

The opening numbers were now in place on the four-square. At a glance, Michael said, you could see the significant numbers of this deal—purchase price of the car, trade-in, down payment and the monthly payments. As you negotiated you could move from box to box, making progress as you went. It allowed you to sell a car in different ways. For example, if the customer was determined to get full value for his trade-in, you could take extra profit elsewhere—in the purchase price or maybe even in financing.

The first numbers that go on the four-square come from the customer. The down payment and the monthly payment are only what they would *like* to pay. Now, it's time to get the numbers that the dealership would *like* the customer to pay. These numbers are called the "first pencil" and they come from a sales manager in the tower. Michael said that the first pencil was the dealership's starting position. "You have to hit them high," Michael explained. "You have to break them inside—make them understand that if they want our beautiful new car, they're going to have to pay for it."

Here's how we were supposed to get the first pencil from the tower. After the customer test-drove the car, we brought them into a sales office and offered them coffee or a Coke to relax them. Then we filled in the information about the car on the four-square. We then picked up the phone and called the tower. Michael held his hand like a phone receiver with his thumb and little finger sticking out. "You say, 'Yes sir. I have the Jones family here with me and they have just driven a beautiful new *whatever* model, *stock number blah blah blah.'* Then you say, 'Is it still available?' Of course you know it is. But you want to create a sense of urgency. So you pause, then say to the customer, 'Great news! The car's still available!' Then the tower will give you the first pencil. Write it in each of the boxes."

I later found out that the first pencil is arrived at by the dealership in a very unscientific way. For every $10,000 that is financed, the down payment they try to get is $3,000 and the monthly payment they try for is $250. In this way, a $20,000 family sedan would require about $6,000 down and a $500 a month payment. (These payments are based on very high interest rates calculated on five-year loans. These numbers are so inflated that a manager I later worked with laughingly called them "stupid high numbers.")

"But here's the beauty of this system," Michael said, "these numbers aren't coming from you— you're still the good guy. They're coming from someone on the other end of the phone. The enemy."

Michael returned to his scenario. "OK, so when you give these numbers to the customer you say, 'Here's a pretty good deal for you.' But Mr. Customer says, 'Oh man! Michael, I told you I can only put down $3,000.' So you cross out the $6,000 you wrote and put down $5,750. You say to the customer, 'Is that more what you had in mind?' And you nod as you say this. Try to get them agreeing with you."

This reminded Michael of something and he laughed. "Here's another thing. Never give the customer even numbers. Then it looks like you just made them up. So don't say their monthly payment is going to be $400. Say it will be $427. Or, if you want to have some fun, say it will be $427.33."

While Michael was training me, he didn't ever say, "Here's how to cheat the customer," or, "This is how we inflate the prices." In fact, he stressed that I was supposed to treat customers with respect to build a strong C.S.I. (Customer Satisfaction Index). But manipulation and overpricing was inherent in everything he said. The reason for this was simple—without overpricing we couldn't make a living. What we were selling was profit. Or, as Michael put it, "This is money for you—money for your family."

At times, Michael became very excited as he thought of new things to teach me. At one point he said, "Oh! This is a good one! This is how you steal the trade-in." He looked around quickly to make sure no one overheard him. "When you're getting the numbers from the desk, they'll ask if the customer has a trade-in. Say it's a '95 Ford Taurus. And say you took it to the used car manager and he evaluated it and said he would pay four grand for it. If you can get the trade for only three, that's a grand extra in profit.

"So what you do is this," Michael pretended to pick up the phone again, "you ask the desk, 'What did we get for the last three Tauruses at auction?' Then they'll give you some figures—they'll say, $1,923, $2,197 and $1,309. You don't have to say anything to the customer. But he sees you writing this down! And he's going, 'Holy crap! I thought my trade was worth $6,000.' Now it's easy to get it for $3,000. That's a grand extra in profit. And it's front-end money too!" (I later learned that front-end money was what our commissions were based on. Back-end money was made on interest, holdbacks and other elements of the deal.)

We talked for almost two hours before Michael finally ran out of gas. He told me that for the next two days I should get to know the inventory and watch the other salespeople. Then I could learn how to "meet and greet." He invited me to check out some keys and test-drive the cars.

"Product knowledge," he said, tapping his forehead. "Very important. You need to get to know these cars inside and out."

I walked outside and surveyed the car lot. The new cars were on our side of the lot—the used cars to my right. Across the street was another dealership, also selling Japanese cars, and up and down the street were still more dealerships. Most of the manufacturers were represented here. Then, in the distance, was the freeway, a solid river of cars. Cars were everywhere.

"What were you selling before?"

I turned to find Oscar, one of my teammates. He had a broad, friendly face to match his incredibly stocky build. Later, I found out he was a high school football star. I couldn't imagine trying to knock him off his feet.

"I used to sell videos," I told him.

"Like X-rated videos?" he asked eagerly.

"Naw. Training materials. Stuff for companies to train the people who work there."

"Oh yeah. We got some like that here." He popped his knuckles. I tried to read the tattoo on the back of his hand. "Michael show you around the lot?"

"No. He was explaining the four-square."

"You never sold cars before?" he asked.

"No. This is the first time."

"It's easy, man. You'll do good. Hey, I'll show you around." He ducked into the sales office and came back with a set of car keys. "Let's take a ride."

We walked through the line of new cars, each gleaming with water droplets from being washed that morning. Oscar showed me how the lot was arranged with the high-end cars facing the street, the SUVs, minivans and trucks along one side and the midsize sedans near the dealership entrance. He told me there was also a back lot with more inventory and even more cars in a rear fenced parking area. As we talked, a car carrier pulled up and more cars began rolling down the ramp.

Oscar opened the door of a high-end sedan in a sport trim. It had a big V6, leather bucket seats, a sunroof and alloy wheels. The sticker showed a total price of $28,576. A second dealer's sticker showed an extra $236 for custom wheels.

"You're walking through the lot with Mr. Customer and he's eyeballing all these cars," Oscar said. "He stops next to this one and *bam!* that's the one you're gonna sell him. You pull it out of the row, open the doors and ask him to see how good the seats feel. When he sits down, you slam the door and take off."

"You mean, you ask him if he wants to demo the car?" I asked.

"Hell no. They never go for a demo if you ask them. 'Cause they know they're weak. If they drive it, they'll buy it. The feel of the wheel will seal the deal, my friend. So you got to kidnap them, man. Just slam the door and take off. Come on, let's go."

We got into the car and he palmed the wheel, backing up, then pulling out onto the street. A block later we hit a light. When it turned green Oscar punched it and I felt the Gs pressing me back into the leather.

"Whoa," I said. "Great torque."

"Strong," he agreed, checking the rearview mirror. We made a right, then another right into a shopping center parking lot. We got out.

"Now you got them away from the dealership, you can relax a little, show 'em how awesome this car is. What you want to do is open all the doors and windows, the hood and the trunk. Then you do your walk around. You start at the driver's door and you point stuff out as you go. 'Mr. Customer, this car's got the highest safety rating because it's got front crumple zones and breakaway engine mounts. It's got a 170-horsepower V6 with four valves per cylinder and *blah, blah, blah.*' See, it doesn't really matter what you say—most people don't even know what the hell you're talking about—but the important thing is to keep talking: 'Here's the headlights, here's the gas cap. Here's the trunk. Here are the tires.' Anything! Understand?"

"Got it," I nodded.

"Good. Now you drive."

"Me?"

"Yeah. You be Mr. Customer. You get behind the wheel. See, you got to be in control on the demo. Because when you get back to the lot, you got to get them in the box and make a deal."

I slid into the driver seat and closed the door. Oscar sat beside me, buckling up.

"Make a right here," he said. "See, the test-drive route is just a bunch of right turns. If you want to go a little farther, go straight there."

"I want to go a little farther," I said, wondering if he was trying to control me. Besides, driving this car felt great. What was it Oscar said about the *feel of the wheel?* We came up on a railroad crossing. The tracks rumbled under my wheels, distant and muffled.

"Point out stuff on the route," Oscar said. "Like those tracks. Like this turn.

Like the way it brakes. Everything. Just keep talking and building confidence in the product."

I looked over at Oscar wearing his white shirt and silk tie. He had slipped on a pair of wrap-arounds and with his black hair combed back he looked very smooth. Later I learned that he came out of a gang-infested area of the city. A job like this allowed him to drive brand-new cars, handle money deals, wear a tie and act like a big shot.

"Thanks for your help, man," I said when we got back to the lot and put the car away.

"No problem, bro." He shook my hand. "You're gonna do good here."

Over the next few days, I noticed that car salesmen shook hands with each other a lot. I shook hands with each of my team members when I arrived in the morning; we shook hands before we left the dealership at night. We might shake hands with each other two or three more times during the day. If I happened to be standing on the curb and if another salesman walked up, I shook hands with him. It was like we were all staying loose, practicing on each other, for that moment when we would greet Mr. Customer and needed to use a good handshake that's going to seal the deal.

At one point, during a sales seminar, I was actually taught how to shake hands. The instructor, a veteran car salesman, said: "Thumb to thumb. Pump *one, two, three,* and out." Another vet told me to combine the handshake with a slight pulling motion. This is the beginning of your control over the customer. This would prepare the "up" to be moved into the dealership where the negotiation would begin. The car lot handshake is sometimes combined with the confident demand, "Follow me!" If you employ this method, you turn and begin walking into the dealership. *Do not look back to see if they are following you!* Most people feel the obligation to do what they are told and they will follow you, if only to plead, "But I'm only looking!"

Besides handshaking, there's a lot of high-fiving, fist-bumping, back-slapping and arm-squeezing going on among the salespeople. Furthermore, there's a certain amount of tie-pulling, wrestling and shadowboxing during the slow periods.

Later that first day, I was standing on the curb outside the sales offices waiting for ups when a voice boomed over the intercom, "All new and used car salesmen report to the sales towers."

I went into the new car tower while the used car guys went into their tower. It was my first time actually going into this cramped room. There was only a small space around the perimeter of the desk where the salesmen stood, all of us looking up at the three sales managers who loomed above. On that shift, the sales staff was made up of all men. In fact, out of the 85 salespeople, there was only one woman working on the floor selling cars. There were, however, several women in the fleet department and working in the finance and insurance department.

Behind the sales manager's desk were three large white boards. The first listed the names of all the new car salespeople. Beside the names was a blue box for each car they sold. Since I started near the end of the month, some of the salesmen had a long row of blue boxes showing they sold as many as 35 cars. Others had only two boxes. This board enabled everyone to see who was doing well, and who was falling behind. The next board showed the number of cars sold by the entire dealership. And the final board listed the names of the salespeople who hadn't sold any cars for three days.

"How ya doin', guys?" Ben asked, looking down at us. He was in his mid-40s with graying hair combed back. His face was thin, his nose pointed, giving him a foxlike appearance.

"Doin' good, boss," the salesmen muttered.

"You lose some weight, Ben?" one of the salesmen asked.

"A few pounds maybe," Ben said, slapping his gut.

"Guess they didn't feed you much in prison," the salesman observed. Everyone broke up.

Ben's face got red. "Will you quit telling everyone that?"

It was an odd response. He wasn't denying that he had been in prison. So I had to assume it was true.

"OK, guys. Listen up. It is slow. *Slowwwww.* You need to start working the phones, get some customers in here. Who's got an appointment today?"

A few hands were raised.

"Here's the deal. No appointments, no ups. You guys each have to have one *shown* appointment or you don't get to take any ups."

I found out that a "shown appointment" was one where the customer actually showed up. This prevented salesmen from putting down a fake name just to fulfill this requirement.

"No shown appointment, no ups," Ben repeated. "Is that clear?"

"It's clear, boss," a salesman mumbled.

"OK. Now here's the other thing," Ben said, looking down at the assembled masses. "The guys in used cars think we're a bunch of wimps. They're going around telling everyone they can sell more cars than us. So I bet dinner, for each guy here, that we can outsell them over the next four days. What do you say about that?"

We all cheered.

Ben looked through the glass and across the dealership at the used cars tower. All the salesmen were in there meeting with their managers, just like we were meeting with ours.

Ben picked up the phone. "Now I'm going to call used cars and we're gonna show them who we are." He dialed the extension for the used cars department. When they answered he yelled to us, "What do we think of used cars?!" He then held up the phone so we could collectively yell into it. We shouted, "Used cars sucks!"

Then Ben asked us, "Who's strong?"

We yelled, "New cars!!!"

Meanwhile, of course, we could see the guys in used cars were yelling and screaming at us, telling us we were a bunch of wimps. The receptionist, who sat between the two towers, looked like she would die of embarrassment.

"All right, guys," Ben said, serious again. "Get out there and sell cars. Let's rock."

The meeting broke up. The salesmen went outside and stood around grumbling. Then, one by one, they went inside and hit the phones.

I was told I was exempt from this no-appointment/no-ups rule, so I stayed outside. I was left virtually alone, which was unusual. At most times, there were from four to 15 salesmen waiting for ups.

A car pulled onto the lot and a young man and woman got out. No one was there to help them. I looked around. Michael was watching me through the plate glass window. He nodded and pointed at the couple. "Go ahead," he seemed to be saying, "Help them."

"Well, here goes," I thought. "My first customer."

As I moved toward them, my mind was crowded with all I had been taught that day. The couple heard me coming and turned. I don't think I'll ever forget the look on their faces.

Chapter 52
Life on the Lot

When I took this assignment as an undercover car salesman, I knew I was agreeing to join the enemy. Everyone knows that the car salesman is the enemy. He is the person we have to do battle with if we want a new car. I had always been on the customer's side of the desk. Now I was crossing enemy lines. But I didn't feel like the enemy until the first time I greeted a customer on the lot.

Here's how it happened. I saw the young couple get out of their car and wander uncertainly toward a row of compacts. They were there to buy a car. I wanted to sell them a car. I walked toward them with the best of intentions.

As I reached the couple I gave them a cheerful, "Good afternoon!"

They turned and, in an instant, I saw the fear on their faces. Fear of me!

Let me quickly add that I'm not the type of person who normally elicits fear from the people around me. I've been called shy, reserved and quiet—all euphemisms for meek, mousy and at times practically invisible. But here I was with my white shirt and tie, my employee's badge hanging from my belt. I had become the enemy. And they were afraid of me.

What were they afraid of? The short answer is, they were afraid they would buy a car. The long answer is that they were afraid they would fall in love with one of these cars, lose their sense of reason and pay too much for it. They were afraid they would be cheated, ripped off, pressured, hoodwinked, swindled, jacked around, suckered or fleeced. And, as they saw me approaching, all these fears showed on their faces as they blurted out, "We're only looking!"

During my short stint as a car salesman, I saw this look of fear from customers many times. It ranged from a mild apprehension to abject terror. Sometimes customers would actually become hostile. I'd cheerfully say, "How can I help you?" And they would lash out with, "Can't you leave me alone for one second? I just want to look! On my own! OK? On my own!"

What the customer didn't realize was that the poor car salesman was not really the enemy. The real enemy was the manager sitting in the sales tower cracking the whip. Suppose for a moment a customer told us they were "only looking," and we said, "Fine, take your time," and went back into the sales tower. Now we find ourselves looking up into the steely eyes of the sales manager.

"That's your customer out there," the manager would say.

"But they said they're only looking," I would answer.

"Only looking? You're going to take that for an answer?" Foam would begin forming at the corners of the sales manager's mouth. "What the hell kind of salesman are you? Of course they're looking! They're all only looking until they buy. You want them to go across the street and buy a car over there? Because they have real salesmen over there. Now go back out there and sell those people a car. And don't let them leave until they buy or until you turn them over to your closer."

So that's why the car salespeople stick like glue to customers. Their fear of their managers is greater than their fear of offending the customers.

Many salespeople find that humor is a good way to overcome objections. If a customer says they're "only looking," the salesman might answer, "Last time I was only looking I wound up married." If a customer objects to being hurried into buying the car, the salesman might say, "The only pressure on this lot is in the tires." These prepackaged lines were exchanged between car salesmen in the slow times with the feeling that the right joke at the right moment could be the ticket to a sale.

Of course, a good joke in the salesman's opinion might be considered the ultimate cornball line by the customer. In one case, a veteran salesman bragged to me that he sold a car to a woman by telling her, "You know, you look great in this car. The color matches the color of your eyes." Oddly enough, that very night I was talking to a woman who told me she had once had a car salesman tell her that the car matched the color of her eyes. Her reaction to this? "Oh, please!"

Car salesmen seem to exist in their own world. What they think is cool is viewed by the public as tacky and obvious. For example, why do they insist on wearing white shirts and silk ties? Or what about gold watches, rings and chains? Who wears that stuff anymore? Don't they realize they are turning themselves into walking clichés? The only answer I came up with was that, as a salesman, I spent all my time with other salesmen. They were my friends. Believe it or not, I tried to fit in, to belong. So I began to develop an interest in gold ties, white shirts and dress shoes. I even grew a goatee because a lot of the guys had beards. And I put gel on my hair and combed it straight back.

During the first week as a car salesman, I used to come home and describe the scene at the dealership to my wife. I told her how we were instructed to follow cars as they pulled onto the lot and stand beside the car until the customer stepped out. She was incredulous.

"Do they think that's going to make people want to buy a car?" she always asked. "If it was me, I'd just keep driving. I'd want time to pick the car myself. To relax and sit in the car and not be pressured." I could only answer that the system was not set up for educated people who thought for themselves, it wasn't to help customers make informed decisions. The system was designed to catch people off guard, to score a quick sale, to exploit people who were weak or uninformed. Those were our buyers.

Let me say that the dealership I worked at was notoriously high-volume, high-pressure. Even so, there were some salespeople there who were relaxed and friendly and treated customers with respect. I also know that there are many good dealerships across the country that are concerned with their long-term reputation. But as a whole, the dealership where I worked encouraged the salespeople to use pressure to speed up a deal, to get a customer to accept high payments, to get the customer to buy a car they really didn't want.

I had been working for several days by now. My manager had trained me on the basics and then told me to watch the other salespeople interacting with customers. Finally, he let me "meet and greet" customers and then turn them over to another team member. Now, it was time for me to actually start selling cars. So I went outside and began waiting for ups.

The dealership where I worked had "an open floor." This meant that any salesman could wait on any available customer. However, if there were 10 salesmen waiting for ups and one car drove in, how did we decide who would help them? In some cases, the salespeople "called" the ups. They would scan the traffic passing by the dealership. If a car turned into the lot, someone said, "Green Toyota!" And this gave him the right to wait on that customer. When you shook hands with the customer you were, in a sense, claiming your territory.

Since I was still a "green pea," the other salesmen tried to push me to wait on undesirable-looking ups—the undesirable customers who the salesmen thought wouldn't or couldn't qualify to buy a car. My manager had, at one point, described the different races and nationalities and what they were like as customers. It would be too inflammatory to repeat what he said here. But the gist of it was that the people of such-and-such nationality were "lie downs" (people who buy without negotiating), while the people of another race were "roaches" (they had bad credit) and people from that country were "mooches" (they tried to buy the car for invoice price).

I will repeat what Michael, my ASM, told me about Caucasians. He said white people never come into the dealership. "They're all on the Internet trying to find out what our invoice price is. We never even get a shot at them. I hate it. I mean, would they go to a mall and say, 'What's your invoice price on that beautiful suit?' No. So why are they doing it here?"

I was already beginning to see the impact of the Internet because of something that happened during my first few days there. I was sent to the service department to talk to customers waiting for their cars to be fixed. Salespeople feel this is a good source of leads to buy new cars. Say a customer has just gotten nailed with a $2,000 quote for a transmission. Now's the time to move in and pitch the virtues of a new car.

There were typically a dozen or more people waiting for their cars to be serviced. They would either watch TV or read while they drank coffee and Cokes from the vending machines. I handed out my business card and chatted with a few people. One young guy was killing time by goofing around with his palm top computer. He was outfitted in designer jeans and a T-shirt, so I wasn't surprised to hear that he had just bought the new youth-oriented SUV our dealership sold. Michael had told me these vehicles were selling for over sticker prices, so I asked Mr. Palm Top how he made out.

"Got an awesome deal," he said.

"How awesome?"

"Three hundred below invoice," he smugly answered.

I asked how he did it. He said he checked prices on the Internet. He then called the fleet manager and made the deal over the phone.

I had a schizophrenic reaction to this. Part of me admired the fact that he had outfoxed the dealer. But the car salesman side of me was angry that I never "got a shot at him." It seemed like just a matter of time before people who, in the past, walked onto our car lot, would be on the Internet making deals.

The salesmen are only vaguely aware of this developing trend. I was standing on the curb next to George, and we saw one of these high-demand SUVs ready for delivery.

"Another damn Internet sale," George said. "Why don't they turn that car over to us? We'd get a grand over sticker. Instead they're selling it at invoice. Does that make sense?" As the days passed I noticed more and more cars marked "Sold: Internet dept." And as I approached people on the car lot, they often informed me that they were here to see the fleet manager. More Internet customers.

Back to that first couple I greeted on the car lot. I don't remember much about them other than the look of fear on their faces. They didn't buy a car from me. In fact, I didn't have a real good prospect for another two days. I had plenty of people who were just looking. Or said they would be back. Or said they had a doctor's appointment. Or had to pick up their kids at school. These were typical excuses they had for escaping. But the salesmen told me to disregard all these stories that customers gave me. As they put it, "Buyers are liars."

Chapter 53

A Tale of Two Deals

In the new car sales tower there was a huge white board listing the names of all the salespeople on the lot. Every time you sold a car, they colored in a blue box next to the name of the salesman. The best salesman on the lot had a row of 15 boxes stretching out beside his name. I had no boxes next to my name. I felt inadequate.

I had been working for almost a week without selling my first car. I had greeted a lot of customers but I still didn't have a single sale to my name. I gazed jealously at the long rows of boxes next to the names of the other salesmen and wondered when I would make my first sale. Then, one morning, I got a "live one."

I had been standing on the curb out in front of the dealership looking for ups. It was funny because, when you looked away, and then back, customers seemed to magically appear. That's because they sometimes sneaked through the bushes. There were hedges bordering the car lot, so we couldn't see people approaching from the street. Often, a shopper might be at the dealership next door. They decided to continue shopping by walking down the street. That's why they came through the bushes.

By the time I reached this customer, he was already inspecting a top-of-the-line minivan. I introduced myself and he told me his name was Randy Park. He was a young Asian man with grease under his fingernails (later, he told me he was a mechanic). At first, Mr. Park was very guarded. But as we walked to the back lot to look for more minivans, he relaxed and opened up a bit.

We found two minivans that were very close to what he wanted but he told me that he didn't like the color of the interior. He wanted beige with a beige interior. I told him that we had yet another lot which visitors were not allowed to go to. He could wait in the dealership while I checked inventory. He seemed to know the game, that once inside we would work him to make a deal. Still, reluctantly, he followed me inside and sat down in a sales cubicle. I had my first customer, "in the box."

I took some basic information about him. He wanted to pay cash for the minivan and trade in a 10-year-old Acura with 160,000 miles on it.

Michael, my ASM (assistant sales manager) came in to meet Mr. Park and he began searching the inventory for a minivan to match his tastes. Finally, we located a minivan that matched the description and we went outside to look at it.

"It doesn't have running boards," Mr. Park said.

"We'll put them on," Michael quickly said.

Mr. Park inspected the minivan carefully, but he refused to test-drive it, saying his brother had the same vehicle, and he had driven it many times. He also said he wanted a number of things added to the minivan besides the running boards—foglights and a rubber scratch guard for the rear bumper. Michael kept saying it would be no problem to add those things.

At this point things got sticky. Michael had to go into a meeting so another salesman from my team, Juan, was brought in to help me with the deal. I stood to the side in the cubicle and let Juan handle the customer. Just as Michael had described, Juan filled in the four-square worksheet with the stock number of the vehicle and the sticker price, $28,318. Mr. Park saw this and began to get excited, saying he would pay only $24,000 for the minivan. Juan ignored this early overture, picked up the phone and dialed the new car sales tower.

"I have a Mr. Park with me," Juan told the sales manager. "Don't call the police but he's trying to steal our car." (Another example of car salesman "humor.")

Juan gave the desk all the extras that Mr. Park wanted added to the minivan. He then wrote some numbers in the boxes and hung up the phone. He told Mr. Park that we needed a $6,000 down payment and his monthly payments would be $523.

"I told you, I will pay cash for this car," Mr. Park said. "But I want your best price. What is your best price to buy the minivan?"

Juan recalculated the prices and told Mr. Park he could have this beautiful new minivan for only $27,500 plus the cost of the extras. Mr. Park demanded to know how much he would get for his trade-in vehicle. Juan told him we would give him $2,500. This sent Mr. Park into a frenzy. He kept insisting the car was worth at least $6,000.

Juan and Mr. Park went back and forth for about 10 minutes. Then, abruptly, Juan stood up and left. I sat down and tried to make small talk with Mr. Park.

This was difficult since I could see that he was upset about the way he was being treated. Juan returned a few minutes later with the four-square sheet on which the sales manager had written, in blue magic marker: "Great deal! $27,150 for our minivan, $2,500 for your trade."

When this was presented to Mr. Park, he became agitated, insisting the trade was worth at least $5,000. Once again, it looked like Juan had gone as far as he could with Mr. Park. He left and came back with a closer who introduced himself as Big Stu. At first, Stu was jovial. He pointed at the list of extras Mr. Park was requesting and asked, "Is there a kitchen sink in here, too?" Later, he began referring to the extras as "Home Depot."

Big Stu was clearly searching for a way—any way—to get a commitment from Mr. Park. At one point, he pointed at me and said, "And this guy here has never sold a car before. If you buy this car, he gets to pop his cherry."

Unexpectedly, Stu suddenly raised his trade-in value to $4,000. He also said our minivan could sell for $26,500. Mr. Park accepted this offer and initialed the sale sheet. He then said he had to go home and get his wife so he could return and complete the credit application and take delivery of his new vehicle.

I walked Mr. Park out to his car and shook hands with him before he left. I noticed that whenever I shook hands with him, he offered me his left hand. All other salesmen he shook hands with right-handed or American-style. I wondered if there was some cultural significance to this. Perhaps he was telling me he trusted me.

Of course, I began thinking that I had made my first sale—or "popped my cherry." Mr. Park's new minivan was still parked in front of the dealership, so I went out to move it back into its space. It turned out the battery was dead. The minivan had been sitting there so long with doors open that it drained the battery. If Mr. Park had insisted on a test-drive, it wouldn't have started. I went into the tower, and told Big Stu we needed a porter to jump-start the car. He leaned over the counter and screamed in my face, "That's not my f—ing job! Call the porter yourself!"

Eventually, a porter with a "jump box" started the minivan. I let it idle for a half-hour, then put it away. Several hours passed, and I began to feel my first sale slipping away. Suddenly, I was paged. When I got to the receptionist's desk, I found

Mr. Park with his wife and baby waiting for me. He looked very excited and happy. Again, he shook hands with me with his left hand. I showed him the minivan and insisted that we take a test-drive. When we returned, we all went back into a sales cubicle.

Somehow, the earlier sales sheet had gotten "lost" and the numbers they had agreed on were "forgotten." The price of the minivan and all the extras shot back up, and the price of his trade-in took a serious dive. For the next two hours, Mr. Park was hammered by every closer in the dealership. I got to watch a variety of styles: impatience, cajoling, begging, threats. Through all this, his wife sat by his side clutching their little baby. Mr. Park began complaining that he had a headache and his manner became increasingly angry. At one point, he ominously muttered, "Don't screw with me."

I couldn't exactly figure out what had happened to the deal. Yes, he had been offered $4,000 for his trade. I knew that for sure. And I seemed to recall that he had been offered the minivan, including the extras, for as low as $26,500. Those extras had not been written into the contract or they had been conveniently forgotten. They reemerged at the end and completely blew the deal. Finally, Michael picked up the papers and walked out of the cubicle muttering, "You're wasting our time."

Mr. Park asked me several times whether I had heard the earlier offer of $4,000 for his trade. I wouldn't commit to this since I knew that I would be fired if it ever came back on me. When I last saw the Park family, they were heading across the street to another dealership.

Moments later Michael appeared and said, "Sorry about your deal, but those people are completely impossible." Actually, he didn't say "those people." He named an Asian country where, he had earlier told me, the people were all "grinders." Ironically, in my attempts to make conversation with Mr. Park I had learned that he wasn't from that country at all. He was from a neighboring country, which wasn't on Michael's list of primo grinders. So here was my boss, adhering to stereotypes—but doing it incorrectly. That struck me as the worst of both worlds.

All week Michael had been telling me about the Friday morning sales meeting. Each time it came up, he would say, "Make sure you're on time."

"What happens if I'm not?" I asked.

"You don't want to find out."

Friday morning rolled around and I made sure I was there in plenty of time. The meetings were held in the lunchroom upstairs and the only way to reach this room was to climb a flight of outside stairs. All the salesmen were gathered at the bottom of the stairs, milling around smoking cigarettes and drinking coffee. Some of the guys were in street clothes, black leather jackets or wearing baseball caps turned backward. That was because they were working the late shift. They had come in just for the meeting and then would go home and come back again later. Those few lucky salespeople who were off on Friday were required to come to the meeting. If they didn't, they wouldn't be allowed to work that weekend.

The rules of the dealership are enforced by threatening to send the offender home. Since we all worked on straight commission, to be sent home eliminated your chances of making any money. The concept of being sent home always reminded me of being in grade school. "If you do that again, we're going to call your mother and send you home."

One day I was standing "on the point" with my hands in my pockets. The point is the entrance to the dealership where cars pulled in from the street. Another salesman came up to me and said, "If the owner of the dealership sees you standing there playing pocket pool, he'll go ballistic. I got sent home one day for doing that." Apparently, the owner felt we looked idle and inattentive if we had our hands in our pockets.

Salespeople also got fired at the drop of a hat. This was known as "getting blown off." I came into work one morning and heard the guys talking about how another salesman got fired the night before. He had done something to a customer that the GM (general manager) didn't like. The salesman was called into the tower and he stumbled out moments later in a state of shock. He said to the other salesmen, "I don't believe it, he just blew me off." The GM saw the fired salesman talking to the other guys and charged out on the lot, screaming, "Get away from them! I don't want you talking to anyone!"

So the salesmen were very careful to show up for the Friday morning sales meetings on time. I was wondering what was going to happen in the meeting when the door at the top of the stairs burst open and loud, pounding music poured out. The general manager appeared and yelled, "All right, guys, get in here!"

We all ran up the stairs, high-fiving the sales managers as we went like we were taking the field in an all-star game. As we gathered in the room, we were all clapping to the music that was booming from a stereo set up in the corner. It was as loud as a rock concert and was playing that music they use at ballparks: "We will, we will, ROCK YOU!"

The music died and one of the sales managers, a short guy in his 40s, with wavy black hair, ran out in front of us pumping his fists and screaming, "Killer, killer, KILLER WEEKEND!!!"

We all cheered.

"What are you going to do this weekend?" he yelled.

"Sell cars!" we yelled back at him.

For 45 minutes we listened to motivational speeches from the managers. Then the GM appeared and told us about the various bonuses. If you sold three cars you got $250, four cars and you got $350, five cars and you got $500. And then he added, "If the dealership sells 60 cars, all the bonuses double. Sell five cars, you get a grand. It's that simple." More ballpark music followed this and we left the room shaking hands and giving more high fives. We were pumped. We ran outside to sell cars. There was only one problem.

Where were the customers?

I had been warned that Fridays were bad because you have all the salespeople on the lot and no customers until late in the afternoon. But still, there was a lot going on. They had set up an inflatable bouncing room for kids, a petting zoo and a grill preparing free hot dogs and hamburgers under a tent placed on one side of the showroom. The smell of cooking burgers began drifting across the lot. Soon there was a long line of salesman waiting for the free chow.

But that wasn't all. In the lobby, a table was put up and "free gifts" (are gifts ever anything but free?) were on display. If you came in and test-drove a car, you got either a key case or a portable camera. I don't think I need to tell you about the quality of these items. The gifts were handed out by young women with bored expressions and tight tops.

Moving back outside, I saw two people roaming the lot dressed in animal suits. One was a brown fuzzy bear and the other was a floppy-eared rabbit. Later I talked to the women inside the suits and they complained about how hot the costumes were and how little kids kept poking them to see if they were real.

It wasn't until the next week that I finally "popped my cherry." It was about 8:30 p.m., and a couple came through the bushes again. Coincidentally, they were also interested in the minivan—the exact model that Mr. Park had wanted to buy. Apparently, they had been at the dealership next door and just decided to stroll over to see what we had.

A truck was parked on the lot shining searchlights into the air to attract buyers. A diesel generator was cranked up to provide power. As I approached this couple, it was very hard to hear what they said because of the roar of the generator. But the body language of the tall, heavy-set man in his 30s was hostile. His wife was shy. I told them we had more minivans in the back, and invited them to come with me to look at them. As we walked together, I was able to shake their hands and get some general information about them.

They found a few minivans that they liked but had questions about inventory—did we have any of last year's minivans still available? This was a good chance to bring them inside. It was also cold out and they were tired from shopping.

Inside, they sat down as I filled out a guest sheet with basic information. They were surprisingly willing to provide their phone number, address and the amount they would put as a down payment.

I brought Michael, my assistant sales manager, into the office, and he met the couple. I noticed that he always began by praising the car the customer was considering, as if they had made a wise decision. He would say something like: "So you're interested in the minivan. Did you know that's our best-selling vehicle here? Everyone loves it. It can hold seven people, but it drives like a car. You can't go wrong with it. And the prices here are the best in the area." Later, I would learn how this was called raising the customer's excitement level. If they were excited about the car, they wouldn't be rational when it came to making a deal.

Naturally, the couple began asking about the price of different models. Michael pointed to me and said, "He'll take you back out to the lot. Find one or two minivans you like. Get the stock numbers and we'll get specific about payments. How's that sound?"

We went back outside, and located a minivan that was buried deep in a row of trucks. The couple made their choice based on color and sticker price. We went back inside, and Michael quoted them a monthly payment of about $550. The man balked at these figures, saying he had been given lower numbers by another dealership. Michael countered by saying it was difficult to compare two vehicles with different options.

"I just had an idea," he said. "There may be a rebate on this vehicle we could use to bring the payment down. I'll go see if it's still in effect." He disappeared into the sales tower.

Whenever someone failed to accept the "first pencil" (the high numbers they begin with) Michael would always "have an idea" or "remember" a rebate or special interest rate program. This avoided the head-to-head confrontation. It also promoted the sense that we were working in the customer's best interest.

When Michael left to go to talk to "the desk" (the sales managers), I sat down with the couple and made small talk. I noticed that the man had his cellular phone out and was punching the keys. I asked if he was playing computer games. He smiled and said, "I'm playing a game called 'calculator.'" I realized he was running the numbers Michael suggested. It struck me that this might be a good way to check numbers at a dealership. If a customer whips out a calculator, it could really tick off the salesman. But we're getting used to seeing cellular phones in everybody's hands.

Michael went back and forth with the guy several times, but they seemed to be settling on monthly payments of $475. Finally, Michael held out his hand and said, "Do we have a deal?" They shook hands.

If the minivan was selling for a sticker price of about $24,000 with options and tax, a 60-month loan at 9 percent interest would be $475 a month. However, I later checked Edmunds.com True Market Value® prices and saw that this van should have been discounted about $1,700 from the sticker price. Then, monthly payments at 9 percent would have been $430 a month. Over the life of the loan this was a $2,520 difference.

The long paperwork process began. They ran a credit report and the couple had a good score. Still, they needed to sign the contracts in the finance and insurance room, or "F&I."

The dealership was closed now, and most of the salesmen and customers had left. But I had been warned that we would stay as long as it took to get the deal done. After about a half an hour, one of the sales managers told me to move the couple into the "fish room." This meant I was to put them into a waiting room built around a large aquarium. Apparently, it was thought that gazing at fish relaxes people.

Later, Michael told me that on weekends he doesn't like people to go into the fish room. "I've had a couple of deals blow out of the fish room. They start talking to each other, comparing deals and payments, next thing you know one of them is pissed off and they leave. I like to stay with the customer the whole time."

Luckily, my customers were the only ones in the fish room. I took the minivan to the service department and told a porter to wash and detail it. Then I took it down the street and bought a full tank of gas. It's funny because, here is a customer who has just spent about $24,000 on a new minivan. But when you tell them you're buying them a free tank of gas, they get all excited.

Back inside the dealership, I checked on the couple in F&I. Apparently, they were having difficulty approving the $3,500 down payment on their American Express card. It was after midnight and the approval office was closed. By now, this poor couple was slumped in their chairs utterly drained. Michael pulled me aside and said, "If their credit card doesn't go through, you're going to have to follow them to their house and get a check." Eventually, the charge was approved and the people were allowed to buy their new minivan. We gave them a short demonstration of all the features, and they drove off into the night.

By now it was 1 a.m., but I still wasn't done. The desk manager told me I had to put up "the blocker"—a vehicle parked across the entrance to prevent the new cars from being stolen. This was part of the nightly ritual called "lock and block." You check to make sure all the vehicles are locked, and then you move a car to block the entrance.

I put the blocker in place, and told Michael I was leaving. He shook my hand. "Congratulations on your first sale," he said.

I asked him how we did on the deal.

"The problem was, he made me bargain against the other dealership. But we sold the car for sticker. That's the good part. There'll be $300 or $400 in it for you."

Actually, when I got my voucher, I made a $501 commission on a payable gross of $1,689—almost the $1,700 discount that Edmunds.com advised. Our commissions were paid twice a month. But we received vouchers within a day or two showing how much we had to look forward to. The vouchers were yellow carbon copy slips from the dealership's books. The salesmen kept the vouchers in their wallets and took them out to show each other like scalps.

A friend came up to me on the lot one day and said in a confidential voice, "Want to see a bomber?" He unfolded the voucher and showed me the yellow slip: $1,274. "Is that unreal or what? What a bomber." If his commission was $1,274 (30 percent of the dealership's profit), the dealership made $4,242. That's a lot of profit to make on a $25,000 car—about 16 percent.

From my commission check, it was clear that the minivan couple could have made a better deal and saved several thousand dollars. So where did they go wrong? Well, first of all, they negotiated as monthly payment buyers, rather than bargaining on the purchase price of the vehicle. When you agree to be a "monthly payment buyer," several variables are introduced that are harder to keep track of: the term of the loan can be extended up to 72 months (six years!) without your awareness and the interest rate can be raised. When you bargain on purchase price, it is a cleaner, simpler way of negotiating.

After my minivan customers left that night, I went back into the new car tower to check out. I looked up at the enormous white board on the wall that listed the names of the salesmen on the lot. The sales manager was coloring in a blue box next to my name. My first sale. I was finally on the scoreboard.

Chapter 54
Learning From the Pros

When I first started working as an undercover car salesman, I was e-mailing my editors every day with accounts of life on the car lot. But as I settled into the job, my e-mails tailed off. There just wasn't much room in my schedule for writing. For example, one night I had a deal that didn't wrap up until 1 a.m. And I had to be at work the next day at 9 a.m.

I must have let several days go by without writing my editors, because I received an e-mail from my boss asking: "Have you gone native on us?" Maybe they thought I was making so much money, or enjoying life on the lot so much that I was going to change my profession. Not a chance. Sales isn't in my blood. I didn't like "tap dancing on raindrops," as one salesman described the sales pitch.

However, I had agreed to work at one more dealership—a no-haggle car lot—before I ended this undercover project. Before I could do that, though, I needed to leave my present job where I had worked for about a month and sold five cars. And I needed to find a way to make a graceful exit. Little did I know the form it would take.

One Friday morning I was trying to sell a pickup truck to a college student. During a break in the dealing, I phoned home to get my messages. I heard my brother's voice on the message machine calling from the East Coast. He said he had sad news. My brother-in-law had died the previous night. It was completely unexpected, and it left me in a state of shock.

I stumbled outside and told my sales manager what had happened. He said to take as much time as I needed and he would hold my job open for me. Later that week, I phoned him from the East to say I would not be returning.

When I got back from the funeral, I began looking for a new job at a no-haggle dealership that sold American cars. This would make an interesting contrast to a high-pressure dealership that sold Japanese-made cars. I called several places until I found one where they were actively looking for salespeople. They asked me to come in for an interview.

It was a small dealership on a busy street filled with storefront businesses and strip malls. The used cars were parked along the front row facing the street with signs in their windshields listing the year, model and price. The new cars were parked farther back in two short rows, and there were about another 40 new cars on the back lot. Inside the showroom, two new cars were on display, surrounded by desks for the "sales consultants"—as the salespeople were called here. I noticed that, unlike at the previous dealership, about half of the salespeople were women. The uniform here was a polo shirt with the car manufacturer's logo on it.

My interview was with the sales manager, a laid-back guy in his mid-30s named Kevin. When I arrived, he was in his office that looked onto the showroom floor. Evidently, there was no sales tower here. Kevin reviewed my application and recognized the name of the dealership at which I had previously sold cars. He whistled.

"How long did you work there?"

"A month."

"You lasted that long, huh?" he laughed. Then he added, "Why did you leave?"

"I got tired of lying."

"Right. When you work here you won't have to lie —." But then he stopped himself, reconsidering what he had said. "Actually, it depends on your definition of lying. But the point is we won't ask you to do anything that conflicts with your core beliefs."

He explained that the way they handled the trade-in is a judgment call for the sales consultant. Say the used car manager appraises the car at $4,500. The sales consultant could then tell the customer that we would give them $4,000 for their trade—thus adding $500 profit to the deal.

But in general, Kevin told me, things were as straightforward as they appeared.

"We don't hit people with stupid high numbers," he said. "We don't pack payments. We tell people we're no haggle, no hassle and we stick to that. It's a good place to work."

He offered me the job starting immediately. But first, he wanted me to attend a four-day sales seminar. I resisted because there had been so much training at my previous job. What I wanted was more of a chance to sell cars. Eventually, though, I agreed to go because I thought it might add a new dimension to the experience.

I attended the seminar with two other salesmen starting at my new dealership. They were both in their early 20s. One was a surfer dude named Al who had long brown hair combed straight back and a big tattoo on his upper arm. He blinked constantly—an affectation either left over from his surfing days, or caused by all the chemicals he'd poured into his bloodstream. The other salesman was Jeff, a sincere young guy who was a real gearhead.

There were a total of about 15 salespeople in the seminar. The others were from a variety of dealerships selling many makes and models of U.S.- and for-eign-built cars. The class was taught by a tall, handsome man named Roy, who had sold cars for 17 years and wore an exquisite suit and silk tie. He told us that when he first started selling cars he was terrible at it. But then he decided to imitate the successful salesmen on his lot. Eventually he said he made a bundle using the skills he would teach us here. I had to wonder just how big a bundle he made if he was teaching seminars like these.

We then went around the class and introduced ourselves. I was struck by how the other salesmen described themselves in ways that revealed extremely low self-images. Most of them were divorced or refugees from other unsuccessful careers. Others were downright bitter and hostile. One salesman, 50-ish with a pink, bald head and white fringe of hair said, "I'm a three-time loser—I haven't kept a job, a wife or kids for more than three years."

I prepared to listen attentively during this seminar since, after my first job, I had questions about how to sell cars more effectively. One thing that baffled me, for example, was how to get people into the sales office after the test-drive. In some cases, the customer loved the car, they felt comfortable with me, but they wouldn't take that big step through the dealership door.

In one case, I had a husband and wife interested in a crew cab pickup. It was obvious the husband wanted to "buy today." The wife didn't. After the test-drive, I held the door open so they could walk into the dealership. He stepped in. She stayed outside. They had a little spat right there. The wife won and I lost the sale.

It didn't bother me that I didn't sell the truck. I wasn't there to sell cars as much as to understand the process. I felt bad about pressuring this couple when it was obvious it was causing conflict between them. But it came at a time when I hadn't sold a car for a few days, and my boss was beginning to give me heat.

The names of slackers such as myself were put on a white board in the sales tower labeled "Three-Day No Sale." This meant you had to meet with your manager to figure out why you were in a slump. Usually they told you the problem was that you weren't taking enough customers on test-drives (called "demos"). The general manager of our dealership was fond of saying that if we demoed three cars without selling one, he would have a "come-to-Jesus talk" with us. This was like being read the riot act. You had to come to Jesus—to give everything to the dealership—or you'd be fired. Then, he added, if you demo-ed another car and the customer left without buying, you'd follow them home (because you'd be "blown out"). He reinforced his point with another of his favorite expressions: "You'll do it my way, or hit the highway."

Roy, the instructor at the seminar, was like the GM at my first dealership. He was filled with trite phrases and platitudes about sales. The difference was, Roy taught a total system for sales, called "Needs Satisfaction Selling." You found out what the customer's needs were, and then you presented the car in such a way as to meet their needs. This meant you needed to know the car's features so well you could present it in a number of different ways. If the customer wanted safety, you had to talk about ABS, airbags and crumple zones. If the buyer wanted performance, you talked about the V8 engine, the turbocharger and the low-profile tires.

The selling system was built around a progression of questions we were told to memorize. That night I took these questions home and my 9-year-old, who loves role-playing, helped me practice using them.

I'd shake my son's hand and say, "Welcome to the dealership! And your name is?"

"Freddie."

"Good to meet you, Freddie. Are you familiar with our product line here?"

"Uh uh," he'd say, trying to be serious like an adult.

"Fine. Do you mind if I ask you a few questions? That way I can better understand which cars on our lot to show you."

"OK!"

"Freddie, let me ask you, what are you driving now?"

"A BMX bike."

"OK. And what do you like about that bike?"

"Goes real fast."

"So Freddie, what you're saying is performance is important to you. Is that right?"

"I guess."

"Well, we have a model over here with a V6 engine that puts out 210 horsepower. Follow me."

He always followed me when I turned and walked toward the imaginary cars. I wished all the customers were like Freddie.

The next day in the seminar I was called up in front of the class to role-play with the teacher. With 14 other salesmen watching and snickering and hooting, it was difficult to remember all the lines I had memorized. But I began to appreciate the way the questions helped identify and address the customer's needs. I thought back to all the haphazard sales pitches I had given at my first dealership. And I was glad I'd have another shot at selling cars in my new job.

During a break in the seminar, I stood outside with my two buddies from my new dealership. Al, the surfer dude, told me his dream was to work at a Mercedes dealership. His father had once owned a Mercedes, and he knew everything about every model ever made.

"Test me, dude," he said to me, blinking rapidly. "Dude, I'm serious. Test me. I know everything."

The other guy, Jeff, started testing him and, sure enough, he did know everything. He could talk forever about how the taillights had changed from one year to the next, how they had added chrome or flashing to such and such a model. Jeff, on the other hand, knew everything about the motors they put in the cars.

Back in the seminar we learned about how to present "feature-benefits." It wasn't enough just to say this car had, for instance, an antilock braking system. You had to point out the feature—ABS—and then link a benefit to their needs—in this case, safety.

The teacher then took out a $20 bill and taped it to the easel he had been making notes on. He told us all to stand up. He then went around the class and named a benefit, and we had to name a corresponding feature. The last man standing (actually, our group included one saleswoman) got the twenty.

As we stood up, I whispered to Jeff, "You're going to win this thing, man."

"I wish."

"You will," I said. "You're like an encyclopedia."

"Economy," the teacher said, pointing at a standing salesman.

"Fuel-injected four-cylinder engine," the salesman said.

"Safety," the teacher said, pointing at another salesman.

"Dual front airbags," the salesman responded.

In the beginning, it was easy. But one of the rules was that you couldn't repeat any features that had already been mentioned. So we began to run out of features for the benefits he named.

Finally, there were only three of us standing: me, Jeff and the salesman who described himself as a loser.

"Performance," the teacher said, pointing at me.

"Twin-cam engine," I said.

"Aaaaant!" the teacher said, imitating a game show buzzer. "Sit down. Someone already said that."

I didn't hear anyone say that. I was disqualified on a technicality!

Jeff and the guy battled it out and Jeff finally won. I had identified Jeff as a winner and the other salesman had accurately described himself as a loser. He took his seat, hanging his head.

Jeff went to the head of the class and got his twenty. As he sat down, he said to me, "Good thing I won. I didn't even have gas money to get home."

An assignment for our class was to go to a dealership and critique a salesman or woman who waited on us. We weren't supposed to tell them this was for a class or that we were car salesmen. We were merely supposed to evaluate their performance in relationship to what we had learned. I chose a German car dealership along a street near my home. As I walked inside, it occurred to me that this was getting complicated. I was an undercover car salesman for Edmunds.com, sent to a dealership, which sent me to a seminar, which sent me to another dealership as an undercover shopping evaluator. I guess that made me a triple agent.

At the seminar we had been taught how to meet and greet, how to shake hands, how to evaluate needs and even how to overcome objections about discounts and pricing. The woman who waited on me at the German car dealership never shook my hand. I had to ask her for her business card. And when I raised a question about the car's performance, she snapped, "Well you obviously haven't been reading *Motor Trend*. It was their top pick in all categories." I left the dealership feeling vastly superior.

We all graduated from the seminar a few days later and received cheesy little diplomas. The other salesmen were psyched up to go out and sell about 10 cars that very day. I went back to my no-haggle dealership and was eager to use my new sales skills. But there wasn't a customer in sight. So I hung around and shot the breeze with the other sales consultants.

In the car business, there's a lot of down time. All you have to do is drive past a car lot in the middle of the week. What do you see? Six or seven sales guys hanging around out front, sipping coffee, puffing on cigarettes and watching the traffic flowing past, hoping someone will turn in. If a customer appears, they park their coffee cups behind the bushes and pop a breath mint. During the slow times, the conversation turns to dealerships where the other salespeople used to work. On this day, a saleswoman asked me about the place I had just worked.

"Was it as bad as that TV news station made it out to be?" she asked me.

"What do you mean?"

"Didn't you see the piece they did on it?" she said. "They went in there with a hidden camera and caught them packing payments and doing the old bait and switch."

I was amazed. "Are you sure?"

"Yeah. It's been running all week."

When I got home I logged onto the news station's Web site. Sure enough, the exposé targeted the dealership I had previously worked at, along with several other car lots across the city. Judging from the dates, they did their "investigation" just after I quit. I skimmed the article, looking for the names of Michael, my assistant sales manager, and the members of my team. As my eyes flew over the text, I realized I was hoping I wouldn't find their names. Why did I feel loyalty to them? When I reached the end, I saw that they had escaped. But the hidden camera had caught a guy I knew vaguely.

The TV news investigation seemed pathetically shallow to me. A reporter went in posing as a customer to see what kind of service she would get. Six hours later they came out with the earth-shattering news that the salesmen were guilty of pressuring customers (you're kidding me!) and also accused the dealership of overcharging the customer (stop the presses!).

It gave me renewed respect for my Edmunds.com editors who had made the commitment to send me into this world for several months. But with my deeper level of understanding, the morality of the issue began to blur. I don't think I'll ever be able to make sweeping generalizations like I once did, by declaring, "Car salesmen are scum!" I knew a lot of salesmen whose skills I admired. Besides that, it's a tough life. The hours stink and you live or die by your ability to sell dreams and move cars. So for the TV reporters to crucify the salesman was a farce. The system was corrupt from the top down. This was proven when the TV reporter went to the owner of the dealership. He told her he was going to launch a thorough investigation into his dealership's practices—as if all this went on without his knowledge. And yet, he had been present in every Friday morning sales meeting, whipping the salesmen into a frenzy, urging them to go for "pounders"—a deal with a $1,000 commission for the salesman.

It was a pretty good bet that we would never be investigated here at the no-haggle dealership. We didn't pressure people, we didn't pack payments or steal trade-ins. The only problem was, we didn't have customers. I found myself wondering whether this phase of the undercover project was going to be a bust. If there's no dirt, what is there to talk about? But that was before the weekend arrived and we actually got some ups. And it was before they sent me into the phone room to drum up business with a technique that didn't exactly fit the company's customer-friendly image.

Chapter 55
No-Haggle Selling

When I was hired at the no-haggle dealership, I was told I would be doing some phone work to build up leads. "Phone work" is a euphemism for calling people at dinnertime and harassing them. I realized I had become one of those people who I despise—a telemarketer. Still, to complete this experience, I attacked it with as much enthusiasm as I could muster.

The leads we were given were names and numbers of people who had bought cars several years ago (and presumably were ready for a new one now) or people who had recently brought their cars in for service since this might show they were beginning to become unreliable. We were given about 20 names a day, and those people who seemed like hot prospects were then called more frequently. Other people who had responded coolly were called again in six months. All our calls were logged into a computer database.

We were given a script to follow when making our calls. To me the dialogue sounded stilted and ridiculous. But I made a point of following it word for word. For example, after we had identified ourselves, we had to ask, "Am I interrupting anything important?" This seemed like a poor strategy to me. I felt they would, without our invitation, tell us if we were interrupting anything. Or we could tell from their tone of voice if they were busy.

Assuming we hadn't interrupted something important, we then explained why we were calling: "We have a shortage of quality used cars on our lot right now and my manager would like to offer to buy your car at above market value. We would like to invite you to come down here for a free appraisal. Is the afternoon or the evening better for you?"

The beauty of this system, the manager told me, was that "they're expecting you to *sell* them something. But you're not! You're offering to *buy* their car!"

Of course, all you're really doing is offering to take their car as a trade-in. Because, when you are appraising their car, it will begin to occur to them that—if they sell their car—they will need another one. So they will begin looking around our car lot and before you know it, you have a sale and a trade-in deal. Nice idea.

But it never worked for me.

Another ploy was to call someone who had once bought a car from our dealership and leave a brief mysterious message such as, "Mr. Jones, I have some information about your 1999 (fill in make and model of car) and I need to contact you as soon as possible. Please call me at—." This method nearly always brought a return call from a customer with visions of urgent recall information or maybe even police trouble. But when they found out that we merely wanted to "buy" their car, they were often quite annoyed.

Still, I was surprised at how receptive most people were to talking with me on a cold call. They were more open than I am to people who call me at dinnertime or while I'm not "doing anything important." I was even more surprised at the loyalty customers showed toward this car manufacturer. Apparently this "no-haggle, no-hassle" style of selling created a feeling of goodwill that lasted throughout the entire ownership of the car. And it was an American car at that! I was filled with patriotic pride thinking how these cars might someday be as popular as the hot-selling Japanese models.

But still, I hadn't sold a car at this dealership. I had attended class, talked on the phone and even taken a few ups on the lot. But no one was buying. When I looked restless, the assistant sales manager, a heavy blonde woman, said: "Please don't quit! I know it's slow, but wait 'til the weekend. You'll sell a car this weekend."

"Wait 'til the weekend," was a popular refrain in the car business. Everything revolved around those two days when ups were supposed to stream onto the lot. One of my other sales managers told me, "On the weekends, we have so many ups, we call it the tuna run."

"Tuna run?" I asked.

"You know—so many fish it's hard to pull them all into the boat. You'll see."

The tuna run never materialized at my old job. I was anxious to see if it would come true at my new job. I made sure I arrived early Saturday morning because, I was told, salespeople took ups in the order in which they arrived for work.

At noon I was still waiting for my first up. I decided I better eat something before the tuna started running. I began walking toward my car when Al called me back, "Dude, where're you goin'?"

"McDonald's. You want something?"

"Dude, dude. You can't leave. You miss an up, that would be like a $300 burger."

Al was very persuasive. We ordered a pizza to be delivered. When it came, it had the wrong topping and Al didn't have enough money for the extra charge. He was going to send it back. I made up the difference, and we sat down to eat in the break room. I never saw food disappear so fast. He hunched over the pizza, I heard muffled grunting noises and it was gone. He belched a few times and headed back outside to look for ups.

One thing I discovered was that car salesmen are easy marks for anyone selling things. That's because they are always hanging around—they're a captive audience. And some of them are flush from a recent sale. At the first dealership, I was in a sales cubicle one day when a guy stuck his head around the corner. "Silk ties, 10 bucks," he said, and disappeared.

Outside I found a cluster of salesmen gathering around the open trunk of a shiny black BMW. In the trunk were boxes packed with ties in protective plastic sleeves. I picked out two ties and gave him a twenty. The Tie Guy (as he was called) fingered the tie I was wearing and then compared it with the two I had selected. He nodded approvingly. "You've, like, got this pattern thing going. Cool."

After the Tie Guy visited the dealership, the salesmen would congregate in the bathroom trying on their new purchases, complimenting each other. Gold ties were the most popular. They went nicely with the watches, rings and chains the salesmen wore.

Besides the Tie Guy, we also had the Sandwich Lady and an older guy who sold golf balls he had found in water hazards. The balls were neatly arranged in egg cartons in the trunk of his car. "Three bucks a dozen. Mix and match," he told me. "Lotta Titleists there." Then he dropped his voice confidentially, as if he was giving me a special deal. "Got a Callaway three iron in the backseat. Ten bucks." I imagined an irate golfer giving it a heave into a water hazard. Little did he imagine that his club would resurface in this way.

Then there was the Chicken Man. You never saw the Chicken Man so much as smelled him. He seemed to appear on weekend nights when it got busy. You would smell fried chicken and see a figure out of the corner of your eye carrying a cardboard box on his shoulder. Then the word would spread: "The Chicken Man's here!"

I went into the F&I office one night and found a sales manager hunched over a chicken dinner with his tie thrown back over his shoulder to protect it from grease splatter. He was eating with great purpose, making *harf, harf, harf* noises.

"Is it as good as it smells?" I asked.

"No. But I was starved," he said, throwing the bones in a trash can. He wiped his mouth, picked up his contracts and moved back into the hallway to a waiting customer.

It was almost 2 o'clock that Saturday afternoon when I got my first up. I saw a man wandering among the new cars. This was the first real up I had gotten since I took my sales seminar. As I walked toward him I began rehearsing all the things I had learned.

His name was Ron and he told me his car was in the service department. He wasn't going to buy a car today, but since he had a few minutes to kill he wanted to see the new family sedans we offered. The top-of-the-line model came with a V6 engine that had been highly praised.

I took Ron to the lowest-level family sedan on the lot. We had been told in the seminar that it was "easier to sell up, than down." This meant that you always started the customer at the least expensive model and let them bump themselves to the more expensive models. The reasoning was that once they had sat on leather and felt the power of a V6, how could you get them excited about driving around in cloth and plastic, powered by a whiny little four-banger?

The strategy worked. Ron told me he liked the roominess of the car and the way it handled, but he wanted power. No problem, I told him. Then, as if the thought just occurred to me, I said, "Tell you what, while we're on the test-drive, I'll have your car appraised. Then, if you decide you want to buy, I can give you an idea of what your payments will be."

He agreed, although he told me he would pay cash rather than finance or lease the car. I got all the information on his trade-in and gave it to the assistant sales manager. She began feeding the information into her computer, then pounded on the keyboard in frustration.

"Damn thing's locked up," she said. "I'll have to do it the old-fashioned way.

She pulled out a small reference book listing used car prices and added the cost of options and the mileage allowance. She gave me a trade-in value of $4,200.

"Great news," I told Ron, who had been waiting in the showroom. Salesmen always return to their customers with what they call "great news." I told him: "We can give you $4,200 for your trade-in. Believe me, that's high. You'd never get that anywhere else."

Actually, $4,200 really did seem like a lot. But I wondered if that was just in relation to the ridiculously low figures we gave for trade-ins at the first dealership I had worked at. Ron seemed encouraged by this figure, so I decided to give him a little sales pitch about leasing I had cobbled together from bits and pieces of presentations I had heard, or overheard, from other salesmen.

For a salesman, the main benefit of leasing is that it is so complicated that the customer sits transfixed during negotiations, unable to defend themselves while the salesman picks the customer's pockets. Usually, the salesman hits the customer with incredibly high monthly payments on a purchase plan. Then, as if the idea just popped into their mind, the salesman will say, "You know, there might be another way to get the payments down... Have you folks ever considered leasing?"

Personally, I think leasing can be a good way to go. For one thing, leasing allows people to drive more expensive cars. But you have to be careful. Some dealers base leases on 110 percent of the vehicle's sticker price. This is called a "full pop lease" and it's what most dealerships aim for. Also, it's easy to disguise the interest rate in a lease because it is expressed as a decimal multiplier called a money factor instead of a more recognizable percentage rate. For example, a 9 percent interest rate becomes a 0.00375 money factor.

At the first dealership where I worked, a veteran sales manager rounded up all of us green peas and taught us how to present leasing to Mr. Customer. He said to tell customers: "In three years, you can turn your old car back in and get one that has the latest technological inventions. And what do you think cars will be able to do in three years? Who knows? Fly in the air! Go across the water! Go under the water! Who knows?"

I didn't give Ron that speech. But I did tell him that if he paid only the drive-off fees (about $650) and gave us his trade-in as a down payment, he would have a $257 monthly payment for 39 months. I pointed out that we offered interest rates of 4.9 percent.

"Why take your money out of a mutual fund at 16 percent when you can use our money at 4.9 percent?" I asked him. "Then, at the end of the lease, if you love the car, you can buy it at about half its current value."

I looked up and saw the assistant sales manager frantically waving me into her office. I left Ron to ponder the advantages of leasing and stepped back into the sales manager's office.

"You didn't give him the price on his trade-in did you?" she asked.

"Of course I did. Why?"

"Damn. The computer just came back up. We're offering him about a grand more than what it's worth." She thought it over. "Look. We have to stand by our offer. But tell him it's good for today only. And if I were him, I'd jump on it, big time."

I walked back out into the showroom and rejoined Ron. "You're going to like this," I said (using a variation of the "great news!" opener). I explained what had happened, then added, "You can tell all your friends how you outfoxed the car salesman."

He chuckled. If you can get people laughing, it gets them on your side.

Still, there was a problem. Of course, there was a problem in every deal. Ron's problem was simple and very common: he had to talk to his wife first. He kept calling her on his cell phone. But she was out with the kids. He confided in me: they had agreed his wife would be the next one to buy a new car. He was worried that she might be upset with his purchase.

By now I had been with Ron for about two hours. It had gone from being a hot, sunny afternoon to a cool, windy evening. Ron was hungry and so was I. But after all this, I didn't want to turn him into a "be-back."

Ron had given up trying to reach his wife. He was about to go home and talk it over with her when his cell phone rang. It was his wife. I moved outside to give him some space. It might sound corny but I began visualizing that I had made the sale. This is a popular technique with salespeople. It just means that you picture the outcome you want before it happens. I pictured shaking hands with Ron and saw him signing the contracts. But life isn't that simple. When Ron was done talking to his wife, his answer wasn't yes or no. He merely said, "She's coming down."

A few minutes later, a van pulled up and Ron's wife stepped out. Before she could speak, I said, "I'm the pushy salesman who's been holding your husband hostage all afternoon."

She laughed. And I knew I had a sale. They leased the car for three years. And I even sold them a service contract.

After Ron and his wife signed the contracts, I led them outside. They transferred all the crap from their old heap to their gleaming new car—cupholders, maps, cassette tapes, Kleenex, flashlights, etc. After they drove away, I pulled their trade-in to the back of the lot. The thing was a real beast. The interior had a moist, funky smell. At this very moment, I thought, Ron was driving home, inhaling new car smell. I enjoyed imagining how happy he must be.

Back inside the dealership, everyone was hurrying to lock up and go home. The F&I manager came over and said, "You did a phenomenal job with that guy. I'm going to break my rule and speak to you before you've been here for six months."

So, did Ron get a good deal? Well, he drove in behind the wheel of an old heap. He paid only $650 out of pocket (drive-off fees on his lease) and he drove out in a more powerful, more reliable, safer, top-of-the line family sedan.

Was the no-haggle method of selling better? From the salesman's point of view, it allowed me to focus on what the customer really needed. Also, the goodwill I built up on the test-drive was preserved during the deal-making process. The only problem I could see with no-haggle selling was with my commission—I made about $350 on the deal. Not bad for four hours of work. But, as it turned out, it was the only car I sold that week.

Chapter 56

Parting Shots

I t was the last day of my career as a car salesman. I was working the evening shift at the no-haggle dealership, on a day in the middle of the week. A typical day. A slow day. I made my sales calls in the "business development center," trying to set up sales appointments I knew I would never keep. My heart wasn't in it and, not surprisingly, I couldn't convince anyone to sell me her "quality used car" for "above market value."

I sat at my desk in the showroom hoping for some diversion to pass the time. I had done that a lot as a car salesman. And on this day, sure enough, something happened to kill a few minutes. It involved a salesman I'd gotten to be friends with, a guy named Craig. He had recently moved from Montana, and true to his roots, he looked like the Marlboro Man—rugged features and a thick graying mustache. Unfortunately, Craig also had bad teeth and was a foot shorter than I imagined the Marlboro Man to be.

Early on, I had been told a good salesman "walks the lot" everyday to check on inventory. Craig did this religiously and memorized the location of every car on the lot. If you were in the middle of a sale, and the customer decided he wanted a white coupe instead of a black four-door, you had only to call over to Craig, and he would instantly give you the location of the car that would seal the deal. I later realized Craig had another reason for walking the lot. He had a bottle hidden out there somewhere. He'd always return from the lot a touch more animated, a glow in his face.

On one return trip from walking the lot, he went to sit at his desk and missed the center of his chair seat. The chair was on wheels and began sliding backward as he continued downward. Despite his heroic efforts—clawing for handholds on a nearby potted plant—down he went. And all this happened right in front of the boss's office window.

There was silence in the showroom for a few seconds, then high-pitched squeaks of laughter from a saleswoman named Allie. Her laughter continued until it infected the rest of us. We stumbled outside to recover ourselves and, as Allie lit up a cigarette, she began regaling us with stories of other mishaps involving the parade of salesmen and women who had worked there during her tenure. I felt odd as she talked about past co-workers since I knew I would soon be joining their ranks, disappearing into the anonymous job market.

Allie told us how she had helped a friend named Mark get a job as a salesman there because, "He was an even bigger klutz than me." One day he took a customer's driver license into the showroom to photocopy before going on a test-drive. Turning back to the customer, he walked right through a plate glass door, saying, "Here you go," and handing back the license as if nothing had happened. As he turned away, Allie saw blood spurting from his knee where an artery had been severed. They wrestled him into the break room and a mechanic in the service bay, who had been a medic in Vietnam, stanched the bleeding. They rushed back outside to tend to the customer and discovered he had a long shard of glass protruding from his foot.

Another time, Mark went outside to "lock and block" and never returned. Lock and block is a nightly ritual where the sales staff makes sure all the car doors are locked and the entrance is blocked by parked cars. In this case, Mark had pulled on a chain link gate to see if it was locked but succeeded in pulling it down on top of himself, pinning him to the ground. When they lifted the gate off him, he had a waffle pattern on his face from the chain link fence.

As we talked, the afternoon turned to night and a chilly wind came up. Allie went inside to make more sales calls, and Craig drifted away to do a thorough check of our inventory and, probably, take another toot off the bottle he had hidden. I leaned against a car and watched the traffic passing in the street. From where I stood, I could see the guys across the street at the Dodge dealership drinking coffee and smoking. It was slow over there, too. I began thinking back on my experiences, summarizing what I had learned from my three months as a car salesman.

Of course, I absorbed a lot I couldn't easily describe, bits and pieces of information I knew would come back while I was at Edmunds.com. But how had my view of the big picture changed?

I know for sure I'll never look at car salesmen and women in the same way. I used to hate and fear them, to lump them all in the same category with sweeping generalizations. Now, I had visited the waters they swam in. I sympathized with them, I pitied them and—in some cases—I admired them.

I saw that many car salesmen and women, like myself, were just moving through the dealership experience, on their way from one point in their lives to another. Most of them didn't have college degrees and were trapped in lives that they thought offered little chance for advancement. The car business offered them a way to use a lot of hustle and a little book learning to make money. I admired anyone who was trying to improve his or her life, particularly through hard work. But making big bucks in the car business wasn't the slam-dunk it was made out to be.

Previously, I had known car salesmen from the outside, as I encountered them while buying a car. Now I had worked alongside them. I had been rejected by customers and bullied by sales managers. I had been excited by a big sale and disappointed when a sure thing fell apart. I saw the same dream they saw: big commissions from easy sales. All you had to do, as my assistant sales manager Michael told me, was get "right in the head."

During the Friday morning sales meetings at my first dealership, the managers tried to psyche us up by saying that we could make more money as a car salesman than a doctor. True, some of the successful salesmen made a lot of dough. But the vast majority of car salesmen were eking out a living, thinking that someday, somehow, their luck would change and the money would begin rolling in.

So, you think I'm romanticizing car salesmen? Trying to clean them up and excuse their evil ways? And, you might ask, if the salesman isn't the bad guy, who is?

Having been a salesman myself, I began to view the managers and dealership owners as the real culprits. While salesmen play people games with the customer, the guys in the tower work the numbers with computers, their eyes fixed on the bottom line. They can see at a glance what kind of profit they are taking from the customer and they do it anyway. Furthermore, they bully the sales staff, encouraging them to manipulate, control and intimidate customers while they take the lion's share of the profit.

Sometimes, the profit a salesman generates is not even pocketed by him. One salesman told me the F&I people can work accounting magic to rob a salesman

man of his commission. They move front-end profit to the back end where it evaporates from the salesman's voucher and returns, over the years, to the dealer in the form of high interest and steady payouts. I experienced a little taste of this myself. I leased an SUV to a single mother at sticker price and expected a nice commission. But on payday, I cashed a $65 check. No explanation. No hint of where my commission had gone.

The management pushes the salesman out the door, lets him meet and greet the customer, then takes the profit. Not only that, but the management also blames the salesman when something goes wrong. I saw this quite clearly when the TV news team did its hidden camera investigation of the dealership. A salesman was made out to be the bad guy. When the camera was turned on the dealership owner, he disavowed knowledge of what was happening in his business and promised a complete review of their practices. This, despite the fact that at Friday sales meetings, the owner was cheering the boys on to get more deals at a higher profit.

Profit. By itself profit is a positive word. But in the car business, the dealership's profit is the consumer's loss. I'm not suggesting that dealerships should be run without a profit, but in one case I heard about, the dealership made a 16 percent profit on a $25,000 car. That means the consumer, the average Joe buying the car, paid about $4,000 too much.

While working as a car salesman, I became impressed with the damage a bad car deal can do to the budget of an ordinary person. In one case, I participated in leasing a car to a couple at well over its value. I was haunted by the thought that this nice ordinary couple had trusted me, and I had let them sign a contract that would bind them for five years to a high-interest lease. I consoled myself thinking perhaps another dealer would have inflicted greater damage.

How did the car business get so screwed up? There's nothing else in our society that is sold to consumers who are so conspicuously unprepared.

During the sales seminar I took, the instructor attempted to tackle the "Why is it this way?" question. He said that just after World War II there were a lot of people who wanted to buy cars, and there were a lot of people who had money, but there weren't enough cars to go around. So the car salesman didn't really have to "sell." Their job was merely to qualify customers, to find out who was really going to "buy today," so they could move on to the next customer. This set the tone for the business, and it is still that way today.

My last day on the job was almost over, the last day of this three-month undercover project. I still had to lock and block before I could go home. Craig and I moved outside. He took the back lot, I took the front. We checked all the cars, then pulled two blockers up and parked them across the dealership entrance. We went back inside and left the keys to the blockers on the receptionist's desk. Just before I left, I put an envelope in my boss's mail slot so he'd get it when he came in the next morning. It was a handwritten note saying I was resigning because it was so slow and I couldn't make a living there. It really was too slow to make a living there. That much was certainly true.

I didn't feel too guilty about leaving. I had sold two cars, made a little profit for the dealership. My departure meant that the remaining salesmen would get more customers and could make more money. The dealership didn't know which salesman would pan out, so they hired too many people knowing some would drop out. I was one that dropped out.

"Give me a ride over the hill?" I turned and found Craig, the Marlboro Man. He took the bus to work everyday. I usually gave him a ride to the bus stop. There was no hill where we worked. It was just Craig's Montana way of talking. We got in my car and started driving.

"I'm gonna have to get me a vehicle here pretty soon," Craig said. "That way, I can get up to the mountains, do a little fishing on my day off."

We drove in silence.

"A nice little pickup would do me just fine," he said. "Maybe, if something comes in on trade, I can get it cheap."

Maybe so. And maybe tomorrow an 800 credit score would walk in and buy a top-of-the-line, fully loaded sedan from Craig. And maybe next month Craig would sell 20 cars and be top man and get all the bonuses. It could happen. You just had to hang in there and wait for your luck to turn.

I let Craig off at his bus stop, and he thanked me for the ride. Now that I was alone, I realized that my undercover project was finally over. I took off my tie, put away my white shirts and, the next morning, shaved off my goatee. The next week I was back in the office, writing about my experiences. But I often wondered if Craig got the pickup truck. And I wondered what happened to Allie or Michael, or any of the dozens of salesmen and women I had met over the past three months. As far as I know, they're still out there, trying to make a living by moving metal, dreaming of good deals with high profits but, all too often, having to settle for long hours and small vouchers. Think of that the next time you go to buy a car. And be glad you are the one buying the car, not the one whose livelihood and identity depend on selling it.

Car Lot Lingo

Want to talk like a car salesman? Or, would you like to know what they are saying when they inadvertently slip into their native tongue? Here is a list of words and phrases salesmen use when the customer's not around.

Be-Backs: A customer who leaves the car lot promising to return later, saying, "I'll be back," or some variation of that statement. "The guy was a *be-back*. But I think he meant it. I'll see him again."

Boss: The typical way that salespeople address the managers or the GM. "Hey, *Boss!* Got a deal for you!"

Bumping: Raising the customer's offer for a car. "If Mr. Customer says he only wants to pay $250 a month, just say, 'Up to —?' He'll probably *bump* himself up to $300 without you doing anything."

Buyers Are Liars: Car salesmen know they have a reputation for dishonesty. But they counter with this claim of their own.

> Salesman #1: "After the test-drive this guy tells me he has to leave 'cause he's got a doctor's appointment. Yeah, right."
>
> Salesman #2: "What can I tell you, man? *Buyers are liars.*"

Closer: An experienced salesman who is brought in to "close" the customer by making them agree to a deal. "If I worked with a better *closer,* I'd have more units on the board."

Demo: This is the test-drive. "This guy comes in, *demos* the car and I think he's ready to buy, right? Then he tells me the car's for his wife and he can't make a decision without her. Same old line."

Desk: This is the sales manager, not the place he sits. "Ask the *desk* if these rebates are still in effect."

F&I: This stands for the finance and insurance office where the documents are signed. The F&I salesman usually will push products such as extended warranties, fabric protection and alarms. "The wait for *F&I* is two hours. Better stick with your customer so they don't skip out the back door."

The Feel of the Wheel Will Seal the Deal: It is assumed that if you test-drive a car, you will buy it. "This prospect was on the fence, right? I get him in the car, he drives the thing, now he's hot to buy. It's like they always say, '*The feel of the wheel will seal the deal.*'"

First Pencil: This is the opening offer from the sales manager, usually written onto the four-square work sheet, so called because it is highly negotiable, i.e. written in pencil, not ink. "I show my customer the *first pencil* and it's so high he nearly dies. I scrape him off the ceiling and make a deal."

Four-Square: As negotiations begin, the salesman pulls out a work sheet divided into four squares which represent the four elements of a car deal: selling price, trade-in value, monthly payment and down payment. "I started working the *four-square* and looked up at the prospect. It was great—they had no idea what the hell I was talking about."

Full Pop Lease: This is when a vehicle is leased at 110 percent of the sticker price—the highest amount allowed by most banks. "I got them into a *full pop lease.* I'll get a nice voucher for that."

The General Manager (GM): The GM is the head honcho at the dealership. He runs the business from day to day. "The guys were standing out on the curb drinking coffee, so the *GM* called them into the tower and read them the riot act."

Green Pea: A new salesman. "The funny thing is, *green peas* can outsell the veterans. That's because they don't know how hard this job is."

Grinder: A customer who negotiates for hours over a small amount of money. "We were only $500 apart but the guy wouldn't sign. Man, what a *grinder.*"

Home Run: This applies when a salesman has taken advantage of every element of the deal: trade-in, sale price and financing. "I stole their trade and buried them in a full pop lease with 9.9 percent financing. *Home runs* like this don't come along every day."

Lay Down (also "Lie Down" depending on usage): A customer who takes whatever deal the salesman offers. "I quoted him monthly payments of $575 and he took it! I wish all the customers were *lay downs* like that."

Mini: The commission on a deal where the car was sold at close to invoice price. "Sure, the deal was only a *mini*. But I qualified for a weekend bonus and made a grand."

Mooch: A customer who wants to buy a car at invoice. "People are spending too much time on the Internet. It's turning them into a bunch of *mooches*."

Packing Payments: Adding extra profit to the cost of a car. "This place I used to work got busted for *packing payments*. Next job I get is going to be in a no-haggle store."

The Point: The place on the car lot where the "up" man stands looking for customers. "The GM saw me standing on *the point* with my hands in my pockets. He went ballistic and sent me home for the day."

Pounder: A deal with $1,000 profit in it. "Doctor comes in and buys the top-of-the-line model, fully loaded—and he pays sticker! That'll be a *two-pounder* for me."

Rip Their Heads Off: This describes taking a customer to the cleaners. "I stole their trade-in, I sold them the car at a grand over sticker—I mean, I just *ripped their heads off*."

Roach: A customer with bad credit. Not to be confused with the "roach coach" (see entry below). "The guy looked good. But we ran his credit and he turned out to be a *roach*. We're talkin' a 400 credit score, repos and bankruptcies out the wazoo."

Roach Coach: The food truck that comes around to the dealership every day. "I shouldn'ta eaten that chili from the *roach coach*. My stomach's killin' me."

Spiff: A tip, kickback or payment of any kind, usually cash which is handed between salespeople. "I *spiffed* the F&I guy 20 bucks, and he took my customers first."

Strong: This has a special meaning on the car lot. It means holding firm on your price and being a tough negotiator. "When they ask for your price, you have to be *strong*. Hit 'em with high payments, then scrape them off the ceiling and start negotiating." (See also "Weak.")

Tower: The office where the sales managers work. This is usually a raised platform allowing the managers to see over the roofs of the cars so they can watch customers and their salespeople. "Attention: All new car salesmen report to the new car *tower!*"

Turn Over: Also known as "turning," this is the practice of passing a customer from one salesman to another. It is thought that this will prevent customers from leaving the car lot. The theory is that the customer might just have bad chemistry with the first salesman and he might like the next salesman. "I *turned* this guy to my partner and he wound up buying. I'll get half of the commission on the deal."

Up: A customer who walks onto the car lot. The term probably comes from the order in which customers are taken, as in: "I'm up next." Many dealerships also have an up system. "We've got *ups* all over the lot, and you're in the back drinking coffee?!"

Voucher: Car salespeople receive a voucher to let them know what their commission was for selling a car. They don't know until the deal is finalized exactly how much they will receive. "Check out this *voucher*. I thought I had a pounder. Instead it's a mini."

Weak: This describes being a weak negotiator or coming down too quickly on price. "The guy was *weak*, so he only lasted a few months. How are you going to make money in this business if you give away cars?"

Glossary

The following list of words and phrases are used in buying, selling, leasing and insuring cars. A glossary of car salesman's lingo is included separately, on page 294.

Add-ons: Items that the dealer installs after the car is delivered from the factory. These are generally high-profit items such as entertainment systems, wood paneling or chrome wheels. Usually, the prices for these things are listed on a second sticker in the car's window.

Allowable Mileage: This is the number of miles you are allowed to drive over the term of the lease, per year. Most leasing companies allow 12,000 miles a year. If the allowable miles are exceeded, you typically must pay between 12 and 15 cents per excess mile.

APR: This stands for Annual Percentage Rate. This is related to, but slightly different than, the interest rate. This is the interest rate multiplied by the number of periods in the year. If an interest rate is 4 percent quarterly, the APR would be 16 percent. The APR supposedly makes it easier to compare different loans because it always translates the loan to a yearly figure. But some experts caution against putting too much stock into the APR, because hidden fees can raise or lower this figure.

Asking Price: This is the price at which negotiations start. It is what the dealer or seller hopes to get for the car.

Balance: The balance of the loan is the amount remaining to be paid. Each time you make a payment, the balance is reduced.

Capitalized Cost: Often called the cap cost, this is basically the negotiated price of the car to be leased and all the options. This becomes one of several figures used in calculating a monthly lease payment.

Closer: An experienced salesman or sales manager at a dealership who is brought in late in negotiations. The closer is used either to persuade hesitant buyers to commit or to try to sweeten the price for the dealership.

Credit: This word is loosely used in a number of ways. In the financial world, it means the ability to borrow money. If someone says, "She has strong credit," it means a lending institution would gladly lend her money. A company might be given a "line of credit."

Credit Report: A document that comprehensively details an individual's credit payment history. Also included is information such as one's name, current and previous addresses and social security number.

Credit Score: A reckoning of an individual's creditworthiness based on an analysis of the data reflected in his or her credit report. This number provides potential lenders with the means to evaluate credit risk quickly and in a relatively objective manner.

Demo: This refers to one of two things: either a test-drive, or a car that has been used as a "demonstration" model for the dealership.

Depreciation: This is the amount by which property (in this case, a vehicle) loses its value over time. In leasing, depreciation is the difference between the new car's cost and the value of the car at the end of the lease (plus tax, interest and various leasing fees).

DMV Fees: When buying a car at a dealership, you have to register it and pay for license plates before you can drive it away. These various fees are referred to as DMV (Department of Motor Vehicles) fees. These costs might also be called "title and license fees." These fees are a percentage of the purchase price of the car and will slowly decrease as the car ages and loses value.

Down Payment: When someone buys a car, and finances it through the dealership, they are usually required to make a down payment of cash. This payment is credited against the balance of the loan. In other words, if you are buying a $20,000 car, and putting down $3,000, the loan will be for $17,000. People wishing to reduce their monthly payments can do this by increasing the down payment.

Drive-off Fees: This is the amount of money you must pay to begin the lease. Typically, this includes various DMV and leasing fees plus a security deposit.

Some people who want to reduce the amount of their monthly payments will also make a cap reduction payment. This is cash, paid up front, and it becomes part of the drive-off fees.

Early Termination: This means you want to get out of the lease contract before all your payments have been made. After 24 months of a three-year lease, for example, you might decide you no longer can afford the car, or you are sick of it. So you decide you want to terminate the lease. This is very costly since leasing companies typically require you to pay a huge penalty. However, some new companies have sprung up on the Internet to help people sell their leases to someone who wants to step into a short-term lease at lower payments.

Equity: This is the difference between what the car is worth and what you owe on it. In other words, the car is worth $10,000 but you still have $6,000 left to pay on the loan. You have $4,000 worth of equity in the car. If this is a negative number, then you are "upside down" in the car.

Excess Wear and Tear: Most lease contracts have a clause which states that the person leasing the car is responsible for the cost of "excess wear and tear" to the vehicle when it is returned. When cars are used, they will eventually show signs that someone has been in them. What is considered excessive? Check your contract for specifics. But keep in mind that it is important to have the car washed and detailed before you return it. This can go a long way toward avoiding having your security deposit revoked or extra charges levied by the leasing company.

Finance: If a car is "financed," it means you are borrowing money—either as a loan or a lease—to pay for it as you drive it. Instead of financing a car, you could buy it outright with cash. When you buy a car with cash, it immediately becomes yours. When you finance the car, the bank owns it, and holds the title, until you've made the last payment.

Finance and Insurance Office: Often referred to as the "F&I office." When you buy a car at a dealership, you negotiate with the salesman. Once a deal is reached, you are escorted into the finance and insurance office where the contracts are drawn up and signed.

Four-Square Work Sheet: A standard form, used at many dealerships, to help the salesman keep track of the four elements of a deal as he negotiates with the customer. The squares allow him to jot down offers and counteroffers for the trade-in, the price of the car, the down payment and monthly payments.

Gap Insurance: If your leased car is stolen or totaled in an accident, there might be a gap between what your insurance company will pay you for the loss and the amount you now must pay to the leasing company. If you take out gap insurance (it is included in some lease contracts), this will cover you for the loss.

Holdback: This is a percentage (usually 2 or 3 percent of the invoice or sticker price) that the dealer is paid by the manufacturer after the car is sold. This is another incentive for the dealer to quickly sell the car, because the holdback diminishes the longer the vehicle sits on the lot. Although you can't easily use the holdback in negotiating, knowing about it might help you get a lower price.

Incentive: An incentive is a general term for anything that motivates a customer to buy a car. The most common incentives are customer cash rebates and low-interest financing. However, hidden dealer rebates are sometimes available.

Interest Rate: When money is borrowed, the lending institution, often a bank, charges a small fee for this service. Interest rates are charged as a percent of the amount loaned.

Invoice: This is roughly what the dealer paid for the car. If you are getting a car for $200 over invoice, then it is assumed the dealer is making only $200 profit. However, other factors enter into the equation such as hidden dealer rebates and holdbacks.

Lease: If you lease something, such as a car, you don't actually own it. You pay a monthly fee to use the car. At the end of the lease, you return the car and owe nothing more (assuming it is returned in good condition and with the agreed-upon mileage).

Lending Institution: Any company that loans money is a lending institution. It's sometimes thought that only banks loan money, but this isn't true. Auto loans can be arranged by credit unions, banks or the auto manufacturer itself.

Lessee: This is the person who has leased the vehicle.

Lessor: The lessor is the party who is leasing the car to you. Even though the dealership is arranging the lease, the lessor is often a bank or the financial arm of a car manufacturer.

Money Factor: Also called a lease factor or even a lease fee, this is the interest rate you are being charged. It is expressed as a multiplier that can be used to calculate your monthly payments. For example, 7.9 percent interest, when expressed as a money factor, is 0.0033. To convert a money factor to an interest rate, multiply by 2,400. To convert an interest rate to a money factor, divide by 2,400. (Always use 2,400 regardless of the length of the loan.)

MSRP: Also called "sticker price" (or even the "Monroney sticker") this stands for Manufacturer's Suggested Retail Price. The MSRP is what a dealer would like you to pay for the car. Most cars are sold below MSRP. Many dealers will try to base their leases on MSRP or above. However, you can negotiate a lower price to base the lease on.

Payoff Amount: Sometimes called the "buyout amount," this is the amount of money you have to pay to own a car you are financing or leasing. In the case of leasing, the payoff amount might be different from the residual value because of a refunded security deposit.

Rebate: See "Incentive."

Residual Value: This is the leasing company's prediction of what the car will be worth at the end of the lease. The residual value is also important because it affects your monthly payment. The higher the residual, the lower your monthly payments.

Sales Tax: A portion of every monthly lease payment is paid for sales tax. However, you pay tax only on the amount of the car's value you are using. In other words, rather than paying 8 percent sales tax on a $20,000 car, you pay 8 percent of the $8,000 the car declines in value as you drive it. People who hate paying taxes love this part of leasing.

When someone buys an item, they are charged a percentage of the purchase as state sales tax. The actual percentage varies widely from one state to the next and, often, within the state. The sales tax is often made up of a state tax and a local tax. These two are combined for one grand total. On small items, the sales tax doesn't seem significant. But when purchasing a car, it can be a large factor that affects the total cost of ownership.

Security Deposit: The security deposit for a lease is usually equal to one monthly payment. However, multiple security deposits can be made to reduce the interest rate charged.

Sticker Price: See "MSRP."

Subsidized or Subvented Lease: To make leases more attractive to consumers, manufacturers sometimes subsidize or subvent the leases. This means that they are either offering very low interest rates or they are inflating the residual value of the vehicle. Both tactics have the effect of lowering the monthly payment for the consumer.

Term: This is the length of the loan, usually stated in months. Common terms for car loans and leases are 36, 48 or 60 months.

Title: Also called the "pink slip," the title is a legal document providing specific information about the vehicle and stating who owns it. If you borrow money from a bank to get a car, the title will be held by the bank until you make all the agreed-upon payments.

Title and License Fees: See "DMV Fees."

Wholesale Value: This is the price at which cars are bought by dealerships so they can resell them and make a profit.

What is the "Kelley Blue Book" Price?

Let's say you are looking to buy a house. You find one in a neighborhood you like, and you know how much the seller is offering to sell it for—its "listing price."

You'd like your broker's help figuring out what that house is "worth"—what a fair price would be for that particular house. So you ask your broker to research what similar houses in that neighborhood have sold for recently.

Suppose your broker came back and said, "Here is a list of comparable houses, and what their listing prices were." "Well," you respond, "that is mildly interesting, but what I need to know is what they *sold* for. Most likely none of those sellers got their asking price. Only if I know the actual transaction prices for the other houses will I have some idea of what a fair price is for the house I want."

This concept may seem self-evident. But if it is, why do consumers forget all about it when they go shopping for a used car? Here is what frequently happens:

You find a used car you are interested in on a dealer's lot, and you need to figure out how much you are willing to pay for it. The negotiation process is about to begin, and you want it to result in your buying the car for a fair price.

All too often, however, the dealer will direct your attention to a printed price guide—and often it will be the Kelley Blue Book. (Kelley publishes more than one price guide for used cars, but the one your dealer is likely to use is the one labeled "Kelley Blue Book Auto Market Report—Official Guide," the version of the book that Kelley sells to dealers.)

The salesperson will look up the car you are shopping for in the Kelley Blue Book, and will point to the "retail" price for that car. And then he will assert that since the price he is asking is quite a bit less, you should rest assured that he is asking a fair price. The implication is: why negotiate further?

But what is that "Kelley Blue Book" value he showed you? Is it the price at which cars like yours have recently sold to other buyers? Is it even an *estimate* of the actual transaction prices?

Surprising to most used car shoppers, it is not! It is only an estimate by Kelley of the "listing" prices being *asked* by dealers—not what dealers are really getting for each car. As Kelley forthrightly says in the book, these are "suggested retail values" (although we bet that your dealer won't show that to you):

> **Suggested Retail Values** represent Kelley Blue Book's estimated dealer *asking price. The actual selling price may vary substantially.* (Italics added.)

Yes, we agree with that: In our opinion, they do vary substantially. And in most cases, they are likely to be *substantially lower* than the asking price. After all, how many sellers of houses, or anything negotiable for that matter, get their asking price?

And as the version of the Kelley Blue Book that Kelley sells to consumers says:

> **Retail Values** represent what a dealer may ask for the vehicle once it has been inspected, reconditioned and possibly warranted. *This is the "Asking Price" and you may expect to pay less.* (Italics added.)

Yes, based on our research, you often may expect to pay *a lot* less.

Our advice is simple: If a salesman whips out a copy of the dealer edition of the Kelley Blue Book and points to one of its retail prices, say to him: "It is nice to know the price that Kelley thinks dealers are *asking* for this car, but can you show me what dealers are *actually selling* this car for?"

And if the dealer says that Kelley doesn't publish those values, ask him to tell you the Edmunds.com True Market Value® dealer retail price for the car. That TMV® price is the estimated average selling price for your car, and it's what you need to know to negotiate a fair price.

New Car Buying Checklist

❏ Decide how much you have to spend on your new car purchase.

❏ Check to see what incentives and rebates are available on the car you want to buy.

❏ Print out the Edmunds.com TMV® price on the car you want to buy (adjusted for options, color and region).

❏ If you are financing the car, use the payment calculators to determine the monthly payment for the car you want to buy (and remember to apply the incentives to the purchase price).

❏ Contact the Internet department and simultaneously solicit quotes from multiple dealers.

❏ If you are trading in your old car, check its Edmunds.com True Market Value and print out this information.

❏ Call the Internet manager to negotiate the best price of the car you want to buy.

❏ Once you've reached a good price, ask the salesperson to fax you a worksheet showing all the prices, taxes and fees.

❏ Bring your worksheet with you to the dealership so you can compare these numbers to the figures on the contract.

❏ Inspect the car for dents, dings and scratches before taking final delivery.

Used Car Buying Checklist

❑ Choose the right vehicle for you by making sure the car suits your needs.

❑ Consider all cars in the class you have chosen (compact sedan, large SUV, midsize wagon, etc.)

❑ Look up the vehicle on Edmunds.com and check its reliability, editorial reviews and consumer commentary.

❑ Check the Edmunds.com TMV® price by visiting www.edmunds.com to get the most accurate price on the car you want to buy (adjusted for mileage, options, color, condition and region).

❑ Decide how much you have to spend on your new car purchase: down payment, monthly payment and purchase price.

❑ Decide how you are going to finance your car. If you are going through a bank, on-line lender or credit union, obtain loan approval before you start shopping.

❑ Using the Internet, including Edmunds.com's Used Vehicle listings, search for the used car you've decided to buy.

❑ Call the seller and verify the pertinent information. Get the VIN. Run a Carfax report on the car.

❑ Test-drive the car under your normal driving conditions. Take the car to a mechanic if it is not certified by the manufacturer or covered by a comprehensive warranty.

❑ Negotiate your best deal.

❑ Read the contract carefully before signing and always make sure you get a clean title.

❑ Inspect the car for dents, dings and scratches before taking final delivery.

Leasing Checklist

❏ Decide how much you can afford to spend on your lease payment. Decide on the right length of a lease for you (Edmunds.com recommends leasing for three years).

❏ Check to see what special leasing deals are available on the car you want to lease.

❏ Print out the Edmunds.com TMV® price on the car you want to lease (adjusted for options, color and region).

❏ Use the leasing calculator to determine the monthly lease payment.

❏ Contact the Internet department and tell them the car you are looking for. Simultaneously solicit quotes from multiple dealers for the best monthly payment (make sure the quotes are for the same length lease and the same mileage).

❏ If you are trading in your old car, check its value on Edmunds.com True Market Value and print out this information.

❏ Call the Internet manager to negotiate the best lease for the car you want to buy.

❏ Once you've reached a good price, ask the salesperson to fax you a worksheet showing all the prices, taxes and fees.

❏ Bring your worksheet with you to the dealership so you can compare these numbers to the figures on the contract you will be signing. Make sure the contract includes gap insurance.

❏ Inspect the car for dents, dings and scratches before taking final delivery.

❏ As you drive your leased car, make sure you perform all the scheduled maintenance and do not exceed the mileage limit.

Selling Your Car Checklist

❏ Consider market factors affecting the sale of your car (don't try to sell a convertible in the winter).

❏ Check local classified ads to see what others in your area are asking for your type of vehicle.

❏ Determine a selling price for your car using Edmunds.com's True Market Value system.

❏ Give your car "curb appeal" by cleaning and detailing it. Fix any problems with your car or drop the price and sell it "as is."

❏ Consider buying a Carfax (vehicle history report), or getting a mechanic's inspection report to show prospective buyers.

❏ Create a "For Sale" sign for your car window.

❏ Post an eye-catching on-line or print classified advertisement.

❏ Make yourself available to answer calls from potential buyers.

❏ Arrange to show the car to prospective buyers.

❏ Get a smog inspection if required by your state department of motor vehicles.

❏ Negotiate your best selling price by knowing the market and not dropping your price too quickly. Be patient. Don't let yourself be pressured.

❏ Collect payment for the car by getting a cashier's check or cash.

❏ Finalize the sale by fulfilling all department of motor vehicles paperwork to transfer ownership and limit your liability.

❏ Get all personal items out of your car before it is driven away.

Financing Checklist

❏ Make sure the car you are considering will fit in your budget. Your car payment should be no more than 20 percent of your take-home pay.

❏ Decide how you will finance the car. Will you pay cash? Will you take out a loan? Will you lease?

❏ Look for low-interest financing or lease specials on Edmunds.com Incentives and Rebates page.

❏ Consider checking your credit with the major credit bureaus. Repair any problems you discover before going to the dealership.

❏ Apply for preapproved financing through your credit union, bank or an on-line lender.

❏ If you plan to lease, calculate your monthly payment with zero down for our recommended term of 36 months. Print out your result.

❏ If you plan to finance the car, calculate your monthly payment with 20 percent down and a loan term of 36 to 60 months. Print out your result.

❏ After you locate the car you want to buy, contact Internet or fleet managers for quotes on the purchase price of the car.

❏ If you go to the dealership to finalize the deal, tell them you are a "cash buyer" and have preapproved independent financing. This will allow you to bargain on the actual price of the vehicle.

❏ In the Finance and Insurance office, tell them what interest rate you are approved at and invite them to beat your rate with a loan from the manufacturer.

❏ Review the contract carefully before you sign it. Make sure no additional services or products have been added and no unexplained fees.

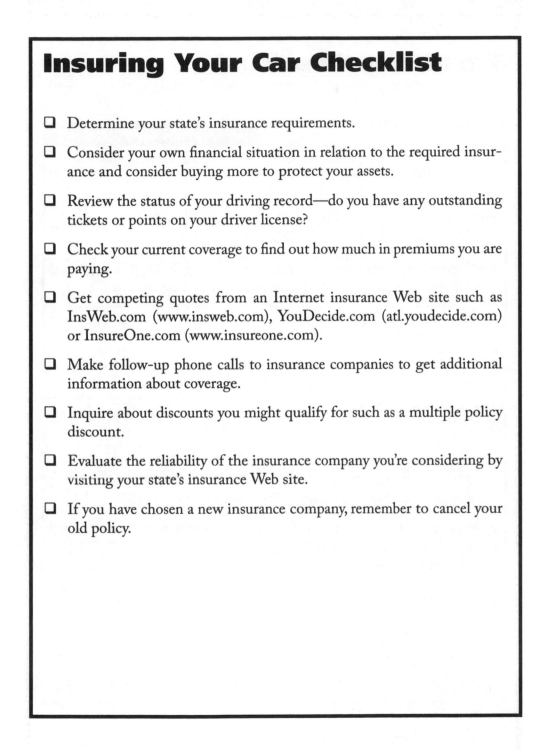

Insuring Your Car Checklist

❑ Determine your state's insurance requirements.

❑ Consider your own financial situation in relation to the required insurance and consider buying more to protect your assets.

❑ Review the status of your driving record—do you have any outstanding tickets or points on your driver license?

❑ Check your current coverage to find out how much in premiums you are paying.

❑ Get competing quotes from an Internet insurance Web site such as InsWeb.com (www.insweb.com), YouDecide.com (atl.youdecide.com) or InsureOne.com (www.insureone.com).

❑ Make follow-up phone calls to insurance companies to get additional information about coverage.

❑ Inquire about discounts you might qualify for such as a multiple policy discount.

❑ Evaluate the reliability of the insurance company you're considering by visiting your state's insurance Web site.

❑ If you have chosen a new insurance company, remember to cancel your old policy.

Test-Drive Checklist

Copy this checklist and take it to the dealership with you when you are test-driving prospective vehicles.

Make/Model:	Good	Fair	Poor
General Impressions			
Exterior: styling, finish, paint, body panel gap tolerances			
Interior: upholstery and ergonomics			
Materials quality: plastics and leather			
Interior			
Ease of entry to front and backseats			
Headroom in front and backseats			
Legroom in front and backseats			
Comfort of seats			
Layout of controls			
Visibility out front, side and rear windows (in convertible, check with top up and down)			
Effective mirrors, both inside and out			
Storage space			
Trunk space			
Convenience features, cupholders			
Drivetrain, Handling and Braking			
Acceleration			
Passing			
Hill climbing			
Engine noise			
Transmission: smooth shifting			
Transmission: downshift without hesitation			
Cornering			
Suspension			
Braking			
General Driving Impressions			
Wind and road noise			
Rattles and squeaks			
Stereo performance			
Safety Features			
Airbags: driver, passenger, side torso, head curtain			
Antilock brakes (ABS)			
Traction control			
Stability control			

Please cut out or copy this page to order subscriptions to Edmunds.com Buyer's Guides.

All prices are in United States dollars.

2005 New Cars & Trucks Buyer's Guide 1 issue per year	Pay Only (includes Shipping & Handling)	Quantity
United States	$13.70	
Canada	$14.70	
International	$16.70	

2005 Used Cars & Trucks Buyer's Guide 1 issue per year	Pay Only (includes Shipping & Handling)	Quantity
United States	$13.70	
Canada	$14.70	
International	$16.70	

Make check or money order payable to:

**Edmunds.com, Inc.
PO Box 338
Shrub Oaks NY 10588
USA**

For more information or to order by phone, call (914) 962-6297. Please pay through an American bank or with American currency.

Rates subject to change without notice.

Name _____

Company/Library _____

Address _____

City _____ State/Province _____

ZIP/Postal Code _____ Country _____

Telephone _____

Credit Card # _____ Exp. Date _____

Cardholder Name _____

Signature _____

About the Authors

Philip Reed is the senior consumer advice editor for Santa Monica, California-based Edmunds.com Inc. Phil is a former newspaper reporter who has also written a number of fiction and nonfiction books.

His first two published books were ghostwritten with a car salesman from Southern California. *Used Cars: How to Buy One* and *Lease Cars: How to Get One* were both published by Book Express and were nationally distributed. Phil then wrote the sports instructional book, *Free Throw*, with world champion free throw shooter Dr. Tom Amberry. He also wrote two thrillers about the car business, *Bird Dog* (nominated for the Edgar Award) and *Low Rider*. His newest novel *The Marquis de Fraud* is set in the world of thoroughbred horse racing. *In Search of the Greatest Golf Swing* is about the world's longest driver, Mike Austin.

Phil was hired by Edmunds.com to work as an undercover car salesman to better understand the automotive retailing business. The result was "Confessions of a Car Salesman," included in this book. After working as a car salesman, Phil returned to Edmunds.com and found himself on the other side of the transaction—buying cars for the company's long-term vehicle test fleet. This dual role has given him a unique insight into the relationship between the car salesperson and the American consumer.

Mike Hudson is consumer advice editor for Edmunds.com. He spent four years covering economics and the automotive industry at *The Detroit News* and *Free Press* before moving out to California with his wife, Rebecca. He graduated from Michigan State University with a degree in journalism with an economics specialty. Mike has won numerous awards, including being named the Michigan Press Association's "Young Writer of the Year" for 2003. His past work has appeared in *USA Today, Boston Globe, Miami Herald, Philadelphia Inquirer, Toronto Star, Atlanta Journal-Constitution, Denver Post, San Jose Mercury News, Seattle Times, Kansas City Star* and *San Diego Union-Tribune*. He continues to write a monthly column for *The Detroit News* focusing on youth and cultural trends in the auto industry.

Index

H

handling 25, 33, 102, 163, 205, 210,
      226, 312, 313
headlights 110, 253
hidden fees 298

I

independent financing 157, 161, 166,
      170, 172
inspecting 89, 91, 106, 108, 118, 173
interest rates 35, 42, 44, 47, 48, 73,
      76, 80, 116, 128, 129, 130, 131,
      132, 143, 150, 156, 157, 158,
      160, 166, 167, 168, 170, 194,
      250, 270, 272, 285, 286, 298,
      302, 303
Internet manager 27, 28, 59, 60, 61,
      62, 63, 79, 80, 90, 135, 136, 137,
      150, 154, 306, 308
invoice 40, 44, 46, 48, 49, 73, 75, 79,
      81, 84, 88, 101, 137, 162, 169,
      171, 261, 262, 296, 301
invoice price 40, 44, 46, 49, 73, 84, 88,
      101, 162, 171, 261, 296

K

Kelley Blue Book 304-305

L

laws 111
lawsuit 188
lawsuits 176
leaks 108, 109, 219
lease ads 130, 138, 139
lemon 91, 106, 108

lender 58, 73, 77, 116, 121, 156, 157,
      158, 159, 160, 166, 170, 171,
      299, 307
liability 111, 178, 179, 180, 193, 216,
      228, 309

M

maintenance 11, 19, 20, 25, 36, 46,
      125, 127, 146, 149, 153, 154,
      189, 203, 205, 221, 308
manual 34, 110, 165
mileage 34, 35, 51, 87, 92, 99, 101,
      105, 115, 117, 121, 125, 140,
      142, 145, 146, 149, 152, 153,
      154, 206, 207, 209, 218
mirrors 30, 33, 189
monthly payment 15, 16, 35, 48, 50,
      68, 72, 83, 85, 90, 114, 121, 123,
      124, 125, 129, 130, 132, 133,
      136, 137, 138, 139, 140, 141,
      144, 148, 149, 152, 154, 156,
      157, 168, 249, 250, 264, 270,
      272, 285, 286, 295, 296, 299,
      300, 301, 302, 303, 306, 307,
      308
MSRP 44, 45, 49, 129, 131, 132, 137,
      236, 302, 303

N

National Highway Traffic Safety
Administration 25
navigation system 73
negotiation 14, 31, 32, 45, 49, 52, 66,
      73, 75, 76, 95, 119, 134, 135,
      145, 152, 157, 168, 206, 212,
      213, 214, 218, 254, 285, 295,
      298, 304

O

odometer 100, 107, 108, 111, 116, 145, 153, 203

on-line 26, 58, 61, 73, 77, 78, 81, 97, 98, 99, 104, 107, 116, 121, 157, 160, 161, 194, 195, 207, 215, 218

option to buy 147

P

paint 33, 57, 80, 89, 110, 142, 163, 164, 172, 173, 202, 203, 210, 219, 221, 312

parking brake 110

penalties 142

pre-qualify 105

pressure 28, 31, 53, 56, 77, 110, 159, 233, 235, 236, 259, 260, 273, 280

pricing 36, 42, 43, 44, 45, 50, 70, 72, 73, 84, 119, 200, 202, 218, 223, 279

private parties 95, 113, 115, 117

profit 14, 44, 47, 49, 50, 65, 88, 93, 94, 100, 143, 162, 164, 169, 171, 233, 247, 248, 249, 251, 272, 274, 290, 291, 292, 296, 298, 301, 303

property damage liability 178, 180, 193

R

radio 30, 37, 110

rearview mirror 30, 253

registration 86, 111, 119, 120, 140, 151, 161, 163, 194, 195, 229, 231

regulation 230

rental cars 101

rental companies 101

repairs 25, 46, 51, 96, 102, 105, 124, 126, 142, 146, 172, 189, 196, 203, 204, 205, 212, 226

resale value 24, 26, 48, 102

S

safety 11, 20, 22, 25, 30, 33, 34, 71, 115, 182, 183, 184, 186, 188, 189, 195, 229, 230, 231, 253, 276, 277, 278, 312

sales tax 51, 87, 88, 124, 130, 133, 140, 141, 149, 156, 248, 302, 303

salvage title 101, 102, 108, 102, 105, 115, 116, 117, 203

seats 33, 110, 117, 138, 210, 216, 252, 312

security deposit 123, 133, 138, 144, 149, 299, 300, 302, 303

security system 163

service contract 89, 127, 149, 152, 164, 287

service records 95, 106, 212, 219, 221

smog 112, 216, 228, 309

smog certificate 216

smog test 112

steering 30, 31, 110

sticker price 44, 45, 46, 62, 68, 79, 80, 84, 129, 131, 133, 162, 248, 264, 269, 270, 285, 291, 295, 301, 302, 303

Notes

Notes